To
so many comrades who share the
bond of commitment to public causes.
I hope these stories will remind you
of the progress achieved in your own
crusades and of the common lesson of
our experiences that when citizens are
informed, aroused and organized,
remarkable change happens for
people, communities and society.

Be encouraged and proud.

Brian

Brian O'Connell
Spring 2005
Tufts University

Prepublication copy from first printing of first edition

FIFTY YEARS IN PUBLIC CAUSES

Civil Society: Historical and Contemporary Perspectives

Series Editors

VIRGINIA HODGKINSON
Public Policy Institute, Georgetown University

KENT E. PORTNEY
Department of Political Science, Tufts University

JOHN C. SCHNEIDER
Department of History, Tufts University

BRIAN O'CONNELL
Civil Society: The Underpinnings of American Democracy

PHILLIP H. ROUND
*By Nature and by Custom Cursed: Transatlantic Civil Discourse and
New England Cultural Production, 1620–1660*

BOB EDWARDS, MICHAEL W. FOLEY, AND MARIO DIANI, EDS.
*Beyond Tocqueville: Civil Society and the Social Capital Debate
in Comparative Perspective*

KEN THOMSON
*From Neighborhood to Nation:
The Democratic Foundations of Civil Society*

HENRY MILNER
Civic Literacy: How Informed Citizens Make Democracy Work

VIRGINIA A. HODGKINSON AND MICHAEL W. FOLEY, EDS.
The Civil Society Reader

THOMAS A. LYSON
Civic Agriculture: Reconnecting Farm, Food, and Community

PABLO EISENBERG
Philanthropy's Challenge: The Courage to Change

BRIAN O'CONNELL
Fifty Years in Public Causes: Stories from a Road Less Traveled

Other Books by Brian O'Connell

America's Voluntary Spirit (1983)

The Board Member's Book (1985)

Board Overboard: Laughs and Lessons
For All but the Perfect Nonprofit (1996)

Civil Society: The Underpinnings of American Democracy (1999)

Effective Leadership in Voluntary Organizations (1976)

Our Organization (1987)

People Power: Service, Advocacy, Empowerment (1994)

Philanthropy: Four Views
(with Robert Payton, Michael Novak, and Peter Dobkin Hall) (1988)

Philanthropy in Action (1987)

Powered by Coalition: The Story of INDEPENDENT SECTOR (1997)

Finding Values That Work: The Search for Fulfillment (1978)

Voices from the Heart: In Celebration of America's Volunteers (1999)

Volunteers in Action (with Ann Brown O'Connell) (1989)

FIFTY YEARS IN PUBLIC CAUSES

Stories from a Road Less Traveled

BRIAN O'CONNELL

TUFTS UNIVERSITY PRESS
Medford, Massachusetts

Published by University Press of New England
Hanover and London

TUFTS UNIVERSITY PRESS
Published by University Press of New England,
One Court Street, Lebanon, NH 03766
www.upne.com
© 2005 by Brian O'Connell
Printed in the United States of America
5 4 3 2 1

Library of Congress Cataloging-in-Publication Data

O'Connell, Brian, 1930–
    Fifty years in public causes : stories from a road less traveled / Brian O'Connell.
        p.   cm. — (Civil society)
    Includes bibliographical references and index.
    ISBN 1–58465–476–7 (cloth : alk. paper)
        1. O'Connell, Brian, 1930– 2. Nonprofit organizations—United
    States—Employees—Biography. 3. Associations, institutions,
    etc.—Employees—Biography. 4. Independent Sector (Firm) I. Title.
    II. Series.
HV28.O33A3 2005
361.7'63'092—dc22   2004028284

For those going forward

on this road less traveled

and

to my grandchildren

and maybe theirs.

Contents

Preface

Two roads in a wood diverged, and I—
I took the one less traveled by . . .
—Robert Frost

I had not thought to write another book and indeed had promised myself
I wouldn't. Changing my mind began when I was working on the eulogy
John Gardner's family had asked me to deliver for his memorial service at
Stanford. In reviewing a great deal of material about him and by him, I
realized how often he advised people to "tell the stories." His advice is almost encoded in my mind, "Tell the stories, Brian, tell the stories." For a
while I didn't connect or perhaps didn't want to associate that thought
with the rigors of writing anything of book length. However, I found myself thinking about some stories, and then many of the unusual situations
of my quite different life and how often telling about those experiences
had been the best way to inform and guide others who were also trying
to understand what it takes to build public causes.

It was also on my mind that young people often talk to me about what
it's like to spend a career in nonprofits, and they want to know if what I
do is within what people think of as public service. Nonprofit endeavor
is still sufficiently vague that even public-spirited young people find it
hard to consider if it's right for them. Our conversations generally lead to
whether I would advise them to follow my path or take a more traditional
route through civil service or elective office. I always encourage them to
think positively about civil service and politics but to realize that voluntary organizations and institutions provide another way by which public
service is performed. I also point out that many people spend parts of
their careers in government, business, and the independent sector, and that
each emphasis or phase is likely to provide significant accomplishment
and satisfaction.

I'd like to think that careers like mine have helped widen the public's
understanding of who and what is included in public service, extending not
only to diverse careers but also to America's vast network of volunteers
and to the concept of citizens as the primary office holders of government.

Whatever and whyever, I gradually realized that such a book should be pursued describing my quite different journey and telling stories from along the way. It's not an autobiography or a study of voluntary organizations or anything else very studious. The closest it might fit in publishing parlance is as anecdotal memoir.

With the forbearance of publishers of previous books of mine, I have drawn on those works to help portray places and episodes along the road. The endnotes and references provide acknowledgement of those writings and of other referenced material, but to keep the book informal and flowing I've avoided extensive notes.

In earlier drafts, several chapters included lists of volunteer leaders with whom I've worked, but preliminary readers advised that such material interfered with the flow and would be more appropriate to an appendix. I agreed only when I was satisfied that this would not obscure a central point of the book, that staff leaders are usually effective to the extent they serve to multiply the participation and impact of the volunteer leaders with whom they work.

Acknowledgments begin with John W. Gardner, who even in death keeps prodding his followers to do more for society and whose wisdom and example continue to guide me.

Other influential helpers included Robert Hollister, my dean at the University College of Citizenship and Public Service at Tufts University, Sharon Stewart, my former assistant at INDEPENDENT SECTOR, and my brothers, Thomas E. and Jeffrey O'Connell. Mary Perry, my assistant, has been wonderfully effective, creative, and patient, even when overworked, inadequately compensated, and too rarely praised.

As Tufts representative to University Press of New England, John Schneider guided the manuscript through early stages, and then the team at UPNE took over with their own personal and professional guidance, personified by Ellen Wicklum, my editor.

I acknowledge The Atlantic Philanthropies, primary supporter of my work during this period, and the Charles Stewart Mott Foundation and Carnegie Corporation of New York, which provided important project support. This gives me further opportunity to acknowledge the founding support of my professorship by the Ford Foundation and W. K. Kellogg Foundation.

Once again, largest thanks go to Ann Brown O'Connell, who has shared the long journey and has given me balance and perspective.

Brian O'Connell
Chatham, Massachusetts, July 2004

« 1 »

WHICH ROAD TO WHERE?

False Starts, Unexpected Influences,
and a Special Mentor
1953–1956

In 1974 I began to hear warnings from government insiders that I had been added to President Nixon's "Enemies List." I never knew if that was really so, but I learned soon enough that somebody very high up was out to get me and the national organization I headed, the Mental Health Association (MHA).

Two years earlier, MHA celebrated victories in Congress that took the form of hugely increased appropriations for mental health research, training, and community services. Those new appropriations amounted to approximately $125 million per year, to be awarded by the federal government to state and local mental health authorities, *not* including the association itself. For an organization that was raising about $25 million a year, those were major accomplishments for the cause we championed.

After succeeding in getting the legislation passed and the funds authorized and appropriated, we were horrified that President Nixon "impounded" the money in further demonstration of his unexplained antagonism toward the subject and field of mental illness/mental health and his abhorrence of aggressive public advocates, particularly those who challenged him. We were absolutely stymied because Congress, having already approved the funds, had no further role. It was a standoff between the legislative and administrative branches of government, with only the federal courts left as possible arbiter.

Our feisty group, struggling with the gigantic but unpopular cause of mental illness, took the lead in suing the Nixon Administration in two class action suits, and eventually we won both of them, and on lopsided votes. It was one of the greatest victories ever for the association.

Not long after the judicial decisions, some of our MHA state affiliates became the subjects of Internal Revenue Service (IRS) financial and program audits. I knew what a financial audit was, but I had never heard of a program one. I learned quickly that it entailed an examination of whether we were exceeding the amount of advocacy activity allowed by what was then a very indefinite formula. At that stage, our state affiliates were trying to improve conditions in state mental hospitals, rehabilitation programs, and the like. It was pretty obvious that the best affiliates would be heavily involved in influencing public policies and programs. Therefore, we were highly vulnerable to a claim that we exceeded the "insubstantial" amount of resources that could be expended for advocacy.

For the MHA organization, the consequences were becoming horrific. One after the other, our state affiliates were reporting that IRS auditing teams were showing up, focusing little attention on financial records, but giving painstaking scrutiny to minutes, correspondence, and anything else that could provide a sense of interactions with government. Within months, we learned that our enormously effective Maryland division would lose its tax exemption, and it looked likely others would too.

We thought we might get relief by using an old contact with the IRS Commissioner, but he rejected angrily any notion that his organization was politicized. Years later, I learned that in fact he was unaware that White House officials had gained considerable leverage over key people in the IRS, particularly with respect to so-called enemies.

In desperation, we turned to influential members of Congress, who fortunately understood that the Administration's arbitrary interpretation of the vague "not more than an insubstantial" investment in advocacy left us at the mercy of federal officials who objected to our efforts to influence them. Congressman Barber Conable and Senator Edmund Muskie took up our cause, and with their help we were able to enlist an impressive group of cosponsors of legislation that would specify what legislative activity was appropriate for voluntary groups and even declare that advocacy was healthy in the development of sound public policies and programs. The legislators made their displeasure clear to the IRS and White House and demanded that during consideration of the legislation, foreclosures of tax exemption should be limited to cases of fraudulent behavior.

After two years of growing support and negotiation, Congress finally passed the law "Lobbying by Public Charities," which clarified and expanded the lobbying rights of nonprofit groups. With our new law on the books, the MHA was free of retaliatory efforts.

On a personal side, the White House continued to go out of its way to undercut me but the IRS had little to go on. It was the only time in my life I was relieved and grateful to have so little money.

In the mental health field we were used to the phrase "I never promised you a rose garden," after the title of Joanne Greenberg's book about a long struggle with mental illness, but for me those words were particularly poignant during the Nixon presidency. His White House Rose Garden was certainly off limits to me, but then again it wouldn't have been a very safe place to go anyway.

My getting involved with the Mental Health Association is a tale in itself, beginning with my realization, after accepting the national directorship, that I couldn't even spell schizophrenia. I knew almost nothing about the field, and in a couple of months I was to head a national organization of 50 state affiliates and 650 local chapters, involving thousands of people who were steeped in a vast and complex subject of which I knew no more than what I had gleaned from one college psychology course. It dawned on me that the only thing I had in common with their cause was that I had to be certifiably crazy to think I could lead it.

To explain our seemingly bizarre interest in one another requires a review of what I had been doing previously that offered any possibility of a match, and that begins with an accidental exposure to community organizing right after college.

After graduating from Tufts University in early 1953, and with six months to go before graduate school, I needed to earn some money and hoped I could find something that would give me experience in public work. The closest short-term opportunity in my home town of Worcester, Massachusetts, was a staff job devoted to what today we call developmental disabilities, such as cerebral palsy. The association was comprised primarily of parents who shared a fierce belief in the potential of their children and a bond forged by pervasive professional advice to put their sorry children away and get on with their own lives. Their relatively new school clinic was struggling to keep open and to provide at least minimal physical therapy and education for about twenty youngsters. As great as the pressure was simply to maintain the operation, it was outmatched by the uproar from the scores of families on the waiting list and by everyone's insistence that the services had to be increased.

Many of the kids and parents were not particularly appealing to this sheltered newcomer. Some of the little ones were often wildly spastic, with more spittle than speech, and some of the parents were so used to fighting and rejection that they were alternately raging in my face and sobbing on my shoulder. The parents were determined that their kids could and would learn and talk and get around. The forces that drove them were not necessarily guilt or blind hope, although there was plenty of both. They knew from daily and hourly attendance on their kids that there was much more within them than professionals saw, and they would not rest until it was coaxed out.

By the time I got there, the association—largely the parents—had convinced the county to lend them a closed wing in a very old and dilapidated hospital, hired a physical therapist to train the parents to work with their children, and convinced the school board and superintendent to assign two public school teachers to work full time with these ragged pupils in a gradually promising effort to test and nurture their learning potential.

Although the operation was still tiny and terribly fragile, what was evolving began to serve as a model providing hope and courage for struggling parents and enlightened professionals in communities throughout the country.

During my brief stay, we—again mostly the parents—raised enough money to maintain and slightly enlarge the program for a year, extended the physical therapy training to many children on the waiting list, stabilized somewhat an association made chaotic by the desperation of the parents, and began to get better media coverage, usually around the "miracle" of such kids walking and reading.

With that fascinating interlude behind me, I was off to Syracuse and the Maxwell School of Citizenship and Public Affairs to prepare for "real" public service. That experience started positively, but I found I couldn't quite shake thoughts of my Worcester school clinic and my increasing examination of such activity as seminal public work. Gradually, I realized I was becoming committed to those prior activities, which represented positive public results and real if unrecognized public service, and that I wasn't going to learn more about them even in a very good school of public administration. Such nonprofit involvement simply wasn't on the radar of such institutions.

I recall the reactions of some members of the faculty when I announced I would be leaving. My recent bride was now pregnant, and although we might have found a way to do without her salary, our revised circumstances hastened my decision to pursue the different track of what I almost alone on the campus seemed to recognize as public endeavor. When I explained the plan to my faculty advisor, he told me with every good intention that I would be a real loss to public service. I was too surprised to express my intuitively more expanded view of the scope of public service. In retrospect, it was a defining moment in my career.

Fortunately, I had been invited back to the association and school clinic to fill the newly created post of executive director, but even as I turned in that direction, I determined to remain in touch with the field of public administration and many years later was elected a Fellow in the National Academy of Public Administration, perhaps the first Fellow who had never been in government. This represented a significant breakthrough in efforts to broaden the definition of public service.

In the course of my second stint in Worcester and with my eye on a career as a community organizer, I realized that I needed far more guidance and training than was possible in a one-person office. Fortunately, we had a great fund-raising campaign, including a telethon involving Ertha Kitt, who was at the zenith of her popularity. The encouraging fund totals justified their gamble on me, but unfortunately the board began aiming immediately for even higher amounts the next year for substantial expansion of the clinic and to start other programs. In addition, the volunteers were so tired and beaten down by their years of struggle that they were all too ready to turn most responsibilities over to me, which compounded my inadequacies.

We had developed a relationship with United Cerebral Palsy (UCP), but it was too new and small to have a staff development program. Its only encouragement to my growth was the compliment of an offer to have me take over the Nebraska affiliate, which I learned was even less advanced. So, despite a real sense of letting my group down but knowing that we were heading for a total mismatch of expectations and talent, I searched for another setting where I might learn and grow.

At first I didn't know how to proceed, and got as basic as checking the Yellow Pages to get a sense of what organizations of size and interest were out there. Then I checked with the local or Boston office of those that seemed like possibilities. After a lot of calling and appointments, I came down to eight that looked significant in both cause and capacity. With contact names from local representatives and good reference letters from my board and UCP, I wrote and called each of the eight to explore traineeships and/or placements with good mentors. To my surprise and delight, three of them, all in New York City, offered to see me. Of the three, the one that seemed absolutely best for what I needed and wanted was the American Heart Association (AHA), which, after all the necessary correspondence and interviews, facilitated my engagement as a field representative with its Pennsylvania affiliate under the tutelage of Charles Mears, who turned out to be the best mentor and people builder I could possibly have hoped for.

So Ann and I and little Todd were off to Harrisburg for a rewarding professional and personal experience, including becoming members of the wonderful nationwide family of AHA.

As a field representative in Pennsylvania, my territory was the eastern side of the state, working with about fifteen chapters and a like number of un-organized areas. I also assisted Chuck Mears with some statewide as-signments, such as our newsletter, annual report, regional and state meet-ings, and some categories of fundraising such as memorial gifts.

At first I worried that I might know less than the chapter executives I was supposed to advise, but I was surprised and relieved how much I had learned in the Worcester job. This, along with my mentor's close guidance and the patient assistance of my much more experienced partner, Dave Foster, who covered western Pennsylvania, helped me survive and actu-ally be useful.

It was also at this point that I began to realize how much I had expe-rienced and learned from my time in the Army. I was in the service for just a year and a half shortly after World War II when the military needed re-placements so badly that it enticed us with eighteen-month enlistments, hoping that many of us would stay longer.

I had gone into the Army after the first half of my junior year in high school, largely to qualify for the GI Bill, and had not really expected much of the experience except as an adventure. On such a short enlist-ment I could not go to Officer's Candidate School, but I did get into Non-commissioned Leadership Training, which turned out to be extraordinar-ily good. Subsequently the Army placed me as an infantry platoon leader in a basic training company, which gave me the leadership advantage of taking recruits through basic training five times and the personal disad-vantage of hating it all five times.

I finished my tour as a sergeant heading our regimental Troop Infor-mation and Education Center (TI&E), where I coordinated the weekly troop information programs for all companies in the regiment and was responsible for education services, including correspondence courses and GED (General Educational Development) testing. The combination of line and staff jobs provided far more leadership experience than I believed could be concentrated in so short a span. It also produced a degree of con-fidence that served as a boost in my later professional challenges.

As an aside, but perhaps a worthy one, my involvement with the TI&E

operation came about because I had been taking correspondence courses to keep from falling too far behind in high school. I was able to earn a year's credits, which meant I only had a half semester to make up when I got out. I do have to confess that I cheated at biology. When the textbook arrived, I started out all right, but when I came to a chapter that began, "Go out into the woods and catch a frog," I was stumped. I was at Fort Dix, New Jersey, which was sixty-four square miles of sand with nary a frog or toad in sight, so I simply went to the base library, found a book on frogs, and did fine. I suppose that if there has to be a lesson carried over into the job world, it would be not to sweat the little things, or, if you're going to cut corners, hold them to frog size.

Let me return to describing my Pennsylvania years, when important lessons were so routine that they equaled the best graduate school imaginable, including field placements with line experts. That period and its significance for me deserve several chapters, but they would come out sounding like a diary or recital of what might seem like ordinary situations. The value was in the consistent and sage advice, gentle corrections, and constant encouragement. I was given my head, but with backup to deal with just about everything that came at me. It was rarely dull but not particularly noteworthy. It was just a lot of trying, doing, tripping, falling, learning, succeeding, and growing, growing, growing.

To keep from telling you more about penguins than you want to know, here are just a few examples of experiences that have stayed with me.

To get it out of the way quickly, let me tell you of a ghastly blunder that should have gotten me canned but that Chuck Mears turned into a growth experience.

I hadn't been in Harrisburg long when he asked me to help prepare the annual report. We talked a good deal about all aspects of it, and he went off on vacation. During his absence I prepared a colossal report, which I was sure would win all kinds of accolades and awards. To please and impress, I had it printed and put the first copies on top of all that was waiting for him when he returned. I expected he would come out almost immediately raving about it, but I had to wait in awful suspense for a couple of hours. He finally called me in all right, but all I had to notice was his uncharacteristic red flush to know he was more raging than raving.

Fighting for control, he began to take me through the report, starting with the errors of fact, names, dates, figures, charts, omissions, size, graphics, and syntax. That in turn led him unnecessarily to tell me that I should never have gone to press without his clearance. He finally ended by asking me what in the world I was thinking of, but there was no defense or even any wisdom in offering one. All I could do was apologize, tell him I was trying hard to surprise and please him, and ask for a chance to make it right. He agreed only that it was a surprise. He did say it was not a good time for him to think clearly but that we would talk again. The only hope I took away was that the strongest thing he actually said was, "Gee willikers, this is awful."

I had to leave for a three-day field trip that day, and the whole time away was dominated by a combination of black worry and trying to find the worst possible descriptions for my stupidity, which definitely did not include anything as gentle as "gee willikers."

When we talked again, he was reasoned and far fairer than I deserved. I repeated my apologies, added shame to it, and waited for his decision. He opened with a review of all my good work and progress, said that I deserved a chance to prove that this serious error was an aberration in judgment and performance, and that, yes, I should work with him to do the report over again.

I've remembered that one, not just because I was so relieved and grateful, but as a model of how to behave toward others even when upset and disappointed.

Another learning experience that has stayed with me was the regular and careful attention the volunteer leaders and Chuck gave to being sure that staff and volunteers throughout the state had opportunities to know firsthand what their efforts meant to the cause. I remember, for example, having the opportunity to take small groups into operating room amphitheaters, where they could look down on the miracles of heart surgery with explanations from renowned surgeons such as Charles Bailey about what the problem was, what the surgery would do to ease or solve the problem, and what the consequences would have been just a year before without these new techniques. It was tough to watch, but those who did became even more dedicated people and more effective communicators of what we were all part of.

Similarly, several other major figures in the field of heart disease, including surgeon Bob Glover, were willing to crisscross the state year after year to report to our chapter annual meetings how readily our volunteers' efforts translated into lifesaving. It was the best of "telling the stories."

I also remember taking thousands of volunteers through a house-size heart replica that we had provided to the Franklin Museum in Philadelphia. It gave members of the public a chance to walk through the heart as though they were drops of blood, entering the heart and going through all the chambers and then passing out again to the other parts of the body. It was an extraordinary success in helping people understand the role of the lungs, heart, veins and arteries. To "Walk Through Your Heart" was such a fascinating and valuable experience that eventually millions of people took the walk, and the thousands of volunteers who did so took away the additional reward of having a far better idea of what they were trying to protect and why.

A third and different experience served to help all of us understand the importance of both tenacity and faith in our cause.

It's fascinating to hear people today speak about the American Heart Association's success. They assume that the organization couldn't help but succeed. They will go on at great length about how the organization had a visible cause, leadership, fund-raising staff, dollars to invest, and a basic fund-raising blueprint; how the total association was organized and dedicated primarily to raising funds; and how, in the early 1950s, there was a wide-open climate for fund-raising. The truth is otherwise.

Fifty years ago, the real picture was similar to that of most organizations today when they are trying to figure out how to raise money. There wasn't a visible cause; heart-attack victims looked so normal that there was no chance to get the kind of sympathy one could generate with a poster showing a child polio victim. We didn't have leadership; certainly we didn't have the community leaders with us. Most of the leaders were physicians, who took little interest in fund-raising. We didn't have a fund-raising staff—most of us were young idealists with far more fire than knowledge. We didn't have very many dollars, certainly not the kind of money necessary to prime the pump of a major campaign. We didn't have a blueprint for campaigning—indeed, we were floundering around trying to figure out whether to sell valentines, raise money by mail, or accept government grants. Everywhere we went, we were told that people were tired of volunteering and fed up with being asked to contribute, and that we should look to the United Fund for support. It was extremely difficult to get local groups interested in fund-raising and convinced that they could do it.

In the intervening years the American Heart Association has gone from that modest beginning to an *annual* income approximating $500 million.

What evolved during the 1950s was, first, that local boards were convinced that money had to be raised; then gradually came the recruitment of campaign chairpersons who were willing to join up and give it a try, and a growing pervasive spirit for making each February's totals better than the year before.

As often happens, the darkest days turned out to provide some very real blessings. Throughout the 1950s and 1960s, the American Heart Association was fighting to survive the United Fund's determination to take the association in or else to dry up our income sources. We lost a good many chapters, and we lost a great many board members. Indeed, we seemed to lose most of the bigger names we had tried so hard to recruit. It turned out, however, that those who stayed with us were a hardy lot.

They were independent souls who were not frightened away and who, by standing up and being counted, brought to the agency a verve, backbone, and determination that have been its making.

I had my own taste of the power that could be turned against us in the form of an ugly confrontation with a daunting figure in Scranton. This was during a trip to work with our Lackawanna County campaign committee. When I checked into the Casey Hotel there was a note—really an order—to meet with William Scranton at his office at 8:30 the next morning. William Scranton, later a Pennsylvania governor, was either the current or recent head of Scranton's United Fund, a leader of the local paper and easily the city's most powerful figure. I'll admit to being scared sleepless and was at his door precisely at 8:30. He didn't stand or shake hands but only pointed to a chair opposite his desk. The only good thing I can say about what transpired was that it was brief. With index finger wagging, arms slashing, and voice shouting, he told me that people in Scranton had decided how charitable funds would be raised there, that only the United Fund would participate, that we were ignoring the will of the people and would pay dearly if we persisted. He said it in about five different ways, which at least gave me time to consider my response and to review in my mind that I must not appear frightened or cowed. In contrast to his verbal bombast, I wanted to come across as peaceably nonviolent or at least not moved.

At the point when he seemed to run out of vitriol, and when I figured it was my turn to talk, he ordered me to call off the campaign, leave his office at once, get out of town, and never come back. Of his orders, I only followed the one about leaving his office, and that happily so.

I proceeded to my campaign planning meeting, where I briefed the group on the warnings and was delighted in their scrappy response of, "Who the hell does he think he is?" I came back regularly to assist with the campaign, which continued but with increased emphasis on our door-to-door solicitation to counter any negative influence Mr. Scranton and others might have on our special and corporate gifts. We far exceeded our goal, and the chapter went on to become one of the best in the state. The people of Scranton were with us, even if Mr. Scranton was not.

In the years that followed I would occasionally hear thoughtful people refer to Governor Scranton as a very nice man, and I accept therefore that he must have been, but on that morning and that subject he was a pompous bully. I had learned in boyhood that usually you have to confront a bully, but I'd also learned in the military that sometimes, as with Scranton of Scranton, you're better off just walking quietly around and going about your business.

Although it was a hard lesson and sometimes still harder to follow, I learned that when it comes to choosing between self-appointed power brokers and the people, I'll choose the people just about every time.

When I called Harrisburg to tell Chuck about the "problem" with Scranton, he was naturally worried about what the consequences might be and said that I should come in to talk about it. Recalling the last time I had been asked to come to talk about unpleasant business, I worried all the way back. When I arrived, he wanted to hear every word over and over again and then called in Dave and others to hear my report. Although they were worried we might be in for trouble, at least in Lackawana County, they were relieved and thrilled that this young field representative hadn't knuckled under and that our cause and resolve were thereby reinforced.

With that kind of support and comradeship, I was ready to settle in for a long stay.

« 2 »

A STRAIGHT-UP LEARNING CURVE

American Heart Association—Maryland Director
1956–1961

Less than two years into the Pennsylvania assignment I received a call from our Maryland director, Clyde Arbegast, indicating that he was leaving the job and recommending me for it. Alarm bells shrieked. I didn't want to go anywhere. I owed it to the Pennsylvania Heart Association (PHA) to stay longer, Clyde hadn't cleared the contact with Chuck Mears or the American Heart Association (AHA), and at a recent regional meeting I had heard that Clyde was facing one important power struggle with his president and another with his fund-raising director, whom he wanted to fire but the board wouldn't allow it. As if that wasn't enough, I figured I was still too new and green to be selected for the job and didn't want to create all the upset and uncertainty a candidacy might entail.

But I didn't say no. I was complimented beyond good judgment, needed time to figure out if there was something going on that I didn't understand, and the first time I had heard the Maryland setup described, I was curious. Because of the size and geography of Maryland, the state director served also as the metropolitan Baltimore director, a twofer in experience and stature.

Before I could settle down and think more sensibly, I received a call from AHA's personnel director, Bernie Kapell, who had steered me to Pennsylvania. Bernie said that Clyde had just called him to report his approach to me and that I hadn't seemed interested. I couldn't read whether Bernie thought I should have said no, should have reported the call to him right away, or, long shot, thought I should have shown more interest. It turned out that he (a) thought I should have called him right away, (b) thought I should at least show some interest, and (c) offered enough reservations about my candidacy to leave me feeling inadequate and confused, a bad combination.

When I talked to Chuck to report the contact and Bernie's reaction to it, he said I should be complimented, was good and getting better, could profit from more time in Harrisburg, and owed it to them to stay longer, so I called Bernie and Clyde accordingly.

A couple of days later I received a call from the chairman of the search committee in Maryland, who said that he had talked to the immediate past president of AHA, who checked me out with National, and reported I was someone to look at. The chairman asked when could I come down to talk. I explained that I was not a candidate and wished him well. But Bernie called again. He had talked to Chuck and they agreed that I should at least go down and look. I reviewed Bernie's prior reservations about my getting the job and he replied that there could well be a fit. I couldn't figure out if they were desperate for anyone or what they were thinking, but I said I'd go to Baltimore, be nice, and come home and get back to work.

I went to Baltimore to talk and we both seemed interested, so I went home to study, talk, and think. When I went back for a full interview they offered the job and agreed to my every important condition, such as total executive control, including hiring and firing. AHA agreed to back me to the hilt. Except for lingering doubts about my readiness, it seemed the right thing to do.

I accepted and we were off to Baltimore, this time with both Todd and Tracey in tow.

I know what I've reported seems a long introduction to the Heart Association of Maryland (HAM), but the tortuous turns and gambles of such transitions are very much a part of my story. It was often what it was like to move around in the nonprofit world. Today it's easier, but still too hit and miss.

At this point it's probably useful to be more explicit on what the Heart Association did. I'll focus on the chapter level, where most of the action was, but also provide some indication of the roles at the state and national levels. In general, all three parts of the organization were involved in research, education—including education of professionals and the public—community services, and fund-raising.

The primary responsibility for research was at the AHA level. At least one half of its income was committed to research activities such as support of career investigators, senior and junior investigators, fellows, and specific research projects. Research was generally focused in such areas as atherosclerosis, stroke, congenital heart disease, rheumatic fever, and high blood pressure.

Most state affiliates and many chapters also supported research, usually on projects in their geographic areas. In Maryland, with Johns Hopkins University, the University of Maryland, and many other fine medical facilities, there was considerable opportunity to support good research, particularly by individuals who had not yet achieved stature to compete for national support. Maryland had also been the focus of major breakthroughs in understanding and treating various heart diseases, most notably the groundbreaking efforts of Helen Taussig and Alfred Blalock, who found ways to correct the inadequate blood supplies in what had been known as the "blue babies," almost always fatal or seriously debilitating.

The professional education activities of the association were focused on putting research findings to work in prevention and treatment. In our years this emphasized education of physicians, beginning with general practitioners, pediatricians, and other primary care doctors.

Public education efforts were organized to provide the general public with information and motivation to help prevent illness or learn to deal with it quickly and effectively. In my years with the association there was a great deal of effort to convince the public about the importance of such precursors to disease as smoking and improper diet. On the diet side, I recall listening to a debate about whether it was really possible to get Americans to change their diet in order to reduce cholesterol. The nay-sayers were convinced that people couldn't be induced to make such a major change in their living habits. At that, Irvine Page of the Cleveland Clinic observed, "Any society which has learned to like the taste of martinis can learn to like anything."

Also at about that time we began to acquaint the public with the risk factors relating to heart attack and stroke. Essentially they were smoking, high blood pressure, dietary fat intake, diabetes, heredity, and lack of exercise.

Community services entailed a broad array of efforts to help individuals and groups minimize their risks of the consequences of health impairments. For example, most chapters had information and education programs to provide up-to-date information about the various heart diseases and where to get more information and help for them.

Beyond efforts to deal with prevention, education, and services, each chapter was involved with fund-raising to support those activities, which in most chapters involved door-to-door solicitations, memorial gifts usually in lieu of flowers for those who had died of heart problems, special solicitations among corporations and well-to-do people, and bequest cultivation programs.

Those examples of activities might give you an indication of what I would be responsible for in Maryland. I was fortunate that we were more advanced than many states, but this only made my challenge more difficult. The expectations were higher, the staff quite sophisticated, and the volunteers were determined to expand the efforts. I was eager to get underway but very aware and concerned about my relative youth. It didn't help when at dinner the night before I was to start, the waitress required proof of age before she'd serve me a beer!

My youth was accentuated the next morning when I met with the staff of about six professionals and four or five support staff and it was painfully obvious that I was decidedly junior to them all. That was exacerbated when someone explained that this group was considerably younger than the twenty or so staff people in the chapters.

The first six months were a blur of getting acquainted, lots of listening, learning the ropes, keeping things going, bolstering the morale of a staff recovering from two years of board and staff struggles, doing quiet appraisals of staff abilities, using lots of AHA consultants, and of necessity giving priority time to a much-enlarged fund-raising campaign that would start in just six months.

It was also a time for similar concentration on the chapters around the state, which involved spending a great deal of time on the road. It looks like a small state until you try to drive it up and down and back and forth.

My toughest tussles were with the fund-raising director, who had been around a long time and had his own definite ways of operating. There had been some dramatic fund-raising breakthroughs in other parts of the country, which I had learned and gained from in Pennsylvania, but he didn't believe in them and wasn't about to try. I had to take the relevant parts of this responsibility from him, but he so poisoned the waters with many of our campaign volunteers that I had to build around them also. It was necessary to live with some of his antics and presence for a while because there was only so much I could take on and there was some institutional memory and experience I depended on.

Fortunately, the campaign went spectacularly well, especially the new categories and strategies. While Maryland hadn't been on the low side of AHA's affiliates in financial development, it wasn't a leader, and in that first year we quintupled our totals and moved into the top ranks.

During the campaign there was one awkward situation that quickly turned from public scare to insider humor. Our Heart Sunday door-to-door campaign turned out to be so successful that we had not distributed nearly enough coin bags to our area captains throughout the city. As a result, they had to stuff overflowing coins into paper bags, old pillowcases, and worse. When it came time for them to turn in their returns at our downtown headquarters, cars were double and triple parked up and down the street. At least twenty or thirty people at a time tried to carry or drag their flimsy overloaded sacks as fast as possible from their cars to our terribly backed up tellers. Inevitably many bags split and thousands of dollars worth of change tumbled out. To make it even worse we were on an active trolley line on a busy cobblestoned street and to make it even much worse than that, we were expecting a *Baltimore Sun* photographer/reporter team to cover what we thought would be good news. We were all imagining what the story and pictures would actually look like the next day and what that would say about our lack of charity stewardship.

The scene was a combination of bedlam, chaos, and terror. There were at least thirty or forty of us trying desperately to pick, scoop, or sweep up the pennies, nickels, dimes, quarters, and half-dollars scattered twenty five yards in each direction. The more we tried to grab hold, the more we seemed to spread the sea of coins farther down the tracks and street. Picking coins out of trolley tracks, gutters, and cobblestones is hard enough, but it was already dark and trolleys were bound to come soon from both directions.

Thank the Lord that Sunday's schedule slowed the trolleys and a fire elsewhere delayed the reporter and we somehow escaped. Our celebration was not spoiled, but there wasn't much clapping. Our fingers and hands were much too raw.

The *Baltimore Sun* article was wonderful, and as time passed our low point became a high point and legend. To this day, when I meet up with some of the old Baltimore crowd, Heart Sunday night and pushing coins down the trolley tracks will inevitably be good for renewed storytelling and bonding.

With a successful campaign under our belt, the board backed me fully in a staff reorganization in both structure and people. Though some members of the board wanted me to find a spot for the fund-raising fellow, I would have none of it. It was the first major firing I had to do so I was very nervous about it, but I moved with dispatch. Later severances in my career were far more difficult but none as obvious and significant.

I organized the staff into the categories of education, community services, communications and fund raising. I filled in as staff to the research committee. Three of the four key assistants I brought in from the outside.

The remaining one, Lee Bowers, who handled the education portfolio, was superb and I was lucky to keep him. Of the others, Gene Taylor from AHA's Philadelphia chapter took over community services, Bob Thompson from the Kentucky affiliate took on communications, and Paul Neff from Maryland's Tuberculosis and Health Association became fund-raising director. All of us also took on a geographic portfolio so that we not only had Baltimore and statewide responsibilities for our specialty; we also had general field responsibility for parts of the state such as the Eastern Shore.

I've had other good staffs, but never was there such a thrilling sense of mutual confidence, teamwork, and the fun of being on a dramatic and sensational roll. Some of the delight was that we were operating in significant part at the local level, able to feel and see the results of our work almost daily. It was the last time I would have that tangible experience of quick results and rewards. The state level is great and provides opportunities for broader impact, and that's even truer at the national level, but the farther one gets from the local level, the harder it is to have the immediate delight of seeing change happen.

I also learned how much teamwork can soften the loneliness of being the director or president. It was shared decision making and shared rewards. Out of that confidence and comfort I learned a very important thing about my own leadership. Up to that time, whether in college or with the school clinic, I almost always felt that I had to know the answers of what to say or do in order that I not appear hesitant or ill prepared when decisions were required. There was so much to be decided and done in those days in Maryland that there was no way that anyone, certainly not I, could have all the answers. If I had pretended so, I would have been tossed out on my ear. It was hard at first. I learned to go into those staff meetings or other settings and say with increasing comfort, "I don't have the slightest idea how we should handle this one. What do you think?" I learned also how very much other people have to contribute. Out of all that shared decision making and responsibility we not only made far more right decisions than I could have ever come close to, but we also had the advantage of shared commitment to follow through.

I knew that in the end I often had to make choices among all the ideas put forward, but knowing that I really cared and that each was a contributor to the best ideas, the staff took the losses in good spirit and moved forward.

That experience was a defining moment in my ability to deal with increasingly complex decisions and the multiplication of them. I wouldn't have survived Maryland without that change and never would have gone on to even bigger things.

I also was able to practice something learned back in Worcester and much more in Harrisburg, which was to maximize the role of board members, committees, and other volunteers so that the overall outreach and impact of the organization was multiplied many times beyond staff capacity. It was there that I even began to do regular measurements of the number of volunteer hours that could be produced by each staff person and by the staff as a whole. That may seem terribly administrative or technical, but it helped all of us to realize that the largest service of staff is usually measured by the performance and impact of the volunteers who are enabled by staff backup.

The depth and quality of volunteer participation in greater Baltimore and throughout the state was extraordinary. There are probably readers who will be curious how those volunteers were arrayed and the kinds of things they did, which might be most easily conveyed by referring to our standing councils and committees: At the top, we had executive, medical advisory, and program coordinating committees. Program councils included the Council on Research and its Research Allocations Committee, and the Council on Professional Education, with committees for health careers, nursing education, scientific sessions, postgraduate courses, medical journal, and regional education.

The Council on Public Education included committees for school health, speakers bureau, health information, and patient education, and the Council on Community Services and Rehabilitation had committees for cardiac-in-industry, home care, and rheumatic fever.

Beyond the program-related councils and committees, there were operating groups, starting with the Council on Public Relations and its committees for radio, television, special events, publications, and press. There was also a Council on Chapter Affairs and then a Council on Administration and Finance with five working committees: for finance and budget, by-laws, personnel policies, organizational structure, and nominating and membership.

Lastly there was a Council on Development, with three committees involving legacies and bequests, memorial gifts, and the Annual Heart Fund.

This structure, along with those involved in chapter activities around the state, represented at least 2,000 active participants, with many additional thousands involved during the fund-raising campaign.

In going through some of the material left over from those days, I came across a 1959 pamphlet headed "The Story of Your Heart Association and Its Advances Against Maryland's Number One Health Problem." It began:

> This booklet describes the life saving and life giving activities of your Heart Association. It is directed by doctors and laymen who volunteer their time

in order to fulfill their promise—and yours—that the staggering toll of heart deaths will not continue.

It also included a quote from a talk that Dr. Paul Dudley White gave at our annual meeting in Baltimore in 1958. White was a founder and past president of the American Heart Association and became a prominent national figure when he was President Eisenhower's doctor after the President's heart attack. Dr. White said to us, "We have made more progress in the fight against heart disease in the last twenty-five years than had been made in all the centuries before."

I added, "Although the advances made in research and community programs in that time are thrilling and far exceed even our brightest hopes, we must still regard our efforts as only a stimulus for the really unbelievable job ahead. With your help, none of us will have to forever face the prospect of so many friends and family dying from heart disease."

It's an absolute thrill and one of the great satisfactions of my life to read so often today about the dramatic declines in death and disability from heart attack, stroke, rheumatic fever, congenital heart disease, and high blood pressure. We've almost forgotten how many people in the 1950s and '60s were described as "cardiac cripples" whose prospects were decidedly limited. Today they function well with the benefit of coronary bypass, valve replacement, pacemakers, medications, and outright prevention. There's still a long way to go, but compared with what we faced in the 1950s, the advances represent miraculous change.

One of our greatest boosts of this period, particularly for our public education efforts, grew out of the President's unfortunate heart attack. The fact that he lived and could return to his demanding job, and his willingness to talk and write about it, provided more education of the public than we could have achieved in decades. His willingness to identify with us as honorary chairman of the AHA Board including providing statements, film clips, and occasional appearances, helped us in about everything we were trying to do.

I always tried to be sure that even the thousands of campaign volunteers felt a part of the association and of the progress they helped us achieve. Each holiday season I sent a card to every volunteer, reinforcing our appreciation. For example, our 1959 card signed by Dr. Helen Taussig, famous throughout Baltimore for her lifesaving work with "blue babies," carried this important message:

> In this season of happiness and hope
> Your Heart Association and I send thanks
> For your own demonstration of
> Good Will Toward Men.

May we all hope for renewed strength
In the coming year to further our joint effort
Against heart disease.

For both Ann and me, the five years in Baltimore, which we learned early to pronounce "Ballmer," were personally delightful. To this day some of our closest friends are still there and we greatly enjoy the visits back and forth. Among our delights were that we shared season tickets for the Baltimore Colts games in the glory days of Johnny Unitas et al. We were so personally happy that we seriously considered staying and even mentioned the possibility to our friend and sponsor, Nelson Offutt. He took it so seriously that he supplied me with two business prospects to look into. One involved an executive role with the Port of Baltimore. It was intriguing because it had the feel of being part of not only the community but an interesting facet of it. The consideration put me to the acid test of what I really did want. Each time I came to such a crucial cross-roads, I had to reevaluate whether to stay on my different course, and that's what I finally decided to do. Nelson was disappointed and a bit hurt by my choice. He read more into my maybes than I intended and had worked hard to line up the possibilities. I wish I'd handled it better. I was lucky that we remained good friends.

Years later, when I reviewed the progress I helped achieve in Maryland, particularly when I compared it to my doubts about my experience and age, I found myself wondering what made the difference. I don't think this was an ego trip. I genuinely wanted to learn what the success told me about myself and my responsibility to those staff people who looked to me for development and guidance.

Those examinations always brought me back to the advantages I had and how much I gained from being a Mear's protégé and to AHA's networks of assistance and friends. I probably drew more from those possibilities than anybody. I also had the great head start of Clyde Arbegast's solid building efforts. He was even better than given credit for.

I realized too, as I had in the Pennsylvania job, that I brought to the table more than I realized, such as a history of hard work beginning as early as grade school, including caddying, newspaper routes, and grocery-store clerking. During college I worked summers as a waiter and bartender and in the school year served nights as a bartender for conventions and events at the Tremont Hotel in Boston. (Although it's often referred to humorously, it really is true that being a bartender is good training for lots of things.) My work ethic and record were both strong. Also, although it seems vain to think about and awkward to write, I benefited from being reasonably presentable, articulate, and I guess imaginative, all of which helped. Maybe I was smart but I certainly wasn't anything approaching brilliant. In a family of six alert kids, my grades were least impressive, only so-so and uneven—A's and B's in English and history, B's and C's in languages, and C's and D's in math and science. I was reasonably strong in extracurricular activities like debating and drama and, although not a natural athlete, won my school and city letters in cross country. As I mentioned before, the brief but packed Army experience helped prepare me for responsibility and leadership more than I realized.

I was also beginning to benefit from a reputation for success and as a doer, which helped with both personal confidence and a perception of ability, often beyond what was truly so. It's important for anyone in leadership to be careful not to exaggerate one's own talents, or the axiom "Pride goeth before the fall" will take its toll.

I couldn't deny and still can't that I profited from a great deal of luck, which came in three types: the kind that occurs when you're ready to pounce on a good break, the accidental kind of luck that happens when everything doesn't go wrong all at once, or blind luck—when great things happen that you couldn't ever have anticipated. I had lots of every kind in Maryland. I certainly needed all of it in California.

RIDING THE GOLDEN BEAR

American Heart Association—California Director
1961–1966

After five great professional and personal years in Maryland I began to receive feelers about moving on. The American Heart Association (AHA) put some interesting prospects before me, including a good national office possibility, but they weren't more enticing than the special situation I already had. A few other organizations also inquired, but my reaction was the same.

In the spring of 1961 I received a call from Fran Chamberlain, a recent AHA president from San Francisco, inquiring unofficially if I would be interested in heading the California Heart Association (CHA). It was by far AHA's largest affiliate with many major chapters, including Los Angeles, and a significant depth of experienced and respected volunteer and staff leaders. I was interested.

What unfolded was not quite as complex and contorted as the Maryland search, but it came close. This time I'll spare you most of the problems but cover some parts that may, in a perverse way, be interesting.

AHA was supportive but couldn't back me because there was a strong inside candidate who had formerly headed the prestigious San Francisco chapter and was strongly favored by the incoming president of CHA and, importantly, was acceptable to Los Angeles. National was also concerned that it had just played a central role in placing one of my top staff people, Gene Taylor, as the new head in San Francisco, and it was their practice not to weaken an affiliate by too many transfers. They were pleased to hear that I might be susceptible to a move and mentioned Massachusetts, which I had previously turned down. It was my home state and a good affiliate but just not different enough. However, I realized that if I was turning down Massachusetts because it wasn't large enough and if California was not going to be open again for quite some time, my options were narrowing.

In the face of AHA's understandably cool reaction to my CHA prospects and in light of the insider's sizeable lead, I decided against it and called Fran to explain. Given the cold realities of the situation, it was an easy decision but still not easy to put behind me.

So much time passed that I assumed the insider had been selected, but something evidently intervened because several weeks later I had a succession of urgent calls from AHA people and the chairman of the California Board, telling me that the search committee wanted me as the outside candidate. They were very fair in telling me that the former San Francisco executive was still a strong candidate but said there would be only the two of us with no favorite. In one way or another, all of my contacts said it was 50/50. I asked for time, but got only two days. They needed to get it settled.

I called Chauncy Alexander, the Los Angeles executive, a good friend, and asked him to level with me, "If I got the job, would we be OK as a team?" I didn't put him on the spot by asking anything more, but he had the opening to tell me not to muck up the search by competing with the insider. Chauncy was appropriately discreet but I got the clear impression that although he favored the other guy, he was hearing that it might not go that way, and if it didn't he would hope very much that I would be the choice.

I also called Fran Chamberlain and others in California. I didn't ask anyone for support but only to clarify that I would not be ill advised to compete and that the contest was really open. Although each had to be careful, I got the message that it was OK to go ahead and that the job was a toss-up between the two of us. I also picked up enough to realize that the insider was not quite as strong as earlier believed, and the president-elect of CHA, a strong leader of the San Francisco chapter, had warned that he would resign if his San Francisco candidate didn't get the job, a threat that seemed to be having the opposite effect he intended.

At that point, and with my two days gone, and a strong base in Maryland, I figured, "What the hell, go for it."

They put the two of us into the same small anteroom outside the conference room where the search committee was meeting. For the first hour and a half we chatted while the committee did other things, and then for the hour and a half each was interviewed we sat alone. After those three hours we sat side by side again for another two hours while we waited. How we found so much to talk about I'll never know, but we sure worked hard at it.

Finally, I was asked to come back in and I figured they wanted to get the bad news over quickly and get on with negotiations with the winner. But no, I got it, and while we started to work on details, someone went and told my friend it wasn't to be. It was hard to concentrate.

The president-elect did resign, but in anticipation of that possibility, the executive committee had asked a former CHA president, John Sampson, if he would be in the wings to recycle and he had agreed. With no disparagement intended to the resigned president-elect, whom I didn't know, getting John Sampson to come back at that important juncture turned out to be the best possible happening for the association and for me.

That night, a Saturday I remember well, I flew from Los Angeles to San Francisco to be ready to meet my new staff on Monday. On Sunday I went alone to the Top of the Mark and with a Bloody Mary in hand looked out over San Francisco Bay, and with absurd exaggeration, but absolute delight, toasted the scene and thought, "This is now mine!"

To provide perspective, it might be useful to view the California Heart Association in 1961 in the context of where AHA as a whole was and where we all wanted to go in the decade ahead.

In 1959, the Rockefeller Foundation commissioned a study of "Voluntary Health and Welfare Agencies in the United States." The task was assigned to a group of twenty-three distinguished Americans staffed by Robert Hamlin, a prominent lawyer, physician, and public health official. Hamlin had been a friend of my brother Jeff's at Harvard Law, which gave me an opportunity to talk to him during and after the review.

At a preliminary stage, Hamlin was so surprised that the Heart Association seemed uniformly applauded that he wondered if he had missed the negatives. He told me, and reported personally to the AHA Board, that in the preliminary survey, "AHA came out better than any other organization and that there was not one adverse comment." He went on to say, "AHA had been successfully combating the problem of bureaucracy and constantly striving to streamline its organization; [and that] in 1957 over thirty million dollars had been given by voluntary agencies for medical and biological research, which was about ten percent of the total spent in the United States for these purposes, and over half of this came from two agencies; the American Heart Association and the American Cancer Society."

The final report, "Voluntary Health and Welfare Agencies in the United States," issued in 1961, did not deal with individual agencies, but it was made clear to me, and again more importantly to AHA's top leadership, that although we were a lot younger as a national voluntary organization than most, we were in the top few in performance and impact on the program side and in structure and management on the organization side.

The "Hamlin Report," as it came to be called, was particularly useful and timely for me as I took over the California responsibilities. For example, it challenged the field as a whole and each organization to strengthen themselves in five categories: stronger voluntary agency leadership, higher standards for local affiliates, increased participation in organized planning, better reporting of programs and accomplishments, and greater emphasis on research and the application of new knowledge.

To address each of the five, the National Board was quick to appoint a "Committee on the Future of the AHA." When that committee was ready with its report, "The Heart Future: The Continuing Obligations of a Voluntary Health Agency—The American Heart Association," the leadership saw the event as so significant that the board of directors went to Gettysburg to be with President Eisenhower, by then honorary Chairman of the Board, for consideration and approval of the report.

The specific recommendations followed the five categories in the Rockfeller/Hamlin document and established special tasks and goals for each. They also examined and spelled out such considerations as program, structure, organizational relationships, fund-raising, and communications, including the role to become the authoritative voice of cardiovascular diseases that "has been thrust upon us by the media stemming from Eisenhower's heart attack."

Essentially the report confirmed that our basic responsibilities and opportunities still rested within the areas of research, professional education public education, and community services. It also provided standards and examples of excellent performance for each.

There were a lot of expectations of the association as a whole, but as the largest affiliate, California carried a particular responsibility for leadership. In the immediate context, those expectations were immense. Two Maryland guys were now in the top jobs at CHA and San Francisco, and people were watching to see how these new "hot-shots" were going to perform. We had both beaten out local favorites, which turned up the heat. The CHA president-elect had resigned in protest of my winning out over his favorite, which played up the fact that I was hardly a unanimous candidate, and the Los Angeles chapter was waiting to see what all this change would mean for it.

In addition, the California affiliate and all its chapters wanted to soar, and a 31-year-old was supposed to make it happen. All I had to do was put a lot of troubles behind us and get the train on a fast track. I was very much aware that without a chapter to run directly, I had much less chance to prove myself. I was supposed to achieve all these results from the affiliate level, where we didn't have direct authority for what the chapters did. I didn't have a Baltimore anymore, and I missed it. I found myself humming "Maryland, My Maryland" a lot.

Fortunately, many of the chapters were already very good and CHA previously had a very positive record of strong relationships and leadership. If I could reasonably quickly establish personal credibility and evidence that CHA was again capable of effectiveness and leadership, I could take advantage of people's willingness to at least wait and see.

There were two areas where I had to establish a foothold fast. The largest and very imminent problem involved the absolutely ugly relationships between the Los Angeles chapter (LA) and CHA. There was also serious loss of confidence in the state staff to provide practical assistance to the increasingly independent chapters, and third, could an Easterner crack a generalized attitude that although California was by far the largest state affiliate, American Heart seemed so Eastern focused and dominated that Californians felt neglected? I realized that this last consideration was endemic to California vis-à-vis the East (usually, east of Missouri!), but woe to a state director who didn't understand how real the isolation was and didn't work like hell to give state and LA their due.

Starting with Los Angeles, I had these things going for me: My reputation for success in Maryland related particularly to metropolitan Baltimore, where, functioning as a chapter exec, we became one of the most respected locals in the country. Chauncy had done the same for Los Angeles, and although his scale was very much larger than Baltimore's, we greatly respected each other's accomplishments. He had also said and meant it that we would make a good team, and I was determined that he would never have reason to question my side of it.

John Sampson, the new president-elect, was a revered professor at the University of California Medical School, where many of the state's cardiologists received their training, including the current president of the LA chapter, Arthur Feinfield. John's willingness to step into the breach was greatly appreciated by all. We also had Harney Cordua of San Diego as the current CHA president. San Diego, from its size and southern base, shared some of LA's concerns about state operations, which made Harney acceptable. The Los Angeles leaders were tired of so much of their time and energy seeming absorbed with state-local battles, and regretted that they were so often and unfairly viewed by AHA as the bad guys.

Even with such advantages, I knew there was such a long history of hostility it would be hard to change, and that because New York City, Chicago, and St. Louis were separate affiliates, not linked to their state organizations, Angelinos would always aspire to that arrangement and chafe under anything short of it.

Although it took some struggles with the national organization, I was able to change the long but absurdly cumbersome and unnecessary arrangement that just about everything Los Angeles did in relation to AHA had to pass through the state. Let me illustrate how easily this could remind the chapter of its subordination: It would have to order all its education and campaign materials through us, but we would rarely have the necessary quantities on hand, so the orders would have to go to AHA, which would then send the materials to us and we would forward them to Los Angeles. Despite warnings that if I pressed for a change, Los Angeles would use the opening for greater autonomy or I would be opening the way for every chapter to want the same treatment, I persisted. And because I was the new guy, AHA agreed to try it. The same roundabout process held true when the chapter wanted to arrange for a national consultant to help it and on and on it went. Breaking those restraints early helped enormously to prove my overall intent and to reduce friction.

I spent at least a day a week in LA, keeping Chauncy in the know about what I was thinking and doing and getting his advice on all kinds of things. It even reached the point that one day toward the end of the first year when I was going through a fairly routine briefing of Chauncy with our AHA regional consultant John Herman present, Chauncy interrupted and said something like, "Brian, for goodness sake, you don't need to take up the time of all of us to tell me what the hell you're doing." Afterward, out of earshot, John burst out laughing and I couldn't understand why. He said, "After all those years of hearing Chauncy complain about never being in the know, it was just a delight to hear him telling you to cut it out."

I was nevertheless careful to be in town for most of LA's key events, including celebrations, launches of new programs, installation of new officers, and on and on. In addition, Harney Cordua and John Sampson were there often, as were heads of state committees, to show their eagerness to learn of the chapter's impressive activities. We made very sure to add their key people, including staff members, to our committees and to involve them in consultations with other metropolitan chapters, and we moved as quickly as possible to place their people on national committees and gradually the national board.

Those placements caused my first really difficult showdown with AHA. I had made up a list of Californians I thought deserving of national recognition in the form of committee participation and in a few cases board involvement, but little happened. I finally had to go to the top to Rome Betts, with whom I had always had a good relationship, and I thought I'd win the day, only to be told that involving West Coast people was too expensive. I absolutely couldn't believe it. At that point we were providing about 15 percent of their budget, later to rise closer to 20 percent. I tried to point out the contradiction, but the closest he came to compromise was to ask if we would pay the expenses for these people or at least share them. In subsequent sessions with him and others, I tried to point out all the immediate and long-term advantages there would be as a result of improved communication and participation, and slowly the spigot began to loosen.

Keith Thwaites, my predecessor in California and now a program director at AHA, was a helpful inside ally, as was John Herman, our regional representative. Both carried our water in battles far beyond what was welcomed by their higher-ups. Lastly, I made the most of Chauncy and his staff's abilities, experience, and willingness to be involved in consultation within the national operation and with other large affiliates and metropolitan chapters around the country.

Even with all of that, there were strains, problems, and occasional serious disagreements between ourselves and LA, but both sides knew that these were inherent in the structural arrangement, and instead of letting situations get out of hand, the mutual effort was to solve or minimize the upsets.

The second area where immediate and continuing efforts were required involved the confidence of the chapters in the state association and me. After a lot of listening and trying to see both sides, including the staff people who had somehow lost the confidence of the chapters with which they worked, I realized I couldn't wait as long as I had in Maryland to make some difficult changes. When I put two and two together it was inescapable. Almost everything that California Heart represented had to occur at the local level, and our primary link to the chapters was tattered.

In fairness to the people involved, I need to say that these were very bright, dedicated professionals, but they were too centered on the theoretical or academic side of the enterprise to be content with or effective at working with even the larger chapters in the day-to-day business. They were enormously stimulating in discussions of research paradigms or the subtleties between primary and secondary prevention, and they all wrote very well on such vitally important things, but there was just no real match between what they cared about and preferred to do and what the chapters needed. Sadly for them, there had to be a wholesale change, which was absolutely awful to go through. Fortunately, two of the people left on their own accord, but four were left to terminate. Even before it was done, I started lining up possible replacements because I knew we couldn't survive a substantial hiatus.

Some of the chapter directors and volunteer leaders who had pressed me the hardest to change things were down on me for doing it pretty much all at once, but I had learned that if I focused on who would be in place and what would be accomplished six and twelve months hence, there was reason to believe my critics would ease up.

I brought in new people for every key slot and, as in Maryland, gave them dual responsibilities, one for their specialty and the other for a region of the state. They included two of the best California's chapter directors, Ruth Morse, who had been director in both Alameda and Santa Clara counties, and John Blum of San Mateo. Ruth had the southern part of the state, assisted me with Los Angeles, and was head of community services. John had the greater San Francisco Bay area and fund raising. Doug Waterstreet came from New York to work with the two great valleys stretching from Sacramento to Bakersfield and with professional education. Bob Thompson followed me from Maryland to continue his outstanding work in communications and to work with assorted chapters that didn't fit neatly into a regional pattern. As with Maryland, I handled the research portfolio.

The new team quickly provided a refreshing new beginning for me and more importantly for the chapters, who couldn't quite believe the early and positive changes that resulted.

Bringing Bob Thompson represented still another person out of Maryland's ranks. I worried a great deal about that, but in conversations with Paul Neff, who succeeded me as executive director, he indicated he was ready to deal with it and had good people in mind. Still, some people held it against me. I'm not sure I should have done it differently, but I still think about it and respect and acknowledge the upset and hurt I caused.

I don't want to leave the impression that our relationships with AHA were primarily difficult or negative. We worked constructively and harmoniously on almost all activities and I continued to value greatly my partnerships and friendships with just about everyone on the national staff and the hundreds of people within other state affiliates and chapters. It continued to be a wonderful experience.

I was asked to chair AHA's Committee on Personnel and Training, and one of our tasks was to deal with ways in which our affiliates and chapters hired their executive directors. On the basis of my own transitions to Maryland and California, you will understand that I felt myself expert on this topic!

The heart of our new arrangement was that the national office, or the state affiliate for chapter openings, should automatically be part of the process. That role began with the makeup of the search committee, a review and development of the job description, consideration of compensation, and other such basics. The core of it was that the national operation should have a prescribed role in presenting two or three candidates, not necessarily within the organization but usually so, who seemed to fit the personal attributes and prior experiences important to the next stage of the affiliate's development. The affiliate was certainly encouraged to put forward its own candidates. The regional consultant would either staff the committee or be a member of it. Each side would have an implied veto if either felt strongly that the individual in the lead just didn't seem right. We recognized that in a crunch the affiliate would have the final say, but at least there would be a process to cause people to think hard about what was needed and who could provide it.

That approach was slow to take hold but was given impetus by an even more complete program we initiated in California. I had been concerned as far back as Pennsylvania that the state affiliate had relatively little to say about the selection of a chapter executive director and that local boards tended to choose local people often on the basis of quick judgments or friendships. Many chapters made bad decisions because the search committee found it awkward to decide against the friend of the president or a person pushed hard by a board member. The smaller the community, the tougher it was. Board members would feel sorry for a woman newly widowed or a county commissioner unfairly defeated, and the search committee would ignore common sense and sound procedures. The result was that too many important board decisions ended up being made badly. Even in larger chapters the process was not really suited to finding the person needed for the years ahead.

I was repeatedly told that it was better to locate a person who knew the local scene, but I gradually realized that was often not the right course. I came to believe that a bright, effective community organizer was going to see the local scene and develop the necessary contacts in lightning fast time. Indeed, he or she would not be encumbered by some of the difficulties that the local resident might have. Those difficulties involved the set ways in which individuals are already perceived, such as being someone's kid sister, being associated with the north side, or having worked for the other newspaper.

In Maryland I learned to step in even when not invited, to try to be appropriately influential in the search process. By the time I reached California I considered this one of our most important services, although not always welcomed, at least in the early years. To try to build the pool of persons ready to step into chapter responsibilities, we worked hard to develop lists of impressive up-and-comers and to even provide traineeships. We recruited young people who received brief training prior to their first job placement at the local level. These individuals grew quickly into significant staff leaders, and their youth proved to be an asset rather than a liability.

The program also allowed us to carefully screen people who had the attributes of success. It had been my experience, born of many sad lessons, that it takes a unique person to succeed in the staff role of a voluntary agency. Over the years, I developed a profile that helped me screen persons who are exploring staff possibilities. My profile of persons most likely to succeed is:

They're committed to public service. This is more than a generalization. The persons who succeed will face many rocky times. They'll be underpaid for their ability, and they'll put up with a great deal of conflict. For these reasons and many more, these persons must have a dedication to public service that will get them over these obstacles and tough times.

They like people and get along well with them. Liking people is often used as the only criterion for selection and therefore can be exaggerated. In carrying responsible positions in voluntary agencies, however, most staff people deal with a wide variety of individuals and must be able to get along with them.

They have a great deal of patience and tolerance. Staff persons work with a wide variety of volunteers who are often at their most excitable pitch. The more vibrant and active an agency, the more this holds true. A staff person must be a stable and patient human being or the emotional aspects of working together for significant goals will get out of hand.

They are mature. Psychologists define maturity as the ability to forego short-term satisfactions in favor of long-term goals. This applies to organizations as well as individuals, and particularly to successful staff persons. Most goals are long range and require persistent, dogged pursuit through all kinds of difficulties. The satisfactions are rarely found on a weekly or even monthly basis. It's only as the agency looks back from a fuller perspective that the attainments are visible and the satisfactions apparent.

They are willing to work hard. Successful people usually work hard, and this is particularly true in the nonprofit field. There is so very much to be done, the dedication of volunteers is so high, and the number of forces to be dealt with is so great that the only way to achieve success is by working awfully hard.

We learned that selecting the right person is so important that we developed a fund that allowed us to sweeten the pot if we had confidence that we had a good person ready to step into an available job but where the local search committee or board felt she or he was too expensive. We would offer to carry the full salary the first year, one half the second, and one quarter the third. In almost every case, chapters large and small accepted the offer. It was expensive but on balance a tiny investment with early payoff and a long-term bonanza.

Another investment was in the development of standards and evaluation. It started out with an invaluable *Harvard Business Review* article I had read, "How Can Businessmen Evaluate the Management of Voluntary Welfare Agencies?," in which Earle Lippincott and Elling Aannestad stated, "If the basic organization components of the agency are operating effectively you can assume that the output is likely to be worthwhile." They acknowledged that this wasn't an exact equation, but they believed, for example, that "if the Board and the basic committees are functioning—including regular meetings with quorums present—it is likely the agency is not wasting its time."

We agreed with the authors that one can be encouraged if the basic operation seems to be functioning, but recognized that this doesn't assure that the end product is really good. Therefore, we added two elements. First, we identified the basic activities that we believed a chapter of the American Heart Association should be handling well. Second, we acknowledged that one of the great things about voluntary agencies is their role as innovators. Certain activities can't be anticipated, so we gave a whopping one-third of the total score to those unusual things that the chapter might be doing over and above the basics.

As a result, the standards we developed were divided into three parts: "Basic Organization" (such as board makeup, meetings, and turnover), "Basic Activities" (such as an information and referral program, and at least one seminar for general practitioners each year), and "Additional Activities." A chapter was evaluated every three years by a peer group of board members from other chapters. This had many intended and desirable results, but it also had a side benefit: The board members doing the evaluation learned a good deal about how to improve their own chapters.

I emphasize organization matters here because program development depended on strong organization. Later in my career I would make it a part of every fund raising campaign to link the efforts in what I would label "Building for greater achievement and achievements worth building for." When I put it that way, I found that even funders who were adamant about not supporting fund raising or what they pejoratively called "infrastructure" were willing to get behind our two-part plan involving investment and payoff.

There were clearly investments that were paying off, and I'll provide five examples that might also illustrate the kind of efforts conducted at the state rather than local level.

The first example relates to research. As part of the Future Role Report, a major responsibility for AHA was to coordinate the research programs of the three levels of the organization. Part of this stemmed from concern that some state and local efforts were of questionable merit and a few even subject to favoritism. The larger effort was simply to be sure we were taking advantage of the three levels to build the strongest possible research program. California, again because of its size including the totals of our affiliate and chapter research allocations, was asked to lead the way. I raised the old question about California representation in the process and this time it was much easier to achieve, including folks from LA and the Bay Area. As the person staffing CHA's research committee, I was asked to be an ex-officio member of the national research committee, without vote. The swiftness with which barriers fell in California reflected not only the inherent desire of everyone to be part of a superior program but also the distinct advantage of including some of us.

I was later designated by AHA's Society of Heart Association Professional Staff to be its representative to the national research committee, where I could help interpret to other affiliates and chapters how unthreatening and rewarding the process of integrating and coordinating research activities could be. Those experiences reinforced all the lessons I had learned about the absolute essentiality of involvement, particularly in federations where gaining cooperation has to be earned.

In professional education, my second example, we undertook an annual scientific session as part of each annual meeting, and we worked hard to make the sessions so appealing that they attracted physicians and later other health professionals from throughout the state. For that same reason, we began to encourage all of our delegates and attendees at AHA's annual meetings and scientific sessions to sit in when professional papers were being presented and discussed. Even when they couldn't understand a lot of the scientific terms and jargon, they could turn to our physician delegates to get the inside scoop and the significance of what they heard.

The third example involved education of the public, which was becoming an increasingly important function for the association as a whole, and we welcomed a growing role in it. Fortunately we had Bob Thompson, who was one of the very best at finding ways to use the media to get our messages across. These were not just one-time stories but ongoing campaigns to inform and educate the public about high blood pressure, exercise, smoking, danger signs, and other critical factors in prevention and early intervention. The papers, radio, and television were initially not ready to consider ongoing or parallel campaigns. The practice and attitude were that they would give us pro bono coverage for some spots during our fund-raising period and for other extraordinary developments, and that we should be happy with these. Bob and our media committees, with the help of AHA, began to break that mold by the combination of strikingly impressive materials and stories and evidence that the public was enormously interested in them. We even began to get science writers and reporters with health assignments to attend our scientific programs.

Our media committee took a look at our progress in 1965 and found that at least two thirds of our placements involved program related messages. At first some on the fund-raising side thought they were getting short shrift, until they realized that the media was all the more interested in us because it respected and welcomed what we provided them throughout the year. It certainly helped our fund-raising greatly that the public knew more about us and saw regular evidence of what we were accomplishing.

My fourth illustration of investments that were paying off involved community-related services which included professional and public education components. For example, in our statewide nutrition program, our largest effort involved acquainting professionals and the public with the importance of sensible nutrition for healthy blood pressure, weight control, and the general maintenance of health. On the direct services side of it, we provided training and assistance to the chapters to set up nutrition counseling classes for persons with heart problems. There were some similar dual roles for direct statewide efforts and chapter programming in such important areas as school health, for prevention and early identification and treatment of rheumatic fever, general heart disease, stroke, and much more. For instance, our school health program was divided between direct state efforts to reach state groups of school administrators, school health officials, medical societies, pediatricians, general practitioners, internists, and others, and the chapters were constantly tied into these and developed their own services. That was so in the early days of local programs to be sure local hospitals and clinics were providing appropriate medicines to children with streptococcal infections, which had been found to lead to rheumatic fever and heart disease in a frightening proportion of cases.

My final example represented an activity that almost overwhelmed us. I mentioned in the Maryland chapter that we had begun to pay attention to what was then called "closed chest resuscitation," now cardio-pulmonary resuscitation or CPR. By the time I got to California the importance of CPR was understood and efforts to teach and learn it were springing up everywhere, and people were looking to the Heart Association for guidance and instruction. We conducted hundreds of sessions for statewide and regional groups of emergency personnel, including police and fire departments, but the largest responsibility went to our local groups to whom the training responsibility was falling. Although the burden was heavy, there was also a sense of satisfaction in providing an important service and being in the thick of a lifesaving crusade.

One aspect of it was certainly tangible and occasionally vividly so. To make the training more practical, some of our people helped to develop a life-size doll that looked like a grownup Raggedy Ann, including the tousled red hair, and was appropriately called Resussy-Ann. As rapidly as they could be manufactured we shipped them off to the chapters, where they got compressed and inflated day and night by people pressing as hard as they could on the sternum and breathing life into the lungs.

The almost too vivid part came one night when a policeman noticed a light on in our San Mateo office and looked in on the space our people used for the CPR training. The patrolman, seeing several bodies laid out on tables and a horrible heap of others around the floor, called headquarters to report a mass murder and that every available backup was needed. Within minutes the building was surrounded with reinforcements from every corner of the county and beyond, all to witness the "saving" of eighteen Resussy-Anns. The media reaction was sensational and the publicity for our CPR efforts couldn't possibly have been better. There was of course the little matter of our relationship with the police, but we figured that also could be resuscitated.

A highlight of morale building for the California Heart family involved our own Eisenhower moment. By then the former President was spending a good part of each year in Palm Springs. With some indication that he might be willing to make an appearance, we scheduled a statewide meeting close by and, without his promise that he would show up, held our breath that it would happen. When the day came I blessed myself and made the call to verify his availability. Having crossed myself, I guess it's fair to say, "Thank God he was on." I was asked to meet him in the locker room of his golf club.

At the appointed time I started down the steps, and before I'd gotten half way, he was coming up all alone. He looked up at me and said, "You O'Connell?" I replied, "Yes, Mr. President," and he said, "Let's go."

He didn't say much and couldn't stay long, but even that brief time with such a hero and icon, who had experienced firsthand our cause and became a champion of it, made those moments magical. He was so warm, smiling, and appreciative and he looked so healthy that everything about the time together was sparkling.

I'll always remember too that when he was ready to leave I said I'd walk out with him, but he told me to stay with my group, and I watched as one of the most important people in the world walked by himself to his cottage.

I was particularly pleased that so many of our staff and volunteers could experience that moment. I'm sure that every one of them remembers that day and has passed it on to hundreds of others as a high point of their volunteering.

Another highlight of those special years is the message captured in the dedication of *Fighting for Life: A History of the American Heart Association 1911–1975* by William W. Moore:

> To the Volunteers, Staff and Contributors:
> the conquest of the cardiovascular diseases may not come in your lifetime, or in mine, but it will come in the fullness of God's own good time. And when it does come, it will be your victory, and the victory of all those who have joined together in this magnificent adventure.[1]

We're not there yet, but oh how special it was to be present in what has to have been some of the very best years.

In my third and fourth years in the Golden State, I began to get some feelers about other jobs, including possible leadership of some national health and welfare agencies and two possibilities at the national level. Although complimented, I was not turned on by them. Two approaches within the Bay Area stirred greater interest, but exploring them caused me to be quite a bit clearer about possible next steps.

One involved leadership of the greatly enlarged Bay Area United Way. As I indicated earlier, I found my years at the local level to be particularly satisfying and therefore a return to the grass roots was attractive. Staying in California was also appealing. Ann was not very enthusiastic about pulling up stakes again. Settling permanently in California seemed for a while to be a natural arrangement for us, as it had and does for so many people who, once there, just don't want to leave. The state was growing so fast that there were good opportunities, so there was little reason to have to pack up. Although top jobs in my field usually involved headquarter operations in New York, Chicago, or Washington, all wonderful places, they weren't a match for what we had in San Francisco. One small example will demonstrate the pull of the state for us. We lived just south of San Francisco, in year-round sunshine, thirty minutes from the spectacular Pacific Coast, and for four or five months of the year this family of skiers would in three hours be into some of the best snow in the world.

I had to be in New York and Chicago a good bit, at least a trip a month. Particularly in winter, I would leave the snow or sleet, or at least the cold, and as the plane returned to California, I'd see the sun sparkling on the Bay and be reminded how lucky we were. As I struggled with the dual considerations of what I wanted to do and where we wanted to live, I hoped the two would coincide right there in the Golden State.

Another test helped focus my thinking and direction. Without participating in any of the preliminaries, I was asked to be one of the finalists for the American or National Personnel Association, which would have paid a strikingly higher salary and probably been somewhat less chaotic, but because it wasn't what I thought of as a cause, my heart just didn't go out to it. In subsequent years I received other approaches from appealing trade associations and professional societies, and while I respected them greatly and worked closely with many of their first rate directors, often through the American Society of Association Executives, the jobs did not fit the niche I was in and wanted.

Several people kindly suggested that I stay put in my job because I would have a good shot at AHA's national directorship perhaps three or four years hence. Although I thought there was a good chance I would be in the mix, I didn't think an offer was likely. Relationships had improved greatly since the early struggles to give California its proper service and recognition, and I had been a regular part of national task forces and committees, but some people, including Rome Betts, felt I had pushed too hard and had demonstrated a lack of teamwork. From their viewpoint they were right, but from mine the uncharacteristic heavy hand had been necessary. In any case, I would probably pay the price and should not count on any such long shot.

A very different form of stimulating opportunity that might help prepare me for the future was suggested by a CHA board member who was head of personnel for United Airlines. He had attended, and thought I would enjoy and profit from, the Advanced Management Program at the Harvard Business School. He wasn't sure if they considered nonbusiness people, although he knew they welcomed military and other government personnel, and he agreed to explore it. He reported back that they had not at that stage considered the nonprofit sector but seemed very interested in branching out. At that point the people in CHA leadership were wary of a three-month absence, but when we considered how the vacuum could be filled with a sharing of responsibilities among the senior staff, whom they regarded highly, they approved the idea. But they didn't feel that it was an expense an association like ours should undertake, and even if they did, they weren't sure the chapters would be very happy about it. I appreciated their approval and although I didn't agree with where they came down on the financial side, I understood it.

I was also pleased that the national organization approved the idea and seemed complimented that AHA might be the first national voluntary agency enrolled. However, it too felt it shouldn't swing the cost, because others in the organization would expect similar treatment and the whole idea was so new it didn't want to establish a precedent. I figured that was the end of it, but my United Airlines sponsor wanted to see if Harvard would provide a scholarship, which he thought would be justified if it helped tap a whole new pool of prospects.

It was while all these explorations and negotiations were playing out that I was approached by a search firm on behalf of the Mental Health Association (MHA), which brings me all the way back to the beginning of this book, which questioned why the Mental Health Association might offer its top job to a person who had no experience in the field and why I might accept when I couldn't even spell schizophrenia. I readily acknowledge that to some it may still seem altogether illogical, but on the other hand, some of you may have begun to see that it was not beyond credulity. At that point MHA lagged far behind other health agencies in fund raising, program impact, and public awareness, and thought it might make sense to hire someone from one of those other agencies.

The MHA search drifted on for about four months. I'll spare you all the twists and turns. Suffice it that many years later I'm inclined to characterize it as colorful, but at the time I wouldn't have. When it began to get serious, I decided I would touch base with some of the top volunteer leadership at AHA. I didn't want to pursue the MHA job if I was in fact a stronger candidate for the top AHA position than I supposed. The reports back were consistent. They contained higher compliments than I expected, which helped soften the other side of the message. Under ordinary circumstances the leaders would have strongly encouraged me to stay because they thought I would by all means be in serious consideration but, though it was a terribly important secret, and needed to remain so for institutional purposes, many of the top leaders had decided that because of long-standing difficulties between the positions of national executive director and medical director, even with different people in the jobs, the only way to solve what they unanimously felt was a serious impediment to future performance and growth was that Rome's successor would have to be a physician. They saw no chance that this solution would be changed. Therefore, I stayed in the running for MHA. I wondered if American Heart would actually hold to the rather unusual step of limiting consideration to physicians, but when the post opened up two or three years later, that was indeed the arrangement.

As to the uncertainties of the Mental Health Association search, I had to prepare for the final stages, including the necessary conditions I would have to require in order to have a chance to succeed in the job. In that regard, and as a courtesy, I went back to my United Airlines personnel expert and explained that even if Harvard came through with a scholarship I would not be able to take it if I undertook new responsibilities. I took advantage of the session to outline some of my reservations and worries about the MHA situation, including the fact that the national president, Mrs. Winthrop Rockefeller, was paying all expenses for the search and chairing it, and it seemed that the search director was having difficulty reading or interpreting what she and therefore the committee wanted. For example, at one point the group had decided they were going to split the executive director and medical director responsibilities, with each reporting to the board. When I turned that down I was yanked from the search, only somehow to be resurrected later. Also I had learned that Mrs. Rockefeller had fired the previous executive director without very much consultation or communication with others.

Having provided the background, I sat back and waited for his sage advice. He looked at me a while, then out the window for a while, and back at me. After even further pause, he imparted his best professional opinion: "Brian, hold on to your balls."

« 4 »

HERDING CATS, TIGER SIZE

Mental Health Association—National Director
1966–1971

From February into April of 1966, the Mental Health Association (MHA) search stuttered and sputtered and I seemed to be dealing with a "good cop, bad cop" team at the search firm. The principal, Mr. Kornfeld, seemed to be encouraging, or at least eager to keep me on the hook, but his associate, Mr. Borrus, kept trying to negotiate downward. For example, he said I would be a shoe-in if I would agree to become assistant or deputy executive director under a physician head, and when I turned that down he came back with the prospect of being co-director with a doctor. I had already told Kornfeld I wouldn't accept that arrangement, but later both asked if I would at least meet with the search committee to explain my reservations. I felt it better to not seem to negotiate what was nonnegotiable. A few days later Kornfeld told me the matter had been settled in my favor, and I agreed to meet with the search committee in Chicago.

The day before the session I learned that there would be four finalists, two insiders and two outsiders. The insiders were the medical director and the head of the very best state division, who looked like formidable opposition except I had heard indirectly that he faced even more of the same kind of out-of-favor problem I experienced at the American Heart Association (AHA). He was also in the even tougher spot of being routinely disdainful of any of the other state divisions and local chapters that didn't embrace wholly the mental illness side of the mental health–mental illness spectrum. He was a finalist because he was one of the most effective community organizers in the business. The medical director was superbly credentialed in psychiatry, had been at the national office for about three years, and was serving as interim director. The other outsider was also a distinguished psychiatrist with good organizing experience in professional societies.

It was interesting and worrisome that Kornfeld had made such a point of MHA wanting someone who had succeeded as an organizer in a setting like AHA and yet there were two physicians in the finals. That, coupled with the fact that they had tried so hard to get me to take the number two position under a doctor or at least share the leadership, was a worrisome contradiction.

By the time I got to Chicago, the outside doctor had withdrawn. It was an all-day event and I was interviewed first, finishing up about 10:30 A.M. After that I waited in my room until about 4:00 P.M., without any word from below. It didn't help my frame of mind that the baseball game I was watching for diversion was tied in the tenth. We were all in extra innings.

When they finally called me in I noticed that Jeanette Rockefeller and Leo Kornfeld were not present, but others stood and applauded and made very clear that I had been selected. With that announcement, several others began to leave, but when I asked the fellow who had made the formal announcement if my primary considerations had been met, the room froze, including those in mid step out the door. Bernie Gordon, who, in addition to being on both the executive and search committees, was legal counsel, stammered something like, "Not quite," but rushed on to assure me that it would all work out. He tried to put it in the context of what was best for the organization and added that the medical director would be responsible for the program functions but that I would have total say about the management and fund-raising ones, and that both of us would report to the board.

Somehow I managed not to seem angry, just surprised and disappointed. I explained that perhaps those present had not been aware of my previous openness and definiteness about the executive authority I required to even consider the job, and went on to thank them for their kind offer but that it was necessary to decline. Others came forward asking me not to be hasty and assuring me that down the line things would work out fine. Once again I simply thanked them for their encouragement but said it was not what I could consider. Sometimes when I look back I think I should have just withdrawn literally, because Bernie then said that if that was my absolute condition he was authorized to approve it. Now I was doubly surprised and doubly distressed by the group's behavior, but the remaining people rallied around with new congratulations and praise for sticking to my guns. Later one of them said prophetically that I probably hadn't heard the end of it.

As quickly as possible I got Bernie aside to tell him that in light of past experience and the way the current negotiations had been handled, I would not officially accept until the arrangements were put forward as a contract and signed by Mrs. Rockefeller. He thought this was not a good idea, and when I pressed him it was obvious he didn't think she would go along. All the more, I held to my condition and he knew I meant it.

I was not happy and distinctly off balance when I picked up the *New York Times* two days later and saw the announcement of my appointment. I had to do a lot of scrambling with my California people and called both Bernie and Jeanette Rockefeller to repeat my conditions and express my regrets that the announcement had appeared. I didn't reach Mrs. Rockefeller, but Bernie, anticipating my call, had talked to her, and although she was very unhappy that he had not been able to conclude the arrangements satisfactorily, she would not contradict the committee's decision to go with the last-ditch alternative and would "sign the damn contract." She did, I accepted, and did indeed hang on to my you-know-whats!

The next thing I heard was that Mrs. Rockefeller had promoted the fund-raising director and added public relations to his portfolio. I called and this time reached her and told her that I really needed to have time to take a look at the operation to decide on the individuals I needed and the roles they would play. To my surprise she was conciliatory but said we were about to lose that individual, who she said I would depend on greatly, and asked that I trust her judgment, promising not to interfere with any other executive authority. She went on to assure me that nothing would ever again come between us, and on important matters it never did.

It turned out that what I had going for me, in terms of at least some security far beyond the paper contract, was that the association had had several executive directors over the prior fifteen years, two during Mrs. Rockefeller's period on the board, and she knew what the message would be if a third left, particularly within weeks or months of appointment. Also, although few, if any, would say it directly to her, there were many on the board and in the organization who admired my spunk and knew by then it was based on important personal and organizational principles.

Mrs. R. gave up attending meetings or at least stayed only long enough to fulfill essential obligations. She announced soon after that she would not accept reelection. We saw each other four or five times in the remaining months of her term, and although I heard many reports of her uncomplimentary opinion of me, our get-togethers were cordial.

The organization lost distinct advantages when she dropped out, including substantial financial support, valuable identification with her name, and the loyalty of the many friends she had made in the several years she was involved. On the other hand, the association was not in good shape, and solutions required broadly shared leadership and responsibility, impossible to address with her in the lead.

The Mental Health Association was in many ways like AHA. Both were organized to pursue research, education, and services for their causes and the people affected. MHA was less organized into a series of scientific councils but nevertheless was closely linked to scientific advisors and to professional bodies such as the American Psychiatric Association and American Psychological Association.

The greatest differences were in size and scope, similar to my leap from Maryland to California, but a lot more so. The forces and the sheer breadth of a coast-to-coast operation looked impossible to master or even keep track of. Also, we had a lot less money and staff to cover all the bases.

Before arriving in New York I did a lot of reading and learning about the association and about mental health and mental illness. I also did a great deal of talking with people, including those involved in the California division and San Francisco chapter and with Earl Warren, Jr., of Sacramento, a current member of the national executive committee and board. In the course of all that orientation and on the basis of earlier experience, I resolved that I must never try to sound or act like a health professional. The leaders had hired me because they wanted a manager and leader of causes, and I would undercut all of that if I crossed the line into mental health expert. I was interested in learning about the definitions and characteristics of diagnoses such as depression and schizophrenia, but I knew I shouldn't ever try to act like a clinician.

Along the way I did learn some interesting things. For example, Jack Ewalt, who I think was Commissioner of Mental Health in Massachusetts at that time, explained that the difference between eccentricity and mental illness was described in a story about a man who puts on top hat and tails to mow his lawn, and therefore is, according to Jack, decidedly eccentric, but if the man crosses the fence and insists that his neighbor also mow his lawn in top hat and tails, he's definitely mentally ill. I also learned that it's healthy to be at least a little bit paranoid because someone is often out to get you. Lastly, a psychoanalyst described that the distinction between genius and madness is that the genius is like a person who can watch six different reels of film at the same time and see the interrelationships among them. Most people go mad trying to absorb all the different sounds and messages simultaneously, and if we add just a few more films even the genius will fold.

There you have the extent of my professional know-how. Now, back to my appropriate layman's role.

Other than being at hand July 1, I can't say I was ready. Almost immediately I attended the annual Staff Institute, which brought together about a hundred of the organization's division and chapter executives. It was the perfect opportunity to get to know people and issues. I was impressed by their professionalism and how much they went out of the way to make this outsider welcome. It was a good beginning.

In addition, I began to spend time with Joe Brown, the Indiana Division head, who had been the other inside finalist, with other local leaders, and with officers, including regional vice-presidents and past presidents of the national organization. And I traveled, oh Lord, how I traveled. I needed to show the flag in so many places, I felt I had been shot into space and had months to go before reentry. I did stay around often and long enough to be sure that the national office was improving, including becoming more attuned to the West Coast, such as keeping the phones open until at least 7:00 P.M.

For the first several months, and a good bit beyond, I was in a miles-high learning curve and continued to feel I was far from ready to make decisions and undertake actions I knew were expected. My compromise was to draft preliminary impressions and conclusions and then test them with scores of people, including the executive committee, staff council leaders, and a good sampling of board members, division and chapter leaders, and others. Then I'd revise my ideas and check again to be sure I was getting closer.

In that way I initially developed a "Determination of the Association's Strengths, Weaknesses, and Problems," which was ready for the executive committee's initial consideration as early as September 9, two months after starting. On the basis of the committee's initial review I redid the report for fuller consideration in October.

Simultaneously, I was developing "General Ground Rules for Reorganization: Identification of the Basic Functions of the National Staff, and Determination of Principles of Operation for the National Office." That report provided standards by which the value of any changes could be judged. This went to the executive committee in October and to the board in November, along with the more detailed plan for reorganization of the national staff. With the board's approval, implementation was begun. It was all too hurried but all too necessary.

In brief, the "diagnosis" revealed the magnitude of the organization's strengths and the seriousness of its problems. I indicated:

> There's no question that the organization is making a contribution and has
> almost endless potential. There's also no question that the organization has

very deep seated problems and is in real trouble. The financial crises faced by many divisions and chapters and the hard-crusted indifference and antagonism which exists among levels of the organization are examples of such problems but by turning all possible resources of the Association to the development of strong divisions and chapters, we can greatly increase the Association's depth of volunteer participation at the local level, and only through such volunteer interest and effort will the Association realize its potential impact at all levels and in all program areas.

Specific proposals included identification of inadequate funding of the total association as the most pressing problem and the achievement of financial development as our most immediate and pressing goal; identification of social action as the basic means by which the Mental Health Association achieves its immediate program objectives; and elevation of the personnel recruitment and training responsibilities in the National Office.

The recommended staff structure followed the successful pattern I had developed in Maryland and California but of course was a good deal more complicated. Essentially I dissolved all departments and created five associate directorships, with each responsible for a section of the country and for coordination of one of five specialties: legislation and public policy; personnel and training; financial development; public information; and program services.

Less than six months into the job and with full authority, I began to make the related staff changes including many terminations. The terminations were excruciating but bearable because I had faith that the new team would prove itself. We kept many key people, but most had to accept changed job descriptions, including more field service. These included very popular people like Don Kenefick, medical director, who became associate director for program and the West Coast; Jane Thomas would work with Don and back him up in the West; Mike Freeland, former director of Childhood Mental Illness, to be associate director for legislation and public policy and for the Midwest; Ruth Sensbach, formerly assistant to the executive director, as the new director of general services; and Dick Hunter of our Philadelphia chapter to lead personnel and training and the East Coast.

From the outside I added Doug Waterstreet and Ruth Morse from my California staff and Paul Archambault, executive director of the Florida Heart Association, as associate director for public information and the Southern region. We still had other important slots to fill, but essentially we were up and running by March. Fortunately, there were already some vacancies and other persons experiencing uncertainty had moved on.

The last step in immediate planning involved the development of what I called the "Administrative Agenda of Major Priorities and Projects," which included seventy-four activities and assignments in the categories of *administration,* such as a talent search to identify national, state and local volunteer talent for the national board, councils and committees, and the national consultation program; *organization,* such as an inventory of divisions to clearly identify the current structure, financing, activities, aspirations, and needs of each division in order to better plan national services and to determine nationwide priorities; *financial development,* such as to organize and execute a national financial development plan for national assistance to divisions and chapters; *public relations* and *public information,* for example, to develop and begin to execute an annual public information plan including details of work with national media; and lastly, *program and research,* such as to initiate a study of the most effective relative roles for the three levels of the organization.

Simultaneous with those initiatives, we had to deal immediately with such obligations and opportunities as a new federal Joint Commission on Mental Health of Children, and assistance to the government in developing plans and adequate budgets for the National Institute of Mental Health, including higher levels of research investment. We also moved quickly in our communications effort, both internally and externally. On the inside we were able to improve and increase our communications within the association so that people felt in the know and much more part of the family. We already had a record of good education materials, which chapters found particularly helpful in responding to requests for information about childhood mental illnesses, depression, schizophrenia, alcoholism, and more. Some of the same was true for our services to newspapers, magazines, and other media.

We were fortunate that there were several new reports underway in our Joint Information Service (JIS), a study and information service operated jointly with the American Psychiatric Association. The studies included up-to-date information on state hospitals, child development clinics, early creation of community mental health centers, general hospital psychiatric units, health insurance for mental illness, and other topics that many of our chapters needed to know about to plan, develop, and evaluate local services. Similarly our 50-year-old journal, *Mental Hygiene,* was retooled and made more appealing to lay leaders without compromising the primary focus on professionals.

If I were going to skip more of this period I wish it could be some of the early crises, but you'd know it could not have been smooth going and I'm afraid this too is just a sampling.

Within my first months, a particularly helpful and personable board member, an executive with a large pharmaceutical company that supported several of our projects, called to say he had been promoted and had to leave us but the company had already selected a good successor. I hesitated and tried to think fast. At its simplest, it was essential for the nominating committee to have a major say about his successor. It also jumped out at me that our relationship with this or any other pharmaceutical company had to be at arm's length. With prescription medicines becoming so much a part of the treatment of mental illness, the conflict was glaring. I tried to leave it with our retiring board member that I was certain the nominating committee would give careful consideration to the company's recommendation but that we would have to go through the normal steps. My supposed new friend lashed out at me as a brash naive newcomer who didn't seem to realize who he and the company were. He ended by saying he would call Mrs. Rockefeller and get it settled. By then we had identified Earl Warren, Jr., as the new incoming president, and Earl agreed to call Mrs. R. to ask that this be left in his hands and she agreed. He referred it to the nominating committee, called our mutual friend and said that was the way it had to be, and accepted the warnings of future regret. In the face of our mutual reservations and the nominating committee's concerns, the nomination did not come forward. The money didn't dry up immediately, but it dwindled, with neither side trying to save it.

There was a far more upsetting matter, involving the American Psychiatric Association (APA) request that we support it in difficulties it was facing with proposed inclusion of autism in its classification of psychiatric disorders. I received a call from APA's executive/medical director, who said almost casually that it would help the group's case if MHA would go along, and I had the impression he wanted a quick "of course" and be done with it. When I said I would certainly look into it and get back to him, he seemed quite annoyed, which caused me to be wary. I held my ground and immediately went down the hall to talk to our director of childhood mental illness, who had been executive director of the National Organization for Mentally Ill Children (NOMIC), which had merged with MHA a couple of years before. I put the question to Mike Freeland, quite neutrally I thought, only to get my second blast in ten minutes. Mike thought my tone suggested I was going along with APA and was aghast. It was already a bad day. In my newness I had not yet learned that one of the principal battles NOMIC had been fighting from their start was to be sure that autism was *not* labeled or considered a psychiatric illness. When Mike calmed down and realized that I was interested in being properly oriented, he explained that psychiatrists, and particularly psychoanalysts, tended to believe that the parents, especially the mother of an autistic child, had somehow caused this frightful condition and therefore it was usually she who needed analysis. Autism, as you may know, is often identified with a child who cannot bear external contacts or stimulation and often just rolls into a catatonic ball.

I had already visited the homes of two of the leaders of NOMIC now on the MHA board and had seen their seriously impaired autistic children in contrast to their other children who were obviously healthy, impressive, and outgoing. Thus I was quickly sympathetic to Mike's briefing and knew that we should not go along with APA. That stance was likely to be such an affront to APA that it could cause a breech in a relationship I knew was important to our board and particularly to our Professional Advisory Council. It quickly got even trickier because I was warned that the advisory group would automatically go along with APA.

One of my supposed attractions in the MHA search was my orientation to consumers and citizens, which began, as you may remember, with the parents of the developmentally disabled children in the school clinic in Worcester. Thus I was instinctively inclined toward the NOMIC stance but had to find my way through the thicket of my new setting.

Fortunately Earl, by then president, demonstrated his very savvy ways. We decided that we would have to take the matter to the Professional Advisory council but we would alert them to the sensitivity of the matter within our own organization and particularly with our important partners from NOMIC. Anticipating that the council would not back us, we agreed that both positions would be put before the board, which was made up largely of laypersons with a good deal of experience at the state and local levels, where the association was more oriented to consumers and the public.

The board members didn't go as far as I expected, but in retrospect it was probably best. They agreed not to take a position on APA's request but did not take the additional step requested by our NOMIC people that we take a vigorous and public position that autism had nothing to do with psychiatry. So one side was furious with me and the other side just angry.

In my follow-up conversations with both sides, I learned something that did not change my mind but helped explain why there were psychiatric considerations. The distinction, important to my later understanding of mental illness, is that the underlying cause of autism seemed certain to have a physiologic or neurologic underpinning but that as a result of how others treated those who behaved so differently, such children developed anxieties, angers, and other behaviors that were indeed related to psychiatry and psychology. I know that sounds as though I'm crossing the line into professional territory but in some cases, such as this, it was essential to figure out as much as I could to be sure that our programs and advocacy reflected the scientific realities.

We lost several members of the Professional Advisory Council, but with the board's concurrence we broadened the group, including even Seymour Kety, who had recently been named head of the psychiatry department at Johns Hopkins, despite the fact that he was a physiologist, a move that distressed psychiatrists in general and caused apoplexy among the psychoanalysts.

Although there were a lot of fences to mend in our ranks, the long-term effect was to move us back toward the roots of the organization, begun by a layman, Clifford Beers, who in 1908 had written the book *A Mind That Found Itself*. We were prepared to provide greater attention to the consumer and some greater caution about being overly identified with or influenced by professionals, pharmaceutical firms, and others whom we respected but whom we did not want to allow undo influence.

The board seemed pleased and even proud to be showing this degree of independence, although some were concerned we might lose our long standing good relationship with APA. Earl and I worried too, and worked hard to continue the relationship without subordination.

There were some early problems also with our relationship to our own Research Foundation, which was fairly autonomous even to the point of having the right to select its own board members. They were understandably upset that we were not providing more money, and there was the awkward, sometimes compromising fact that their part-time research director was our full-time medical director who by now had even taken on some field service responsibilities.

After our difficulties with the Professional Advisory Council, which had some overlapping membership with the Research Foundation, entertaining any tinkering on our part with the existing structure was viewed as serious incursion. Despite those stresses, it was fundamentally and operationally necessary to give the MHA Board responsibility to appoint the foundation's trustees. There was no suggestion that we would compromise their final say on all grants, but the governing policies would have to be approved by our board and the director of the foundation would have to report to the MHA executive director. With Don Kenefick's cooperation and his comfort that his situation would be clearer under this new arrangement, the changes were made and worked well.

The early crises certainly included abundant evidence of the ongoing horror of arbitrary determination of dues by many divisions and chapters. Similarly, there was growing awareness of how differently board members, divisions, and chapters viewed what we should be doing and even what their and our missions should be. Heading the list was whether the association should be dealing primarily with mental illness or mental health and within those two, what was most important to address. Some were interested only in mental illness, including the hospitalized mentally ill, schizophrenia, or depression, and others were concerned only about mental health, such as school health education, child guidance clinics, or abstinence from alcohol. On and on it went. We were hardly in lock step and at times seemed not even to be moving in the same direction.

In addition to such large crises, there were all the smaller upsets that seemed to require my presence everywhere. In ordinary times these might not have required immediate intervention, but people knew I wanted to demonstrate my concern and ability to help and they were more than willing to test me.

One thing I learned in all of this is that there are indeed only twenty-four hours in a day and seven days in a week. For example, when I was in New York, I tried getting up earlier and earlier to be at the office to get caught up and be available. For a while I was getting the 4:35 A.M. train from Long Island to be in the office a little after 5:00, but I learned that although I'm an early riser there was a limit to how early I could be alert. I found I made more mistakes before 7:00 or 7:30 than I could correct all day.

There was a larger personal crisis that hovered over me after about eighteen months into the job and finally swept over me like an avalanche. I was on the train coming home one evening and with no immediate crisis or worry on my mind and with no sign, not even a hint of being close to the edge, I suddenly began to cry uncontrollably. It wasn't just weeping, it was loud guttural "oh my God" sobbing as though I had just been told that Ann or one of the children had been killed. It was so engulfing that people on the train tried to calm and console me, but I couldn't talk or communicate except to wave off the idea to have the conductor call for an ambulance to meet the train at the next stop. By that time I could tell everyone thought I had totally flipped and needed restraint and care.

With help, I managed to get off at my stop, still sobbing, but able to walk and wave off help except to get down the steep steps. With the train gone, I sat on a bench outside the Manhasset station and gradually the crying subsided. In the very cold air, I began to get a hold on myself and to start to figure out what in the world had happened. There was no tracing it to anything that had happened that day or recently, and I had never before experienced anything even approaching it.

By the time I had walked the half mile home, the brisk air helped steady and quiet me and my more immediate concern was that I couldn't hide my condition from Ann and the children. She knew instantly that something was very wrong. Leaving the children to eat alone, we went to our bedroom and talked and worried together. By then I began to realize that in the absence of any other sign of physical or mental breakdown and with my quick recovery, that it must have been a pretty shrill alarm signal that I was emotionally exhausted to the danger point. Ann agreed and

ing which they talked about their common concerns and impressions of their leadership experiences. To a person they regretted not having prior experience as managers and each thought this reduced her credibility and effectiveness, particularly at a time when women in the executive ranks seemed to be what counted.

Up to that point in the discussion I had been a listener, but on this point I interjected that in the performance experience of all five there was more management and leadership preparation and performance than in any group of people I had ever known. They were schooled and skilled in finance, planning, communications, and all the other organization-building skills, and they were successful leaders of far more complex institutions than almost any women in business. I added that because they were successful *volunteer* leaders they could range over a broad spectrum of societal needs and goals, which gave them even more scope and accomplishment and greater significance and recognition than the role models they had in mind.

As we talked about specific skills of managers and leaders, they began to recognize for the first time that their leadership profiles were far more complete than they had given themselves credit for. It was a good moment.

Also during this period, we, like many national organizations were forming or being forced to form all kinds of caucuses or interest groups, dealing with minorities, gays, lesbians, big cities, rural areas, and other important groupings. In our case we also had caucuses for subject areas, such as childhood mental illness, depression, rehabilitation, and child abuse. These usually led to resolutions mandating the establishment of a national department or at least a program director position relating to the area of special interest with progress reports back to the annual assembly.

Each of these demands for new or expanded priorities represented a crisis, including a crisis of confidence when a year later we had to acknowledge little progress and the sponsoring divisions would threaten to withhold dues "until you deal with our priority."

Although each of these mandates was tough to deal with, by far the hardest was a resolution that required us to identify "racism as America's number one mental health problem [and] that all appropriate national resources including dollars and staff be assigned accordingly." The board, which was responsible to review all resolutions and provide a recommendation for the assembly's action, felt that the proposal was too sweeping, and directed that a paper be developed to acknowledge that racism was certainly a serious mental health issue but that the organization could not turn away from its history and mission and abruptly drop or greatly reduce attention to the mental illnesses that so many of our units then emphasized, such as schizophrenia.

When the resolution, even with the board's recommendation, hit the field, the reactions bordered on violent, with all the proponents for other priorities pointing out what a devastating impact it would have on them. On no issue did I ever get so many angry calls, most sharply critical of our letting the resolution even get that far. My worry was that the issue might get so soundly criticized and defeated that it would trigger charges of institutional racism.

Perhaps it was fear of that, but more likely it was that people would not allow themselves to be identified with opposition to the resolution, but whatever, the resolution essentially passed. Hundreds of those who told me I should never have let it happen supported it. Even most board members and some officers voted "aye."

What happened then was equally bizarre, because in essence, little happened. Even our Minorities' Caucus didn't expect it would pass and had no idea what to do about it. The divisions and chapters, so solidly on the approval side, didn't intend to desert the people and programs already supported, and the national leadership was already overwhelmed with the scores of sweeping mandates previously approved and impossible to implement.

Another year the annual meeting faced three resolutions, each calling for the establishment of a national department or program directorship, in childhood mental illness, alcoholism, and prevention. The board's recommendation was to explain that until financial resources improved it was not possible to fulfill the mandates and that all three should be tabled or rejected.

All three passed, and with the support of the current president who had taken the lead in the board meeting to recommend that they be turned down or at best tabled. There was enormous celebration on the floor that these important areas would become so much more important in the national operation, and almost despondency for me, knowing that we couldn't begin to fulfill those promises and that the burden would rest with me to either produce or face the music a year hence.

Later that day I asked the president how he could possibly support all three resolutions and he said he didn't want to disappoint so many delegates. When I asked him how we could possibly fulfill the expectations, he stunned me by replying, "Brian, that's what we pay you for." It was a black day for me, and very shortly I went off on a solitary "retreat" to decide if I could or should try to keep at it.

For three straight days I struggled to identify and analyze the things that were terribly wrong in the association and what our reliable assets were to confront these problems or at least to work around those that were almost surely insoluble.

Among our most important pluses were impressive program activities that were growing and spreading. The list I compiled covered many pages, and when I studied it (and even weighed the relative significance of each) I was more than impressed, I was elated. I knew there would be some people all over the organization who would emphasize that this one or that one shouldn't count because it focused only on mental health or mental illness (or vice versa) or dealt with bipolar depression, which was a far less serious condition than schizophrenia (or vice versa), but my reaction at that moment, and for the rest of my service, was to accept that we were one umbrella of very different priorities, but whatever we favored there were exciting and important things going on in each of the areas of interest, and the composite of all of these impressive efforts was rewarding to the point of thrilling.

I'll limit myself to a paragraph of the examples of focus and impact: depression; schizophrenia; autism; attention disorders; racism; alcoholism and other addictions; child abuse; emotional development of youth; parenting skills; hospitalized mentally ill; education of professionals; danger signs of mental illness; insurance coverage; rehabilitation; halfway houses and group homes; sheltered employment; deinstitutionalization; suicide prevention; research; recognition for "at-risk" periods such as death of a spouse; patient education; education of the media; education of the public; information and referral; reduction of stigma; dealing with tensions; anger management; patient's rights; and on and on and on.

Some of our 650 chapters concentrated on only one or a few of those activities. Others tried to tackle several, but none of our units could do it all, although we and often their peers seemed sometimes to suggest that each activity was an essential responsibility. As I analyzed it, I figured that about one third of our local chapters, and perhaps one half of our state divisions, were performing well for what was realistically possible at that stage. Most of the chapters were too small to expect very much of, but we didn't have time or resources to deal with that problem and, at a period when rural legislators dominated most state legislatures, it was helpful to have those small chapters to call on when needed.

We may have been all over the place, programmatically and geographically, but we were at least all over the place and had enough common interests and identification to be a national force. That we were organized nationwide and had a structure that provided opportunities for communication provided at least some cohesion. There were a national assembly, board, office, executive director, and staff, and there were annual and regional meetings, regular communication of new developments and special activities from the field, performance awards, training sessions, and mutual dependence for nationwide education and advocacy efforts. Almost all of our units even had the word "mental" in their names, and although many were far from just the Mental Health Association, there was at least a commonality in our identification. As I watched other national organizations struggle to get anywhere close to where we were in nationwide organization and identity, I realized we were better off than our problems and frustrations led us to believe.

The *degree* of our problems and frustrations was a great source of our difficulties. The field was so vast and the human and social toll so agonizingly large that all of us, at every level, were constantly upset that we couldn't get our act together for what was really needed. That led to blame and anger that reduced us in performance and behavior, bordering on dysfunctional.

A core contradiction between what we expected of ourselves and what we could actually do was the persistent overexpectation of what the national level should do in furtherance of all the different program categories such as suicide, autism, racism, and so much more, and all the different support functions such as training, public relations, fund raising, and more. There were a great many specific obstacles that needed to be sorted out and addressed, several of which were intertwined:

> *The awful schism* between divisions and chapters in at least half of the states contributed to breakdowns in the financial support policies to the point that states had so little money they were considered inept. This just compounded the problem of loss of respect from the chapters, further cuts of support from them, and further cuts of the national operation because our support came from divisions.

> *The loss of support* for the national office meant that the primary investment level of the organization had little money to devote to building for greater achievement.

> *Chapters* were becoming increasingly attracted to and dependent on government contracts and grants that would not allow financial support for divisions or the national level and that caused an increasing number of chapters to be less inclined to engage in advocacy and empowering efforts.

> *A little more than half* of our local units were a part of the United Way, where it was not possible to change things quickly. When most of those chapters had joined it was at a very low level, and most of our groups had not been able to match the increases of more popu-

lar agencies. Also, most United Way groups limited or prohibited their money being sent outside the community. Even where this was not United Way policy, many of our chapters preferred to interpret it that way.

On balance most of our local chapter execs were program oriented and reluctant or even disdainful about larger commitment to financial development.

Most of our solutions to deal with these problems had been rejected, including cutting divisions or make them field offices of the national organization; getting out of United Way altogether; focusing all units of the organization on the same basic programs and goals; and disaffiliating all divisions after a certain period of financial non-compliance and concentrating on the remaining divisions and chapters that were in compliance. But none of these was possible. The National Assembly and the board were controlled by the state divisions, and it was not in the cards to make such fundamental changes. The organization wanted to be pulling together and surging ahead. The time was right for our cause, but the organizational strictures and wildly different programmatic commitments were just too unyielding. All that seemed possible was to accelerate the positive forces and try to minimize the negative ones and settle for modest progress.

I had gone into the retreat prepared for the negatives to win out so handily that I would have to decide to withdraw and thus become the latest of five executive directors in fifteen years to be defeated. By the end of my review I knew more about the towering obstacles than before, but I also saw that the assets were impressive enough to be at least a match. Although it was discouragingly clear that major breakthroughs were unlikely and that the best one could hope for was more of the two steps forward and one backward that we had already been experiencing, I concluded that if I could live with that and not be brought down by fairly regular defeats and criticism, the results could still represent important progress for a cause that needed all the hope it could garner. I decided to stick it out, but with quite a different outlook, including:

No longer being intent on major turnarounds.

Greater focus on helping the organization to understand the same realities that I was coming to accept.

Fuller understanding and tolerance of criticism and controversy.

Making the most of what we could accomplish together.

Concentration of the national operation on those things that would make the greatest difference in the development and impact of the whole organization without being thrown off course.

Being prepared to step aside if things didn't keep getting at least marginally better, and quietly hoping that down the line we could achieve far greater impact.

It was good for my own mental health that I stopped worrying that we couldn't take each idea and program to national scale or rollout. At the next annual meeting I laid out the absurdity of resolutions that required us to do what we couldn't do, in large part because chapters and divisions paid on average only one-third of what they had voted to provide us. I achieved passage of a resolution that in the future any resolution mandating program expansion at the national level had to provide a realistic price tag and identify sources of funding. That quickly reduced resolutions by at least half, and almost all of those that were submitted got shot down by delegates who saw that the required funding would come out of their priorities. We usually advised against resolutions that required the national operation to raise the money, but if they passed, the delegates were advised that such approved resolutions would be put on the waiting list behind all previous approvals until the money was provided.

People cried "foul," but we responded that passing resolutions hopelessly beyond our means or reach was not fair play either, and with most of our affiliates not paying fair share dues, that was the greater foul.

At a subsequent annual meeting we were even able to pass a resolution calling for every unit of the organization to use the common name, Mental Health Association, such as Mental Health Association in Indiana or Mental Health Association of Fulton County. It took a while to take hold, but it was a symbolic and practical step in the direction of unity.

Not long after, there was a different kind of resolution, this one calling for the national office to be relocated, supposedly closer to the middle of the country. Somehow the resolution got around the stipulation of where the money would come from, but when the dust settled we began to determine where, not if, we should go.

It was never dull.

« 5 »

SURVIVAL, SUCCESSES, AND ENOUGH

Mental Health Association—National Director
1971–1978

The committee on the national office location completed its work in early 1970, and Washington, D.C., was the choice. We knew the decision would not sit well with some affiliates that had sponsored the resolution for a move out of New York, because they assumed we'd be going to the Midwest. However, the committee, including representatives of some sponsoring divisions, voted unanimously that it should be Washington, where we would be in a better position to have influence on national policies and programs and where a good many related national agencies already were located.

In June 1971, what was left of the national staff set off for Washington in cars, trains, planes, and buses, with about a dozen moving vans following with our personal and office belongings. Our own family now traveled with a caboose in the form of three-year-old Matthew, born twelve years after Tracey, who enjoyed the excitement much more than the rest of us, particularly living in a hotel for five days, complete with pool and room service, while our lost van was located.

Less than half the professional staff decided to come along and only Max Meyerson and Bob Carter from the support staff. Thanks to the two of them, at least our warehouse, mail, and shipping services were in veteran hands. For the rest, we didn't have a single secretary or clerk who knew anything about MHA, including our lists and files and all the other rudiments of internal patterns and style. Fortunately, Ruth Sensbach, who for personal reasons had decided to stay in New York and had been director of general services, agreed on a three-month assignment to provide orientation and training to help the new people and systems become reasonably operative.

In connection with the move, we not only lost Ruth but other long-term contributors and stars like Don Kenefick and Mike Freeland and even some of the terribly important newer members of the New York team like Paul Archambault. Although they were all hard to replace, we were able to make some promotions and attract other able people from outside the organization. By Labor Day we were functioning pretty well, and by year end we were in good shape.

The transition was more than a physical move. There were important changes in emphasis and staff structure. Perhaps most important was my mind set, and gradually the board's, that we must use our limited resources at the national level to concentrate on those activities we knew were our primary obligations, including the organizational development and basic programs of the divisions and chapters. That meant we would do everything possible not to be diverted from those primary efforts by the whim and demands of every faction in our midst.

A related change that got us, principally me, scorched but at least not skinned was to develop, with extensive field participation to be sure, a listing of the most important basic functions for any division and, in turn, for any chapter. We soon added "next steps" for both levels, which we presumed the middle-sized chapters would already be prepared to provide. Like the California Heart experience from which I drew, the listings also included a great deal of space for unspecified add-ons once the basic and immediate functions were in place. We focused our ongoing attention on the first two levels, but provided plenty of room for units of the organization to exchange information on almost every possible supplementary activity.

We didn't have the resources to add the peer-to-peer evaluation process that had worked so well in California, but at least our initial stages set out the basics, provided plenty of room and encouragement for extras and innovation, and gave us protection from those who wanted us to be all things.

Although it hurt, we also faced up to two other realities that caused us to give up programs that were good talking points but not really as important as they seemed. We had made a big thing of research, including the Research Foundation, and we liked to think of ourselves as similar to American Cancer and American Heart, but our expenditures had never been greater than $250,000 and had shrunk to less than $100,000, with almost all of that coming from one donor-designated bequest. The research advocates inside the organization and others outside, who had regularly and appropriately criticized our poor performance, were now particularly critical and derogatory. We decided to take our lumps and close down our research operation except for targeted ways to make the most of the designated bequest.

Another example of tangible realities and painful decisions involved our long-standing publication *Mental Hygiene*, which might have propped up our image but was overshadowed by several new journals and suffering increasing losses. Although rated highly for visibility by some of our chapters, it was not subscribed to by a great majority of them, so it was discontinued.

With support of the board, I eliminated the position of medical director, while simultaneously revamping the Professional Advisory Council to give it a larger role in advising and guiding us on professional matters. All program functions were put in one department under Dick Hunter, who you may recall had come to us five years earlier from the Philadelphia Chapter. His earliest orientation to our cause came during World War II, when he was a conscientious objector (CO), whose alternate service assignment was working in mental hospitals. He was joined by another CO, Bob Smucker from the Pennsylvania Division, whose specialty was government relations with an emphasis on the kind of advocacy that would be getting much more of the national group's attention. The role was not new, but the degree to which the national operation and the divisions would be emphasizing this way to serve our mission was a major shift.

Our intention was not to become like a law firm providing direct lobbying services, but rather to be the eyes and ears for the total MHA, involving all levels in determining how we wanted to change public laws, policies, and programs, and to be part of a new nationwide legislative network at division and chapter levels to make the case for change with their own U.S. senators and representatives. Some of the best of our divisions had been doing this on statewide issues for years. What had evolved was that volunteers who had served regularly in state hospitals and other mental health facilities and who knew the conditions and needs firsthand became ideal witnesses for telling these sad stories to their state legislators and the media.

Even chapters that were moving toward a direct service role saw the merit of this nationwide network and from their provider experience were also good at telling the stories. They had the additional motivation that some of our work involved getting increased state and national appropriations for research, education, and service, which indirectly increased their likelihood of grants and contracts.

We became much more aggressive on court issues involving the rights of the mentally ill, and even though our advocacy efforts along these lines sometimes got us into trouble, such as when President Nixon tried to cut us down, surviving such challenges and achieving clear-cut license for the legitimacy of our advocacy provided the whole organization with a new sense of unity and power.

A major factor in our effectiveness with advocacy and empowering efforts, especially having the capacity and power to effect change in government, involved our absolute determination that at least at the national level we would never accept government funds. A lot of us had learned that once you go down that road, independence is compromised almost in proportion to the degree of government money in your budget. That's because the government agencies most likely to provide support are almost certainly in the same field of endeavor, such as mental illness, and when push comes to shove it's awfully hard to be an independent critic if it involves the agency that's providing even 20 percent of your budget. We probably would never have gone after Nixon if we had been dependent on the federal government for significant support, and even if we had, our efforts would have been attacked as suspect if part of the money we were trying to free up was for us. I know there are readers who will argue that just because their agency accepts government contracts, grants, and the like doesn't mean the agency can't be an effective advocate. To some extent that's so, and I certainly encourage them to be aggressive, but I submit that on the toughest issues when one needs to put the organization on the line for major reform, it's not likely that the subsidized organizations will be out front.

A brief aside will underscore the importance of a voluntary organization being free to battle with government. Shortly after the Nixon-related court decisions, when I visited my counterpart in Britain, and naturally told her about our stunning victories, she responded not with shared exhilaration, but with alarm. She even asked me to promise not to mention those matters while in her country. At first I thought she was kidding, but it became obvious how deadly serious she was. She explained that more than 90 percent of her national annual budget came via one annual grant from the Ministry of Health, and she was terribly concerned lest there be any interpretation that she had invited me to her country to try to win its mental health community to our "radical and confrontational ways." Because the MHA in the United States was a consumer-oriented advocacy group, I took it for granted that to exercise our independence we had to avoid any reliance on government funding, but she argued that the services her organization provided justified a very different approach to government finances and relationships.

Preoccupation with direct services can also deflect an organization's activities from advocacy and empowering pursuits. For example, several years ago, I served as a member of the board of a large city's Family Service Agency at a time when the community's public welfare system was coming apart. Despite the surrounding chaos, the agency's board meetings remained totally devoted to the direct services of that one agency. Finally, some of the board members were able to persuade the staff and other board members that our knowledge of human needs, community organization, and the welfare system should be used to bring about a humane and sensible public assistance program. The staff and board finally accepted this view, and all were amazed how quickly we exerted influence. We were moving from a preoccupation with service to a use of our knowledge to represent those in the constituency who were public assistance clients.

Even then, however, we were still a giant step from effectively involving public assistance clients in dealing with their own destinies, a pretty basic community organization principle that we community organizers constantly have to relearn. The next step was to form parents' and neighborhood groups and to use these consumers increasingly as the spokespeople for their own views about public assistance. We were beginning to move toward empowerment.

At MHA we beefed up our already good efforts to inform and educate the public about mental illness and mental health. Although we'd lost Paul Archambault, we gained the team of Bill Perry from the civil rights movement and John Thomas of our Columbus, Ohio, chapter, just the right ones to take this function to an even higher level. We realized that to make a dent we needed to develop long-term strategies to deal with specific problems. The first of these programs involved educating the public about depression. This had been an emphasis all along, but surveys made clear that the great majority of the public still had extreme misperceptions about depression. For example, most people thought that once you had it, particularly if you were hospitalized, you were impaired, probably seriously, for the rest of your life. I remember very vividly, for example, that my mother experienced a serious bout of depression for which she was hospitalized, and long after she was discharged there continued to be a silent stigma reaffirmed by such public stipulations that automatically denied her the right to vote or drive an automobile. It was no wonder so many people would not seek treatment.

Bill and John, along with an ideal committee and much help from the Ad Council, developed a multimedia effort to get the facts across to reduce the stigma, encourage care, and improve that care. The latter shouldn't have been a surprise to me for we had found in the Heart Association that educating the public is often an important way to educate the professionals who also see and hear the messages.

About half of our film *Only Human* was devoted to helping people understand that depression is very much like a physical problem for which you seek help and get better. We also emphasized that for most people who seek help, particularly if they seek it early, there is little disruption in their normal routines of work and family. In almost all cases of depression, treatment is by family physicians and rarely involves hospitalization. At about that time, we learned that even where hospitalization was indicated the average stay was less than seven days and was in a community facility, not a distant state hospital. Through every communications angle we pressed these points and backed them up with materials that our national network of chapters could use, including putting their names on most of the releases and reports to give them local credit for being part of the service.

By far our toughest challenge in dealing with public attitudes about depression hit us in mid 1971 when it was reported that Senator Thomas Eagleton of Missouri, who had just been nominated by the Democrats to run as vice-president on the McGovern ticket, had undergone hospitalizations for depression. That alone caused many people to question his qualifications to serve as vice-president, especially to be that heartbeat away from the Presidency, but it was also made known that his treatment included electroconvulsive therapy (ECT), generally referred to as shock treatment, which was unfortunately interpreted by some in the media as causing brain damage. It was not the kind of glaring public attention from which to pursue improved understanding and attitudes about depression.

In our scramble to respond to public curiosity and confusion about both the diagnosis and treatment, we focused on what depression is, what role ECT plays in recovery, and what if any side effects there may be from that treatment. We provided early and full access to many professionals so that accurate information about various diagnoses and treatments was communicated. That alone helped us get by the early assumptions that Eagleton was automatically unsuitable because, as early stories reported, "his brain had been fried!"

Our purpose was to provide both the McGovern and Eagleton camps and especially the public with objective information so that attitudes and behavior toward individuals who had undergone treatment for depression, or any mental illness, would be sensible and fair. There remained a good deal of skepticism about his qualifications to be President, but the public was helped to realize that Eagleton had functioned impressively in the Senate, even to the point that he was a particularly strong nominee for the ticket.

Within a week of the story breaking, the focus shifted to whether Eagleton had responded adequately to requests for full disclosure during interviews leading up to his nomination. That concern plus rapidly deteriorating relationships between the McGovern and Eagleton forces contributed to the decision to drop him.

Given the climate of those times, I'm afraid Eagleton would have been passed over if he had initially revealed his condition or would have been dropped even if relationships had remained cordial after his condition had been reported. However, I also think that this searing episode contributed to the public's awareness that those who have been seriously depressed can return to normal living, heavy responsibilities, and remarkable performance.

A third nationwide emphasis for us was to accelerate the development of community mental health services, including centers for which the National Institute of Mental Health (NIMH) and other federal agencies and most states and some communities were providing funds. Sometimes they were part of broader community health services, but wherever they were located, our object and theirs was to have five basic services available in all communities: inpatient care, partial hospitalization, outpatient services, emergency services, and education programs.

To increase the number of comprehensive centers and to be sure they lived up to their responsibilities provided MHA with healthy teamwork opportunities. We all had important parts of the job. For example, at the national level we prepared several guidelines, trained division and chapter leaders, achieved more adequate federal appropriations, and provided for evaluation of the services. At one point, for example, we did a nationwide test by telephoning a very large sampling of centers, including some in every state, to determine if centers were in fact providing the required twenty-four hour emergency service. Calls went to more than 500 centers on evenings and weekends, and the number and proportion that didn't answer calls at all, or had only a recorded message that didn't relate to emergency care, was staggering. Another substantial group had someone on hand to answer the phone but they were not equipped to deal with emergencies. Less than one third were in compliance. There was a lot of hell raising at all levels, including plans to withdraw or limit funds for breaches of contract. It was consumer activism or at least alert advocacy at its best.

The only down side was that although NIMH made good use of our information, people at NIMH were upset that they were not part of the project. We knew from experience that some of those down the line in NIMH who were responsible for center development would have protected their baby. Not too happily, we also heard from some of our own chapters that were involved with some of the noncomplying centers and in a few cases were running them.

The movement toward community care was part of a larger initiative toward "deinstitutionalization," the rapidly developing trend to down-size patient loads in large state hospitals. In this process, we and others came across thousands of patients who no longer needed hospitalization but who were assumed to be incapable of independent living, without any effort to test the accuracy of that lifetime sentence. In far too many facilities, large numbers of patients were heavily sedated to keep them quiet and easier to care for. We knew that medications were a great boon for certain aspects of care, but they were grossly overused. The responsible officials would say things like, "At least it keeps them happy." As some of these patients moved back into the community, they began to form various patient rights groups to expose what they had been through and to force changes in the systems.

Many of our locals reported that their information and referral programs were flooded by discharged patients who needed a constellation of services, such as medical, dental, subsistence, housing, job training and placement, and much more. Most former patients hadn't the slightest notion how to find any of these services or deal with the maze of them. This led to the development of far more comprehensive referral programs, such as two pioneering efforts, one in Oakland and the other in New Orleans. In Oakland, our Alameda County chapter created a program called "Community Friends," which involved a very large number of volunteers who were carefully trained to understand and work with community agencies. These volunteers were then partnered with newly discharged patients and became "friends," responsible to see that their partners got the services needed and were assisted toward maximum self-reliance.

In New Orleans, our chapter convinced city government officials of the need to establish a place where people could go to learn about services and how to access them. What evolved was an information and service desk right smack in the middle of City Hall, staffed by trained volunteers who were available throughout the day to be helpful to people who didn't know where to turn and who needed to be kept track of so they didn't fall between the cracks. Programs like these spread throughout the association and added considerably to our awareness of how important the information and referral service was for all of us.

Some of the discharged patients told their horror stories in articles and books, and several times we helped put these authors on extensive tours to spread the word. This also gave local chapters a chance to help the authors interact with local media and public officials. We even named some of these former patients as national spokespeople, and many of them won our highest annual award, named after our founder, Clifford Beers, given each year to a former patient who symbolized recovery and willingness to tell his or her story to help others and to advance the cause of humane treatment of patients.

Gradually, the patient's rights movement developed into its own crusade. At first it was difficult for groups to coalesce because of lack of funds and a diversity of messages and strategies, ranging from the quiet voice of the patient as an advisory member of a community mental health center all the way to targeting specific superintendents for legal action. The things patients had in common were their awful experiences, their determination to put the spotlight on how egregiously they had been treated, and a drive to achieve a revolution in care for the mentally ill.

One of my hardest lessons about inclusiveness involved the formation and activities of the National Committee on Patients' Rights. Describing it will certainly demonstrate that the necessary partners of a coalition can sometimes view each other with suspicion and even hostility. To succeed in establishing the principle of patients' rights, achieve articulation of those rights, and foster practice of them, we needed to have at the organizing table the full range of providers and consumers. That included psychiatrists, psychologists, social workers, mental hospital administrators, state mental health commissioners, and an equally varied group of patients, former patients, parents, and other advocates.

The Mental Health Association and I had been asked to call the first exploratory session—not because we were necessarily trusted by all sides, but because we were at least not viewed by anyone as an enemy. It took a great deal of work to get most of these groups to send key representatives to the session (itself a lesson in coalition building), but out of respect for the role I'd been asked to play, or curiosity, or a desire to protect their own interests, all of the parties showed up.

Initially I was curious about the fact that many of the patient-related representatives arrived quite early. I thought they might have misunderstood the starting time, but they said they hadn't, and I figured they just wanted a little advance time to get to know each other and compare strategies. The next arrival, unfortunately, was the key representative of the American Psychiatric Association, who went into the meeting room and immediately stormed into my office with an almost hysterical protest. By the time I got him calmed down, a number of others had arrived, and when we all got to the room, it was obvious we had a problem. Screaming at us from the blackboard was the message "PSYCHIATRY KILLS." Around the room, the accusation was repeated, along with other pungent summaries of what the patients thought of providers and provider groups.

My first thought was to try to meet with the patients as a group and then separately with the providers, but I decided that what needed to be said and worked through required the participation of everyone. I even started with the deliberate but almost absurd banalities of introducing ourselves and indicating what we hoped might come out of the session. Fortunately, that round robin produced a sense of some shared hopes, and by staying within them, we gradually achieved enough trust to widen the path a little. In subsequent sessions we were able to have some mixed subcommittees, carefully chosen to utilize representatives who had credibility with their groups and who were most likely to struggle to produce something constructive. In the end, we produced the Code of Patients' Rights that today is likely to be found visibly displayed in every inpatient mental care facility and most outpatient ones.

After leaving the mental health field, I learned that the group had tried to stay together, at least for periodic sessions or other projects, but it didn't work. Sometime later the National Alliance for the Mentally Ill and other organizations developed, to be as certain as possible that the patient's point of view is never left out.

Although community care was universally applauded, there were several problems in achieving the goal, and sadly, many of the worst of those problems are still with us. The most serious initial problem began when the money did not follow the patients. As the big mental hospitals shrank or closed, the state money that was saved did not flow to communities, which inherited responsibility and were not prepared for it, including the financing. The second problem was that there were few if any facilities at the local level to deal with those who still needed longer term institutional care. Years later, I was told that the largest such facilities evolved not into hospitals but as part of the county or state prisons, where so many of those who now need such care are locked up, usually with little care.

The very large third problem with which societies, particularly democracies, have struggled for so very long involves the civil liberties of patients, including freedom vis-à-vis the state's responsibility to protect the public from those whose behavior may be considered dangerous. The quandary is predicting danger without being so broad that we incarcerate a great many who are not a real threat, including those whose aberrant behavior just makes us uncomfortable.

A very different set of problems that loomed in the 1960s and '70s involved what many people considered bizarre activity that threatened generally assumed distinctions between acceptable and unacceptable behavior. Hippies, runaways, pot smoking, and even long hair were interpreted as signs that essential values were coming apart. Fractured families resulted in terrible pain for everyone. Frantic parents turned to professionals, if only to figure out how to get their kids into counseling or at least to get advice on how to get the kids back on the right track, but the kids fought all the harder to resist conformity.

This was also a period of marked increases in depression and crippling loneliness. People were swamping our information and referral services, reporting a sense of powerlessness or of being overwhelmed. Everywhere there was evidence of a ubiquitous search for new schemes, philosophies, and lifestyles that might help people cope and maybe even be happy. At MHA we were besieged by our own volunteers and the broader public for guidance about coping, tolerance, and values. Society seemed to be in agonizing flux.

In trying to find out what was happening and what could possibly be done to regain some sense of stability, it was helpful to have at hand some of the very best professionals and sage civic leaders, who could put our awful crises into historical perspective, separate out what was truly healthy and unhealthy in what was transpiring, and advise friends and communities how to get a handle on their situations. For example, the larger view helped the association to identify those who recognized the broader context of so many gargantuan shifts in what we had accepted as normal. John Vasconcellos, then a young California legislator, contributed to my understanding of the chaos of those times by describing it as a period of "human revolution." In Vasconcellos's terms, the revolution involved a change in our basic assumptions and a challenge to many of our basic institutions. He said that the encouragement is "not so much that institutions are breaking down, but that people are growing up."

Through the smoke of the revolution, we were beginning to realize that many of these so called iconoclasts had in common a casting off of what they deemed to be repressive shackles, and a common search for a more contemporary alignment of acceptable mores to deal with the vast changes that had been occurring probably since at least World War II.

Among the lessons they were learning were that freedom in the form of vulgar excesses didn't get them very far and that the intelligent use of that freedom was to allow individuals and communities to find the more enlightened discipline they would be willing to accept. They understood that fulfillment relates to a values system and that independence ultimately relates to the worth of our interdependence.

Among the abundant evidence that people were seeking ways to achieve stability and personal growth were the best-seller lists heavy with self-help books, many new groups organizing to help expand the human experience and our coping mechanisms, new religions and old religions reorganizing to find better ways to reach out, and more people experimenting with transcendental meditation, biofeedback, relaxation response, assertiveness training, mind control, reality therapy, psychocybernetics, transactional analysis, Zen, the primal scream, and *I'm OK—You're OK*. Individuals were also turning to altogether new lifestyles, such as a return to nature, communes, voluntary simplicity, and other arrangements in which they might find greater stability, peace, and fulfillment.

The common denominator in all of these experiments seemed to be that people were searching for better ways to identify for themselves what the basic values are, and to build support for their own efforts to live by those values. They would no longer blindly accept the dictums of their forebears without at least checking them against their own experience. This made for painful searching and even sadder confrontation, but that was part of the process of growing. For those who persisted, the reward was a set of values that provided sustenance and direction.

Although each search produced an individual framework of values, the end result was that individuals were finding their own understanding and their own articulation of such basic values as honesty, kindness, loyalty, service, fairness, sacrifice, discipline, peace, and love. The new religions, at least those not representing radical extremes of religious and political control, had in common with Jesus, Moses, Muhammad, and Buddha that whether it's the Bible, Old Testament, Koran, Commandments, Torah, or contemporary equivalents, the makeup of goodness remains basically the same and provides the greatest opportunity for personal fulfillment. In essence, most of the previously lost or alienated souls were discovering in their own experience that the common thread of healthy behavior, ancient and modern, is a natural law of goodness.

Sometimes our job in the MHA was as basic as trying to help people know what mental health was and to figure out where they fit. We said that the reasonable goal toward which we're all struggling is "to feel comfortable about ourselves and to feel right about others," and that the fastest way to join the ranks of average and coping people is to realize that we're probably already there. Normal human behavior covers such an extraordinary range of attitudes and actions that there is ample room for the inadequacies, worries, quirks, and habits of almost all of us.

It was a relief all by itself just to have the burdens of our differentness suddenly shared by so many others, and it was a comfort to know that we are all fragile human beings striving toward a relative degree of stability and hoping for a reasonable amount of happiness. We are making it, coping, having some good days, experiencing some blah days, but coming through all right and striving for better. One of the association's best films had the simple title *Only Human*. It tried to get across the basic message that we are all only human and that we shouldn't punish ourselves trying to be perfect or trying to be something we can't be.

I learned from the famous Menninger brothers, always referred to as Drs. Will and Karl, that the soundest among us are those who fit the fascinating description of stability developed at their renowned Menninger Foundation. Many of their most experienced professionals were asked to describe the positive characteristics of the individuals they considered most mentally healthy. Fourteen staff members put together a list of eighty such people and then attempted to determine why these individuals qualified for such a select circle. Their results were summarized by Dr. Will in a booklet called "The Criteria for Emotional Stability," which identified five basic characteristics:

1. The best adjusted people have multiple sources of gratification. They derive pleasure from their work, family, recreation, friends, volunteer jobs or other activities. They're not dependent on just one part of their lives to provide emotional sustenance. If one part isn't going right, they draw on the others;

2. They respect others as individuals. This respect goes beyond day-to-day courtesy and understanding. It extends to an appreciation of human differentness. These individuals accept and respect that individuals are different in culture, ability and all the other ways we can be different, and they are comfortable with a broad spectrum of differentness. They are not off balance because everyone else does not think or act the same way they do;

3. They are flexible. Particularly important is the fact that they are flexible under stress. At times when they may be terribly disappointed that something hasn't worked out as planned, they back away and are able to give it up or start in a different direction. They are able to step back and look at things imaginatively; they are not in the kind of rut that so many of us get into, which forces us to try to make the impossible work or to force it to work our way;

4. They accept their limitations and assets. This is not to say that these individuals are necessarily totally happy with the way they see themselves, but they do have a realistic impression of both their limitations and assets. This allows them to capitalize on their assets and to deal with or at least accept their liabilities;

5. Not surprisingly, these people are productive and active. These are the kind of individuals who are active in their jobs, their communities and in helping others. They obviously have a zest for living and the capacity to pursue that zest.

Most of us are below the ideal represented by this extraordinary group, but at least we are making a go of it. It's helpful to our egos to realize that a lot of people who seem to parade around as superior beings are probably hiding as many or more of the same worries and insecurities and phobias as we have.

Whenever the subject of mental health was discussed, it was important to acknowledge that there are always some whose minds are in fact shattered and who are looking for much more help than a description of normal behavior, however broad. At any one time there are many people with very real psychic pain who need more than good words to help them turn the corner.

I heard many professional descriptions of those who need help, but they seemed to boil down to the individual whose condition has reached the point where she or he can't function effectively in the normal circles of family, companions, fellow employees, and friends. When the ability to function in those significant surroundings is severely impaired, it's time to get help. Many of our public opinion surveys pointed out that most of us identified mental illness with the individual who has really flipped out and is acting in a belligerent manner. Much more often, those who are in trouble are people who have withdrawn to the point where they are unable to deal with others. For example, the most natural slide into depression results from prolonged and penetrating loneliness.

Perhaps the single most important message to be communicated to those who needed help seemed to be that seeking it made sense and was by no means a sign of weakness. Indeed, the person who knows he or she needs help but will not seek it is the weaker individual, literally and figuratively. It is also helpful to know that even the most stable among us can experience severe problems of coping. The most common form of depression, for instance, is called "reactive depression," and it occurs in otherwise normal, stable people who just can't cope with a sudden change of events or downward turn of fate.

Increasingly, we learned that there are times when all of us are likely to be "at risk" of coming unglued. One of the most common periods of "risk" occurs during times of intense grief. It's natural for anyone to come apart when we lose someone particularly close, but for a very real percentage of us the grief spirals downhill into clinical depression, with which it's hard to deal without professional help. Among the other natural periods of risk are when we're fired, when we retire, or even entering school for the first time. Most people meet those challenges and grow by them, but for many the hurdle is more than they can handle without help.

For those who still worry about what people will think if they seek help, the MHA message was simple: "Go get the help." We liked to add that they'd be in the good company of Abe Lincoln, Winston Churchill,

Buzz Aldrin and Betty Ford. We couldn't guarantee that after treatment they'd be elected President or Prime Minister, but we were pretty sure they'd feel better, and at that point feeling better was most important.

In the mid 1970s a special kind of hero came into our midst in the person of Rosalynn Carter, who had been a board member of the Atlanta and Georgia MHA units and who had chosen mental health as her area of concentration during her husband's governorship. During that period she began to attend our annual meetings as part of the Georgia delegation. She always did her homework and participated, but never with any expectation of special recognition. Georgia was a strong division and she made it more so, including helping quietly and appropriately to be sure that the state of Georgia's own mental health program was substantially strengthened during her husband's term.

She had already been elected to our national board before Jimmy Carter became president. At first we wondered if she would stay with us, but within days of his election, when she was trying frantically to deal with all the new attention and obligations, she nevertheless attended our annual meeting. With cameras, lights, and microphones at every step, she went through just about a normal schedule for delegates, including the assembly, which as usual struggled through lots of resolutions. I noted though that while she was present and the cameras were whirling, the delegate body was all sweetness and light. For this reason alone I was thrilled with her presence. She had to leave a couple of hours before we were finished, and when the spotlights went dark and the room seemed suddenly deadened some unpopular resolutions were revisited and it was business as usual.

For the first year in the White House Rosalynn attended board meetings, but it became obvious that things couldn't be normal. We tried to keep media out but it was hard to do, and she, with some embarrassment, decided it was better for her not to be there routinely. She assured me that when the association needed her she would be available to help in other ways, and she held to that promise.

Right from the start she and the President began to plan for a major Mental Health Commission and soon asked a small group to help put it together, including membership, charge, her role, and other important considerations. John Gardner, whom I had known slightly, chaired that committee. I was pleased to be appointed, except that I soon learned I was expected to be absolutely sure that hundreds of my associates would be named to the commission. Several very good MHA leaders were appointed, but I still went into hiding when the list was announced.

Both the commission and the First Lady's other mental health-related activities provided greater attention, credibility, and momentum to everything we were trying to do. For example, she wanted to do a nationwide tour of mental health programs and welcomed our help in identifying possible sites. John Thomas was our representative to the project and helped produce a film from it. That film and media coverage of the tour provided enormous publicity for good programs, many of which were part of our organization, but far more importantly, the public gained greater understanding of the causes we cared about and ways by which communities could address them.

The President appeared at sessions the First Lady organized at the White House involving Mental Health Association leaders and others. In many other settings they also referred regularly to their joint interest and work in the mental health field. Anyone who's ever been involved in public causes will know that the ultimate boost is to have the First Lady, supported strongly by her husband, so deeply committed and involved. It was thrilling and the benefits lasted a great many years, probably still continuing.

Another break and boon was when Buzz Aldrin joined with us as a very active partner in the understanding and treatment of depression. Shortly after his spectacular trip to the moon with Neil Armstrong and Michael Collins and during the following year of endless celebrations and tours Buzz found himself slipping into black periods, which he thought he'd snap out of but which gradually became so serious that he sought help and was diagnosed with serious depression. From the start he was wonderfully open about the diagnosis, and because of his prominence people were given the opportunity to know that even one of the strongest figures in the country could become depressed. His willingness to seek help and to have it known was a strong boost to one of our most earnest messages. About that time, Buzz wrote his book, *Return to Earth,* which for the most part was about his life as an astronaut but which, as the title implies, dealt a good deal with his life after walking on the moon, including a good deal of attention to his depression and recovery.

For years, the MHA had been using pictures and stories of President Lincoln and Prime Minister Churchill to try to make the case that even the most prominent people could suffer and survive depression, but now we had a contemporary hero with whom living Americans could identify.

Buzz came onto our board, frequently made speeches for chapters and divisions, and came to annual meetings to mix and encourage. He seemed to find it rewarding and satisfying to be part of the group. Within the grounds of fairness and propriety, we made the most of his story and participation to help underscore that even superhumans can be depressed, talk about it, and move on.

We tried to capitalize on his interest by making him the head of a new nationwide drive we had been thinking about but had not gotten going. With Buzz Aldrin in partnership, we figured it was time to move. The plan followed a pattern of successful fundraising efforts by other national groups to call on all parts of the organization to be engaged in a significant activity in the same week or month. Such an event would represent a unified effort to bring the cause to the public's attention and ask support of it. In this case, we wanted to ask a large number of people to become members of the association, starting with people who had been involved with us, served by us, or were on lists of people who had in various ways shown an interest in mental illness or mental health.

We set goals for the first, second, and third years, aiming eventually toward 1 percent of the population as members. At an average membership of $50, this would produce $500,000 in a community with 1 million people. We were offering our members an opportunity to tap into a lot of fascinating information about mental illness and mental health and guidance as to danger signs, seeking treatment, and so on.

We consulted with a large sampling of division and chapter leaders, who responded with overwhelming enthusiasm; secured a grant to be able to do it right from our end; hired as staff director one of the most respected division leaders; prepared all the sample materials so that divisions and chapters could see the tools they would have to implement the effort; and to be absolutely sure that any chapter's United Way affiliation did not thwart their participation or even give them an excuse not to join in, we cleared the project with the Committee on National Agency Support of United Way and with its national director.

A television show had been done of Aldrin's book, and we had been able to coordinate the premier of it with the kickoff of our drive in May, traditionally Mental Health Month. To the extent reasonable, we sent Buzz on the road. With all that and one of the most extraordinary periods of attention to the cause, the climate could not have seemed better.

After further months of preparation, some warning signs began to come through: "Our United Way won't let us do it," "The timing doesn't seem right," "Our board is not enthusiastic," and so on. A lot of us were on the road almost constantly, trying to line up support or counter reservations and to remind reluctant chapters that this was a great time in the organization's history and it was important to take advantage of it.

Finally the week arrived, and for us it was the combination of Kentucky Derby, World Series, and Super Bowl. This could be the time the organization had waited for more than seventy-five years.

Unfortunately or maybe fortunately, we didn't have to wait more than a few weeks to know that it had failed—completely.

Early indications and later evaluations could be summarized in such reports as "too busy," "fearful of the United Way's reaction," and "not our cup of tea," which, based on my experience, translated into "fund raising is not our bag." With all our extraordinary achievements and thrilling developments of the prior few years and such a chance for greater visibility and impact for all that we were trying to do, the field was just not willing to raise money even for a membership approach that United Way endorsed and that would not have required serious diversion from existing program activities.

About that time I was approaching my tenth anniversary with MHA, and the board was trying to figure out something special to do to recognize the anniversary. I had been doing my own thinking and when I was asked if there was anything special they might do, I said I'd like to take a short sabbatical to back away and renew. I had asked my two academic brothers whether three months away might be long enough for perspective and refreshment, and both said, absolutely as long as it is *really* away, literally and figuratively.

Like the California board, the MHA group was concerned about coverage during the absence, although it too became convinced that things would hold together, but it vetoed the idea of a small project grant to help make it happen. Contrary to my brothers' advice, I had indicated a book I was thinking of making a go at during the period, but the board was still uneasy. Once again I found myself pondering the contradiction between an organization needing and wanting able staff leadership but not being willing to invest in the very people who have proven their worth. I don't say this in bitterness but only as bewilderment that nonprofit boards seem to believe that stewardship is related only to protecting the finances of the organization and doesn't include wise investment in the organization's ability to expand its capacity to fulfill the mission. These were wonderful people, mostly good friends, and enormously able board members, who were enjoying the results of what might well have been the most spectacular years the organization had ever seen, but they were worried what the field and the public might think of their giving $3,000 to $5,000 for my work/study project. That, along with the field's reluctance to ride the wave of so many current breakthroughs, sent such mixed signals that I wanted all the more to get away.

Eventually some of the board members contributed generously from their own funds to help make it possible, so Ann and I and young Matthew began preparations for our trip to Ireland for writing, thinking, and recharging. In the subsequent three months, I did my book on values, explored almost every corner of Ireland, had long-overdue quality time with Ann and our youngest, and felt that I was on a glorious and never-ending holiday. That brief respite will always stand out as a high point of my personal and professional life.

Although I didn't dwell on it while away, I found myself pretty much deciding that I shouldn't stay very much longer with the association. From the distance of time and space, this was not arrived at with negatives in control. Indeed, I was able to reflect on and enjoy the good memories and pride that filtered through. I knew it would not be right to come back from even a short sabbatical and announce I was leaving. We were still in such a joyous and productive period, including the Carters' involvement, that it was positive and right to stay to capitalize on it, but I knew I should be contemplating a change not too far distant.

When I returned, things were in very solid shape with lots of good things underway or unfolding, which made it a positive period organizationally and personally. The positives continued to build, but so did the contradictions between those strengths and the underlying condition of the organization. The chapters were increasingly pleased with the progress but lacking in financial support. They welcomed and profited from our influence on government policies and programs, but drifted toward service projects dependent on government funding, which I knew would limit our advocacy potential.

The progress buoyed me but the contradictions dismayed me, and I began to face the inevitability that I had given it my all and that on balance it had been an enormously productive period for the organization but that I was not the one to crack the resistance so necessary to sustain and build on our possibilities. So after two more years of rewarding program highs and discouraging organizational lows, in the spring of 1978, almost exactly twelve years since my hiring, I announced I was stepping down, with eight months notice, so that both of us would have adequate time to prepare for our futures.

I said to the board in June and repeated to the delegates in November:

> The clearest way I can express myself is to say that I'm terribly proud how far we've come, disappointed but accepting that we didn't move even farther and resigned to the reality that I don't have the fresh perspective, the patience, or the stamina to take it the next giant steps.
>
> Twelve years at the head of this dynamic, diverse, demanding, passionate, disparate, quarrelsome, loving, caring federation is as long as any one person can pretend to have the vision, the patience, and the luck to lead successfully

After referring to some of the problems such as fundraising and fund sharing I summed up my concerns:

> I do have one very great worry about the organization which I present with misgiving because I really shouldn't be negative at a point like this, but I do

have a moral obligation to share it with you. I worry greatly about whether it will hold together. We are a fragile federation, too ready to criticize, or to blame, so it's only honest to put forward the consideration. . . .

There's still not enough awareness of the mutual responsibilities, not enough awareness of the interdependence, of the absolute need we all have to make it work. Somehow the common sense and the simple reality of that doesn't penetrate and permeate. Too many differences are still too easily and badly escalated by the threat to walk away. It worries me to the point that I have to say it. It's the thing you have to work hardest at.

I ended:

But the concentration in these remarks and in your thoughts should be on the joy. That is what's carried us so far; the progress, the exhilaration over these twelve years; I think we've been able to do a significant amount of good and along the way I think we're had some sparkling good times and a great deal of satisfaction at being citizens who do make a difference. It's time to go, but I go with a depth of love, gratitude and admiration.

As with my partings in Pennsylvania, Maryland, and California, it was appropriate to end my swan song with an emphasis on the people, including what we did together and meant to each other. Because there were far too many people deserving my thanks and praise, I singled out just one person, who although not an officer or staff director symbolized the kind of people who populated MHA. I referred earlier to Max Meyerson, head of our warehouse, but it's fitting that I do so once more.

Max became very ill during my last year on the job and finally was not able to come to work. He had delayed giving in to the inevitable so long that it was almost as painful for me as it was for him to be in the warehouse as he struggled to carry on. He was hospitalized for a while but then came home for the end to be with his wife Hattie. I had asked Hattie how soon I could see him, and she called me to say that Max wanted Ann and me to come for lunch the next day. I thought the invitation a positive sign, and the visit seemed more of the same. Although Hattie had said Max wasn't supposed to, he insisted on getting out of bed and coming to the table. He looked awful but was in such control that I just welcomed the signs of strength. We even had a glass of very strong brandy, with a toast by him to the association and all his friends, and looking straight at me, he asked me to promise to say goodbye for him to everybody. He took his last sip, clinking his glass with mine, and asked Hattie to help him back to bed, where he died just a few days later.

My weekly memo to the field that week consisted only of the one message, under the heading, "Max Said to Say Goodbye."

On New Year's Day, Ann and I visited a rapidly weakening Max Meyerson, who was clearly reaching the end of his two-year struggle with cancer.

Max, as many of you know, was head of our warehouse for many years, and is fondly remembered for his annual "Max's Warehouse Sale." I presented Max with one of our new medallions, and was struck by how terribly much it meant to him.

As we were about to leave, Max put his hand on my arm, and in a cheerful tone, said to say hello to everybody—and then he squeezed my arm a bit and added, "And say goodbye to everybody, too."

It was said with such strength and naturalness that it was not a painful moment.

It was only later as I began to realize the full import that I couldn't quite handle it. Max and Hattie have always represented a model for me. We often look to leaders to provide the models we attempt to follow, but Max and Hattie have taught me that the simplest people can qualify too. Those two have represented dignity, loyalty, and goodness, and have thereby set an example for all who've had the privilege of knowing them.

Just one week after our New Year's visit, I joined Hattie and her children, Saul and Ida, and hundreds of friends in the funeral service for Max. The brief eulogy stressed two points. The first, that he was so valued as a member of the staff of the Mental Health Association, that when the headquarters moved to Washington, the Association asked him to come along. And the second point was that it was typical of the loyalty Max exhibited in everything he did that at great sacrifice he accepted the call to move. It was a beautiful service, but oh so sad!

On a cold, clear Sunday in his native Brooklyn, just a week after he said to say goodbye to everyone, I carried back to Max everybody's goodbye to him. That special human being is gone but the life model I found in a warehouse will be with me forever.

Max was the embodiment of leadership from the bottom up and of the dedication and spirit that qualifies him for my MHA all time hall of fame.

I went into the Mental Health Association with many people wondering if I was balmy, and I left with as many questioning my state of mind. I had two kids in college, no job in prospect, and very little to tide us over. In retrospect, my action was pretty far out, but with a solid record, a good bit of notice, and a variety of interests, I figured it would work out. About my only condition was that this time around I wanted to do something less chaotic. And look what I got into.

« 6 »

"IT WON'T FLY, ORVILLE"

Creating INDEPENDENT SECTOR

1978–1980

I began my job search in earnest in April 1978. I knew I wanted something cause oriented and related to citizen participation and influence. I also preferred that it be different from a health association. I had done that for more than twenty-five years and it was time for another experience.

To locate my next job I talked to at least thirty people who might steer me to possible opportunities or to other individuals who might have leads. In that way, I was brought to the attention of Ken Albrecht, head of contributions and public service at Equitable Life, and Bayard Ewing, volunteer head of the National Information Bureau and a significant leader in many national voluntary efforts. I had known both, but not in their current leadership roles, Ken with the National Council on Philanthropy (NCOP) and Bayard with the Coalition of National Voluntary Organizations (CONVO). It turned out that NCOP's president had recently died and CONVO's board felt it needed to change executive directors. Both Ken and Bayard expressed interest in exploring my possible candidacy, but from what I knew about each organization, I didn't feel either was what I was hoping for.

I had known that when CONVO was formed a few years earlier, there had been some consideration of establishing it as part of NCOP, but nothing came of it. When I learned each was searching, I asked permission to let the other know, just in case that might lead to reconsideration of a joint effort. I didn't do this with my own situation in mind. My memory and notes remind me that I didn't think even a merger of the two would offer sufficient opportunity or the more sensible setting I was looking for.

Subsequently, Ken and Bayard, after discussions with others, asked if I would help examine what they might do, separately or jointly, in their next stages of staffing and programming. Because I was still in a more than full-time job and facing the stark reality of being off the payroll by year end, I was reluctant to take on even that much, but I thought the examination could be done part-time over several weeks, and it appeared important and fascinating to see if I could help facilitate what might be a sensible amalgamation. I don't remember if I had any sense that Ken and Bayard hoped I would become more interested in their prospects, or if somewhere in the back of my mind there was a glimmer of interest, but if either was the case, it was subliminal.

At that point, Bayard and Ken were eager to make decisions. Each board was engaged in its staff search, and each was facing organizational uncertainties that seriously threatened financial support. For these reasons, each of them hoped I could come forward with clear recommendations fairly quickly so that action might be taken shortly after Labor Day, not many weeks away. As I should have expected, any review of such serious and complicated issues had to be intense, and the challenge of the task was compounded by the very tight timetable.

I interviewed twenty-five people, including leaders of the two organizations and other prominent and informed figures, and I corresponded with about fifty others. (One of the people I interviewed was John Gardner, who demonstrated such interest and knowledge that I asked him if I could stay in touch in the course of my study, and thus began a regular consultation and eventually our partnership.) Early in my interviews, it became apparent that my review would involve three levels of examination, ranging from very specific and immediate to very general and long range. First was the immediate futures of CONVO and NCOP. Second was a grasp of current and prospective issues and activities within philanthropy and the broader voluntary sector, including questions of who was already doing or planning what. The third concerned what, if anything, was needed and could be done to strengthen giving, volunteering, and the overall worth and impact of philanthropy and voluntary action. It was obvious right away that the study had to start at the broadest level and work backward to organization specifics.

The post-World War II period marked the establishment of a staggering number of associations and institutions through which people could express their collective views on what society should be, and to exercise their power to bring it into being.

By the 1960s participatory democracy had begun to include all parts of society. Americans were organizing to influence every conceivable aspect of the human condition. They were also willing to stand up and be counted on almost any public issue.

A few examples may help to emphasize what an empowering period this was: The civil rights battles of the 1960s provided the model and the courage for a great many other groups determined to be empowered and included in the freedoms and opportunities of democracy; the success of the March of Dimes and then of all the other major health organizations, including the American Cancer Society and Mental Health Association, created a new effective force of ordinary citizens, as described in the title of Richard Carter's book *The Gentle Legions;* and the moral indignation of individual parents of retarded children achieved blistering force through the National Association for Retarded Children and set the organizing example for everyone else determined to provide better services and understanding for people with autism, spina bifida, dyslexia, and hundreds of other seemingly insurmountable conditions.

Given this burgeoning of all forms of civic engagement, it was perplexing, bewildering, and frightening for those involved to find themselves and their institutions increasingly questioned, criticized, and attacked. Explanations came slowly but would have profound influence on the future of nonprofit endeavor.

Waldemar A. Nielsen was the first to grasp the reasons and consequences of this alarming development. Author of the seminal study *The Golden Donors,* Nielsen had been the sector's foremost observer and chronicler. Beginning in the mid-1970s, he began to sound warnings that reached the alarm stage in 1979 with publication of his book *The Endangered Sector.* It presented a chilling picture of government's increasing control of the activities of voluntary associations and institutions through money, mandates, regulations, penalties, political influence, and intimidation. The threatening title of the book and the enumeration and elaboration of danger signs drove even the most ardent supporter of nongovernmental activity into confusion and defensiveness. All this was compounded by three developments: a Congressional investigation, a U.S. Treasury *Report on Private Foundations,* and the Tax Reform Act of 1969, all of which cast doubt on the degree of independence that voluntary institutions should be allowed.

The criticisms and concerns came from more than government. Many grass-roots groups, emerging leaders, and unpopular causes were aggressively hostile to both grantmaking and voluntary groups considered to be elitist or indifferent. In just one example, the Donee Group, which described itself as a "coalition of public interest, social action, and volunteer groups," was able to force its way into the activities of the Filer Commission (Commission on Private Philanthropy and Public Needs,

1973–1975), and even issued a report of its own that was distributed with the Filer Commission's report. The donee document, "Private Philanthropy: Vital and Innovative? Or Passive and Irrelevant?," concluded that the Filer Commission was too focused on "preserving the status quo," and that it had failed to adequately "assess public needs."

It wasn't only liberals and the new crop of activists who were critical. From the conservative and establishment side, people like Richard C. Cornuelle of the National Association of Manufacturers expressed their own alarm about voluntary groups surrendering to government many responsibilities that belonged best to private initiative. In his book *Reclaiming the American Dream*, published in 1965, Cornuelle presaged the Republican revolution of the mid-1990s, called "Contract with America," when he proposed that the independent sector take back its traditional role and responsibility for community service. His call for reclaiming the American dream concluded: "Through it [the independent sector] we can restore the supportive circle whereby America originally put its unique emphasis on personal dignity. We can again insure our freedom by limiting the powers of central government. Being free, we can move to ever higher planes of prosperity and ever greater human aspirations. We can, as we learn how, focus our growing prosperity directly and imaginatively on real human needs."

In my own study of the state of things, reported more fully later, I found a litany of concerns and criticisms, including the degree of government funding and consequent influence; government rules and regulations that went far beyond any contracted obligations of voluntary organizations to perform specified services; challenges to advocacy rights; reduction or removal of exemption from property taxes; proposed taxes on endowments; limitations on deductions of contributions; and concerns about unfair competition between businesses and nonprofit organizations.

In addition, I listed other factors that provoked criticism of our organizations, including the illegal and irresponsible behavior of some groups; general questioning of the effectiveness of philanthropic and voluntary organizations; and the growing skepticism in the country about all institutions, including church, government, media, politicians, and big business. I said, "It is to be expected that institutions which perform public functions will receive a great deal of scrutiny. Even when they perform openly and effectively, they will not escape suspicion, and when they are perceived to be secretive, unresponsive, or ineffective, there will be cynicism and scorn."

Much of my review pointed up the pain felt by leaders of philanthropy and voluntary action who believed deeply in the importance and worth of the sector but recognized that all their experience and conviction were being challenged by skeptics who questioned whether giving was a loophole or charity a rip-off. They also had to acknowledge that they were the object of criticism from emerging groups that couldn't get a fair share of the charitable pie and from reporters who were looking behind the tired rhetoric used to rationalize tired programs. They recognized also that the number and intensity of such criticisms caused a lot of people to wonder whether the assumptions that volunteering is good and that voluntary activity is better than government were perhaps themselves worn-out generalizations.

Faced with all these attacks, the sector found there was little research to bolster a factual case for its worth, and there was no clear and pervasive voice speaking on its behalf. People in the sector believed passionately in the value of what they were about and its relevance to a free society. They also agreed that despite the obviousness of the good their sector did, many policymakers and opinion molders increasingly put them on the defensive. There was a consequent assumption that if someone could just better organize the sector to tell its story, the wind would shift. In a very short period of time, those involved in voluntary action went from an acceptance of the inherent goodness of giving and volunteering to an awareness that that appreciation was far from universally shared.

I didn't quite agree that we were "the endangered sector," but I did agree that unless we could improve ourselves, strengthen public perceptions of us, and educate people about the importance of this voluntary, independent sector, our unique contributions to the American experience would be tragically reduced. At that point, like many others, I turned to considerations of whether anything could be done about it.

Many people pointed to the Filer Commission for evidence of the importance of the voluntary sector. Officially named the Commission on Private Philanthropy and Public Needs, and known for its chairman, John H. Filer, CEO of Aetna Life and Casualty and later a chairperson of INDE-PENDENT SECTOR, it began its work in 1973, and in 1975 issued a report and book, *Giving in America: Toward a Stronger Voluntary Sector,* which began: "The *voluntary sector* is a large and vital part of American society, more important today than ever. But the sector is undergoing economic strains that predate and are generally more severe than the troubles of the economy as a whole. . . . Giving in America involves an immense amount of time and money, is the fundamental underpinning of the voluntary sector, encompasses a wide diversity of relationships between donor, donations, and donee, and is not keeping pace" (p. 11).

The Filer Commission recommended "that a permanent national commission on the nonprofit sector be established by Congress to examine philanthropic priorities, determine ways to increase private giving, and establish means of insulating voluntary organizations from political and bureaucratic pressures." Half of the new commission's membership would be named by the President and the other half by the presidential appointees themselves. Half the funding for the commission would come from government and half from private sources.

Less well known than the Filer Commission was the Peterson Commission, which dealt largely with the giving side of the sector. That group was formally named Commission on Foundations and Private Philanthropy, and its report and related book, *Foundations, Private Giving and Public Policy,* were issued in 1970. It was known for its chairman, Peter G. Peterson, CEO of Bell & Howell and later Secretary of Commerce.

This study also chronicled the benefits of private philanthropy and the threats to it. For example, the report stated: "We believe that government should not venture to do those things which private citizens and private institutions can do as well or better. . . . Our society, therefore, is in obvious need of private philanthropic institutions standing outside the frame of government but in support of the public interest" (p. 14). The Peterson Commission focused on ways to stimulate an increase in charitable funds, with an emphasis on strengthening foundations. It, too, proposed the establishment of a governmental body to pursue those ends.

Although it's hard to determine just why the kinds of commissions called for by both groups never came to pass, I believe an important factor was that the permanent bodies as proposed would have been part of government or likely controlled by it, and there was an instinctive reaction that what was needed for this sector had to be largely independent of government.

The Filer Commission (with its related Donee Report) and the Peterson Commission provided observations, criticisms, and recommendations that represented valuable guidance for my immediate study, and later for the organizing committee that created INDEPENDENT SECTOR. Through all my reading and interviewing I heard four critical needs expressed repeatedly: greater influence in Washington; research to prove their case; capacity to get that case to the American people; and a meeting ground and communication mechanism so that those working in this vast and disparate sector would have a better grasp of who was doing what. Of these four, influence in Washington was by far the top priority.

The second part of my study considered whether anybody could really do anything to vastly improve the climate and resources for private initiative for the public good. This in turn led me to study past and current efforts organized for those purposes. I identified twenty-one such groups, such as:

The 501(c)(3) Group, which was formed in the late 1950s to bring together nonprofit leaders concerned with tax policies.

For a brief time the Treasury Department did have an advisory committee on private philanthropy and public needs in response to the two commissions, but quickly dropped it.

In response to Treasury's dropping its advisory committee, United Way of America took the lead in forming the "Coalition for the Public Good" which later joined with the 501(c)(3) Group and others to form CONVO (Coalition of National Voluntary Organizations).

An Advisory Committee on Private Philanthropy and Public Needs was formed by several of those involved with the Filer Commission.

The National Center for Voluntary Action (NCVA) had retreated from an earlier very ambitious role and was concentrating on consultation and technical assistance to voluntary groups.

The Center for a Voluntary Society had recently run out of funds after identifying major research issues that needed to be addressed if the sector was to be understood and strengthened.

Even the fuller listing of twenty-one didn't cover the waterfront, but I hoped it was sufficient to delineate some of the principal players and to highlight concerns about proliferation and competition. I commented, "It is surely an indication of the intense needs that are perceived that so many groups are trying to find a place in that sun."

The third part of my study dealt with the National Council on Philanthropy (NCOP) and Coalition of National Voluntary Organization's (CONVO) histories, missions, governance, members, funding, budgets, staff, programs, similarities, differences, and my candid view of their strengths and weaknesses.

NCOP was twenty-four years old and was made up primarily but not exclusively of funders, especially from the corporate side. Its programs, including an annual conference on philanthropy, involved both donors and donees. Its mission was "strengthening and enriching private resources to better meet public needs." It was housed in New York City.

CONVO was just three years old, having grown out of the Coalition for the Public Good. It was made up primarily but not exclusively of leaders of voluntary organizations, but its programs related to both voluntary and philanthropic groups. Its mission was "to maximize the contributions of the voluntary sector in meeting America's human needs, and to enrich the quality of American society." It was housed in Washington, D.C.

Although my section on similarities was much longer than the one on "differences," the latter were significant, including the different locations; NCOP's almost twenty-five-year history versus CONVO's newness; and CONVO's priority of government relations contrasting with NCOP's aversion to it.

My assessment of the prospects for closer collaboration was based on a number of findings: There was a distinct impression that the two organizations were compatible, but although a few of my interviewees favored immediate merger, most preferred something short of that, at least for a while. Because most of those interviewed hoped that something significant could be done in and for the sector, they believed that whatever happened between CONVO and NCOP should represent important steps in the right direction. Despite CONVO's false start, many people believed that it had the broader constituency essential to national impact. NCOP had the forum (the national conference), the potential for more such communication, and the important interest of many corporate givers. Even those who were critical of one or both organizations agreed that there was a job to be done. They concluded that the two didn't have too much to lose by trying some new arrangement. Overwhelmingly, those interviewed believed that the coincidence of the vacancies in the top staff jobs of the two organizations should be viewed in the perspective of the larger needs of the field, and that therefore this rare opportunity should be seized to try to build something better.

As I came down to the wire, I was far from confident that I had explored all aspects of the situation, but I was nevertheless able to draw up a list of options that the organizations, and the sector as a whole could consider, ranging from continuing as is to creating an altogether new entity. I recommended that they establish a new entity with two principal functions: to serve as secretariat for both organizations, and to determine ways by which the two organizations and the whole voluntary sector might best pursue the protection and enhancement of giving, volunteering, and the worth and impact of the sector.

Responding to Ken Albrecht and Bayard Ewing's request for candor and a definite recommendation, I bit the bullet and summarized my conclusions: "Philanthropy and the broader voluntary sector do need to do something better to protect and enhance giving, volunteering, and the tangible and intangible contributions of the sector to our democratic society. . . . CONVO and NCOP should use the coincidence of their current situations, their similar missions and their shared conviction that something better is needed, to take the first steps toward creating a vehicle for closer organizational cooperation and for fuller pursuit of their common ideals."

Perhaps more important than anything else, I articulated some of the aspirations and dreams I had been hearing in many of the contacts I had made. Examples included: a public affairs network spinning a web of caring and influential constituents around every member of Congress; an information resource to which the media would turn for information, facts, and background; growing impact on public instruction, for instance, such that books in history, civics, and public affairs would include information about the role and contributions of the voluntary sector; a research effort that was respected as objective and contributory to sensible public policy; and the ability to set standards and to create mechanisms by which boards and others could measure performance according to those standards.

Responding to the highest ideals and aspirations I had heard during all those interviews, I said: "Aside from all the fact finding, alternatives, conclusions, and recommendations, the larger message is that we just might be in on the ground floor and at the threshold of building what John Gardner [by then prominent in the process] described as 'an enterprise . . . encompassing the whole fascinating universe of the voluntary sector and addressing issues infinitely broader and more varied than any organization in the sector has grappled with before.'"

I concluded, "There are decidedly good things about CONVO and NCOP. However, their immediate problems and shortcomings and the coincidence of their staff openings, along with their similar missions and shared desire to build a more effective instrument, suggest that to try to bring off the larger collaboration is the most important thing either organization could ever do."

That was all communicated very early in September in the report "Feasibility Study of Closer Collaboration Between the Coalition of National Voluntary Organizations (CONVO) and the National Council on Philanthropy (NCOP)." The reader will understand that when dealing with not one but two voluntary boards, agreements don't come crisply and without a great deal of discussion. There were objections, amendments, and meetings—oh, were there meetings!

After those discussions were successfully concluded, there was a final four-part dance that was slow to execute. The maneuvers involved three intertwined issues and four participants, and none of the parties wanted to be first on the floor. The issues were: Would I be the interim head of the two organizations and the staff director of the planning stage? Would John Gardner chair the planning stage? Would CONVO and NCOP agree to the report with full understanding that what John and I would be working toward was a new entity, much larger than the sum of the two parts?

I didn't want to get involved if we didn't have a real shot at something equal to the needs and dreams of the sector, and John didn't intend to be limited to or preoccupied with a coordinating role between the two players. For each organization, the reality was that this was the real moment of truth, rather than a postponement of it for a year or so down the line. Granted, if we couldn't bring it off, the two organizations could retreat, but they had to be in it just as completely as we were, or we wouldn't stand a chance.

To this quadrille, we shuffled rather than glided. Maybe I said first that I'd do it if John would, or maybe he said first he'd do it if I would, or it may have been that Ken said he felt secure about NCOP if John and I would tackle it and if CONVO responded in kind, or maybe it was Bayard who . . . but whatever and whomever, we finally bowed as partners, joined hands, and moved out in almost practiced rhythm. For the good times and the rough ones ahead, it was extremely fortunate that we were all responding to the same beat.

So I had a job (actually three of them!) that related to my core interests, but it sure wasn't the less chaotic one I had in mind.

Even before the next and even more crucial phase of the effort, Bayard Ewing and Ken Albrecht rotated out of their top roles with CONVO and NCOP. John and I worried what that might do to solidarity, but it turned out that their successors were equally committed and effective. The new top volunteer officer at NCOP was Jim Lipscomb, executive director of the George Gund Foundation in Cleveland, the original home of NCOP; Jim had served for many years in national and international assignments with the Ford Foundation. Phil Bernstein, CONVO's new principal volunteer, had just retired as staff head of the Council of Jewish Federations after a lifetime of leadership roles with that organization. With Ken Albrecht and Bayard Ewing still involved and committed, our core team was considerably enhanced.

Our intention to create something larger than the sum of the two parts became all the more obvious when we deliberately labeled the exploratory and planning body the Organizing Committee. We realized such labeling would cause discomfort among some who were still tentative, but it was consistent with the degree of commitment we had been assured.

Another important early consideration involved the makeup of the committee. Very deliberately, I had recommended in the feasibility study that the body that would plan for the future would contain a significant proportion of individuals who were not on either board. It had not been an easy condition to sell, but was essential to the objectivity and credibility of the group finally selected.

I had recommended that the chairman and I would propose the members, and that our nominees would need to be approved by the two top officers of the sponsoring organizations, now Bernstein and Lipscomb. We all had to take a lot of heat, primarily from those who weren't appointed. There were only three official representatives selected from each organization. The distinct majority did not have formal affiliation with either group.

Anyone who has ever tried to put together a group representative of a diverse constituency or reflecting a broad cross section of the country will recognize the complexity of our task. At first, there were strong pressures to keep the committee small, but even when we settled on what was interpreted as the unwieldy number of twenty-one, it was excruciating to try to hold to it, and in fact, at the first meeting of the group, the members of the committee insisted we had to go to at least twenty-five to correct weaknesses. We ended up with twenty-seven, and many complaints that we hadn't begun to be representative enough, or, on the other side, that we were too big and diverse to get anything done.

The first meeting of the committee would have been a delight to all those who predicted that such a group could never agree on anything. People felt a need to stake out their territory, establish their independence, express their distrust, and insist on adjustments. And that was just in the formal sessions! During the breaks, people wanted to be sure that I knew where they stood, and why the whole undertaking was starting out poorly. John also got a lot of this, but as we sorted it out, we realized we had just experienced a predictable, although unusually intense, first meeting of any truly diverse coalition, in which many of the participants need to say what they came to say, and to be able to go home and say that they said what needed to be said.

Although we continued to meet and to make some progress, we couldn't seem to make headway on the central issues, especially whether we really had enough in common as a group and as a sector to make it possible and worthwhile to try to organize around it. We were into the third meeting, and the go-around was bordering on fruitless, when Sara Alyce Wright, national head of the YWCA, pointed out that the only way we could determine our commonality or lack of it was to see if we felt that we and our institutions shared important core values. I could tell that some felt such an exercise a little mushy, but everyone agreed to give it a try. When we were finished, we had found our common bond and made rapid progress thereafter, even on the difficult questions that had stumped us earlier.

After several rewordings, we stated our common values this way:

The independent sector is so vast and diverse that it reflects an enormous range of values. Using the wide angle lens, we constantly have to remind ourselves that we were dealing with the motivations and values inherent in such different institutions as garden clubs, schools for the blind, scientific laboratories and patients' rights committees. We are also trying to encompass groups that are sharply at odds with one another—the devoted and the iconoclastic; those who are pro nuclear energy and those who are anti; and protectionists and free traders. One might argue that in the face of such infinite diversity the Organizing Committee would do well to pass discreetly over the whole subject of values. But, without denying the diversity of the sector and without proposing to set limits to that diversity, the committee felt impelled to identify and state certain values that it regards as central to its own efforts—values that the proposed new organization should seek to foster.

The listing underwent several changes, especially shortening, and covered commitment beyond self; worth and dignity of the individual; individual responsibility; tolerance; freedom; justice; and responsibilities of citizenship.

It was important to add:

We must be very careful not to seem to suggest that everything done in the sector is necessarily good. It is a common fault of supporters of nonprofit initiative to attribute to the sector a role often romanticized and overblown. We need to acknowledge that the very pluralism that provides the freedom for a lot of good things to happen also allows a lot of activity that some might describe as counterproductive or foolish. As long as neither infringes on the rights of others, no one should have official authority to judge which is which, and all in the sector should recognize a responsibility and mutual benefit in protecting the rights of everyone.

We had an easier but not an easy time defining the sector, at least as we experienced and wanted to relate to it. Most of us began the process with a view closely determined by personal experience, and some were not altogether comfortable with what they were being asked to embrace. The activists among us wondered why they should have to worry about Harvard and Stanford, and the people interested in dance or opera were not quite sure that public interest lawyers or the Flat Earth Society really represented affinity groups.

We also described two of the sector's most salient characteristics: "*Diversity* which encompasses virtually the whole range of human purposes . . . from religions to bird watchers' clubs; [and] *Independence* as seen in the whole range of human activities, they are remarkably free of any but self imposed constraints."

It was the point about independence that eventually led to the recommendation of the name, but there were miles and curves before we got that far.

In the course of the examination, we became even more aware of the overwhelming obstacles that had stalled or negated all earlier efforts to pull the sector together. There was the sheer breadth and complexity of the sector. The broader we stretched, the harder it was to imagine an organization encompassing it all. We had to allow for the fierce independence that exists in so much of the sector. Who could ever get many of those independent individuals and causes working together on anything? There was also suspicion—and actual antipathy—which characterizes so many relationships in this disparate, quarrelsome, and competing world. It was the ultimate in presumption and optimism to think we could pull together the consumers and providers, the donors and donees, the pro-choice and prolifers and many other groups that seemed to be natural antagonists rather than allies. Furthermore, we faced the danger that any organization seeking to retain the support of so many diverse constituencies would end up serving the lowest common denominator of self-interest and not the highest public interest. Finally, we would be operating with a scarcity of hard data about the overall sector, which meant that many of our plans would be based largely on guesswork.

As we addressed those questions and other realities, we concluded:

> Despite how very real these problems are and with full respect for them, they are nevertheless constantly countered by an impressively pervasive conviction that if the independent sector is to continue to serve society well, it must—to the extent possible—be mobilized for greater cooperation and impact. Despite all the differences, antipathies and antagonisms that may exist in this quarrelsome, competing and truly independent sector, there are even stronger forces pulling it together. However different all the other beliefs, there is a shared understanding of the sector's capacity to serve human needs and there is a shared stake in the fundamental relationship between the freedom of citizens to organize themselves and the freedom of citizens. As narrow as those common bonds may be, they are strong enough to jus-

tify the possibility that an organization loyal to them and to nothing else might rally the sector around them.

With that possibility in view, we proceeded.

Although the principal story of that crucial year and a half concerns the work and results of the Organizing Committee, what was happening with the two sponsoring organizations and their common secretariat had an impact on what a new entity might be like and whether an even broader coalition could work. Each time a doubter claimed that donors and donees couldn't be joined in the same organization or that the sector was too diverse to decide and pursue common strategies, we had the great advantage of pointing to breakthroughs already being achieved within our existing operation. That was not a period of drifting, but of expanded activity for both organizations and of deliberately shared efforts to achieve cooperation and collaboration.

Almost immediately, the National Council on Philanthropy took the gamble of going ahead with its annual national conference, which had been handicapped by lack of staffing and funds. Giving up on it would have demoralized an already discouraged organization and would hardly send a message of hope and vitality. So we decided to go forward. With only a couple of months to go, programming, fundraising, and promotion were put into high gear, with enough progress to assure at least a decent showing. Midway to deadline, all our frantic efforts received a rocket boost when the First Lady, Rosalynn Carter, agreed to participate. Late registrants, previously undecided speakers, and delayed support decisions suddenly came through, and our anticipated so-so event turned into a new standard for spirit and value.

Right after the conference, we reinstated NCOP's popular quarterly newsletter, *Voice of Philanthropy*, which hadn't been issued for more than a year, expanded its coverage, and enlarged its subscriber base. There were also bolstering developments in our international project, including publication of the book *International Business Philanthropy*; cosponsorship of a major conference on international education; and a joint NCOP–Woodrow Wilson Center dialogue on "The Role of Philanthropy in International Affairs." NCOP's board members appreciated these clear indications of expanded activity and seemed assured and informed by the new and frequent "Board Memo" that kept them briefed on NCOP and the work of the Organizing Committee.

There was one scary episode during this period that related to international activities. It involved a visit from a delegation of badge-flashing intelligence agents who demanded, on the basis of a small grant NCOP had received from one of their organizations, that I include some of their people in our delegations to international meetings. When I refused, I was told that in a study of my record, it had come to light that as a sophomore in high school, I had been a member of the United World Federalists, which they implied could ruin my career.

I told them two things: One, I was proud of being a student member of that idealistic organization, about which I had never seen or heard a hint of unpatriotic behavior (indeed, always the opposite); and two, I had been enlisted into that group by a famous badly wounded Marine officer named Cord Meyer whose career I had followed and who was at that point the second or third highest official in the CIA. I never heard another threatening word. It's been a lesson ever since that if such an experience could happen to a generally moderate change maker like myself, then the tales are not exaggerated for what happens to those raising a ruckus in such controversial areas as civil rights or control of nuclear power. I have become a true believer in Lord Acton's conclusion that "power corrupts and absolute power corrupts absolutely"; and I believe all the more in Alexander Hamilton's dictum that "the price of liberty is eternal vigilance."

On the Coalition of National Voluntary Organizations side, progress was equally impressive. Initially, CONVO faced a similar need to restore morale and momentum, but once those were developing, our greatest challenge was to try to keep up with expectations, aspirations, and legislative crises and opportunities.

If the annual conference and international program were NCOP's major responsibilities, CONVO's were government relations and research. For urgent government relations matters, CONVO was fortunate to attract to the staff Bob Smucker, who had handled similar responsibilities so very well at the Mental Health Association. Within the first eighteen months, the government relations efforts increased tenfold. For example, the organization successfully fought any use of the term and concept "tax expenditures," which was associated with the argument that because government loses money when people deduct contributions, government should control how those lost revenues are spent.

CONVO also launched its first court test of arbitrary limits on fund-raising costs. The Village of Schaumburg had established a limit of 25 percent on fund-raising costs for organizations that could receive a permit to solicit support in that community. We recognized that unpopular and new causes might exceed that limit, at least in initial years of operation, and therefore communities could use the fund-raising limit to squelch their critics. We argued for full disclosure but not foreclosure.

We were successful in defending the right of voluntary organizations to publish the voting record of legislators on issues of concern to the voluntary groups. We never challenged the legitimacy of the law prohibiting nonprofit organizations from engaging in partisan activity, including telling people who to vote for or against, but we felt it was within an organization's right to reveal what a legislator's voting record had been.

To mobilize CONVO's members and others to advocate for sensible public policies relating to the sector, we began to develop a vast network of sector representatives who could explain to their elected officials just what the impact of proposed legislation and regulations would be on causes within those officials' communities.

After government relations, the next most important concern for CONVO—and one of great interest to NCOP—was research. By early 1979, the research function, including the research committee, became a joint activity of CONVO and NCOP. There were three major research projects during that interim year.

First, we contracted with Martin Feldstein, head of the National Bureau of Economic Research, to determine the current economic significance of the charitable deduction. That important study confirmed that as a result of the opportunity for individuals to deduct contributions from their taxable income, charitable organizations received far more income than the government lost. This proved that the deduction achieved its intended purpose of stimulating private initiative for the public good.

The second project, which was larger and even more significant than the deduction study, was our public opinion survey by the Gallup Organization "to determine the giving patterns of Americans." The gamble paid off, proving for the first time that "tax incentives are an important determinant of the levels of charitable giving." The hundred-page report also provided important baseline data about the charitable habits of Americans by age, income, gender, education, and many other characteristics.

Third, the joint research committee began to report to the members and supporters of both organizations on other research being conducted in and on the sector that could help philanthropic and voluntary organizations be more effective in their own programming and fund raising.

As with NCOP, CONVO sharpened its own internal and external communications. In 1979 we took what was then a major step by hiring John Thomas to help strengthen our ability to communicate within the sector and beyond.

In addition to all of these, John Gardner and I had kept Rosalynn Carter and the White House informed of the work of CONVO and

NCOP and prospects for the even larger entity, and she had said to let her know when she might help. We suggested that one of the most important things that could occur would be for the White House to send a clear signal to the government and the American people that giving and volunteering are activities to be applauded and encouraged. It took a couple of months of planning, but in mid-1979, 250 leaders of the sector, starting with the leadership of both CONVO and NCOP, came together for a very special celebration at the White House hosted by the First Lady and attended by the President. It was an important step in our efforts to encourage and educate the public about the importance of personal participation, and it also added timely visibility and credibility to what these two organizations were doing and what the Organizing Committee might achieve.

Anticipating that the White House session would be significant to share as fully as possible, John Thomas arranged to have a film crew present. He also gained permission to have the same crew go along on the First Lady's visits to some excellent volunteer projects that we had helped identify. With all that footage, we were able to put together a film, *Salute to Volunteering,* which was used extensively by our members and others to reach millions of Americans.

One of the decided benefits of the dramatic expansion of effective activities on the part of NCOP, CONVO, and the combination of the two was that we were able, even during this tenuous period, to significantly expand financial support for both groups. Because of all these advances, when the Organizing Committee began to firm up its recommendations and clear them with the two sponsoring organizations, there was a great deal of positive experience to draw on.

With progress in the first phase of its work and encouragement from the activities of NCOP and CONVO, the Organizing Committee turned to some pretty basic considerations, such as who might support a new and larger organization, what it would actually do, and how it could be protected from control by larger organizations such as United Way or by parts of the sector such as health and hospitals.

The most important consideration was what the organization would actually do, and after months of subcommittees, discussions, and debates, we decided on the following essential functions: *public education* to improve understanding of the sector's role in giving people alternatives and greater opportunities for participation and the creation of a more caring and effective Society; *communication* within the sector so that shared problems and opportunities would be identified and pursued; *relation-*

ships with government to deal with the infinite interconnections between the two sectors, but particularly to ensure the healthy independence and continued viability of nongovernmental organizations; *research* to provide a body of knowledge about the independent sector and about how to make it most useful to society; and *encouragement of effective operations and management of nonprofit institutions* to maximize their capacity to serve individuals and society.

Almost as important as what would be done was the how, and for this we emphasized the creation of a "meeting ground." We saw the new entity as that place where the diverse elements in and related to the independent sector could comfortably come together to discuss common purposes, learn how to perform better, and use their opportunities to contribute to the common pursuits of research, public education, and relationships with government.

We found that the term "meeting ground" helped to convey what we wanted to see developed and also helped indicate what we didn't want, as we put it: "Any new entity must not diminish the very pluralism which it was created to serve and enhance."

A principle important to the committee was that any such enterprise could effectively address its mission only by working through a vast network of organizations. "Existing independent organizations already involve millions of people and are in touch with every community in the country. To the extent that these organizations are brought into the common tasks, the new organization can accomplish a great deal. To the extent that the new organization tries to overreach these groups and build separately, it will have neither impact nor future."

Another rule that became a lifesaver early and often in the life of IN-DEPENDENT SECTOR stipulated that the organization had to stay within the narrow core of common interests in preserving and enhancing the impact of the sector. "The more effective the organization becomes, the more tempting it will be for various groups or interests to try to use the organization and its influence for their own purposes, drawing it into issues and battles that do not cut across the broad spectrum of the entire sector."

A pretty basic consideration was how the organization should be funded. Having decided fairly quickly that it should not be dependent on government or even accept government funding, we had to explore and question whether sufficient support would come from private sources. Here too, it won't surprise any reader experienced in these matters that it is one thing to get agreement on what should be done and quite another to go back around the table for fair shares of support.

When I was a young man, my grandfather used to tell a story that in later years came to mind whenever I was involved in dues debates and collections.

> Two old Irish friends were into their third jars of stout and had reached the sentimental stage. Pat indicated to Mike that they were such very dear friends that "if you had two bicycles I'm sure you'd give me one." Mike, caught up in the spirit, responded, "I would in a minute, and it would make me happy to do so." Whereupon, Pat said, "I'll even bet that if you had two automobiles you'd still give me one," and Mike assured him it was so. With that, Pat leaned a bit closer and said, "I'll bet that if you had two goats . . . " but got no further. Mike straightened and looked Pat clear in the eye, and ended the conversation with "I would not, you SOB, you know I've got two goats!"

I wish I had a goat or even a dime for every time I heard someone extol the mission or even the accomplishments of INDEPENDENT SECTOR, only to object to the dues or renege on them.

Most of us had had enough experience in membership organizations to be cautious in the extreme about financial prospects, but in the end, a number of tests and decisions worked in our favor. During the eighteen months that the Organizing Committee functioned, there was a four-part fund-raising effort that in several ways tested whether the new enterprise could attract private support.

First of all, it had been necessary to maintain and increase support for our two organizations. CONVO had been concentrating on holding its members and attracting new ones. Despite previous organizational problems and the staffing hiatus and change, the organization held all but one of its forty-four members and attracted twenty-five new ones. Similarly, NCOP was able to hold its regular supporters and add twenty-two.

Second, we were encouraged by our efforts to secure short-term funding to help sustain the collaboration and, if appropriate, launch the new operation. Our minimum need for short-term funding was $550,000 and our goal was $1 million. By completion of the Organizing Committee's work, twenty-eight grants had been received, totaling $745,000, a particularly encouraging result considering that we aimed for a broad base of support, both by setting a ceiling of $60,000 from any one source and by reaching out to all regions.

Third, after long testing and debate, we agreed on a dues structure that spread the load among prospective members, including a sliding scale based on ability to pay. Although even realistic dues arrangements are hard to sell, we successfully made the case that all of us had a stake in the operation, and we persuaded members that this could not be another effort that started big on soft money, and then zigged and zagged its way downward searching for project funds wherever they might take us.

Lastly, fund raising and membership development were accepted as high priorities for the organization, including board and president.

Along with the dues, nothing took more of our time than issues related to membership, beginning with: Who? Should there be individuals? (At least not at the start.) Did business corporations really fit? (Their philanthropic/public service arms certainly did.) What about local organizations? (At that stage, we were trying to deal with national forces such as Congress and the media, and most of the national organizations that were likely to be involved were membership federations involving millions of local groups.) Should and could we seek the membership of an organization that was already an affiliate of one of our umbrella groups, such as the Council on Foundations or the National Health Council? (We agreed that a foundation or national health agency should belong first to its natural umbrella group, but that our new organization could not survive simply as an umbrella of umbrella groups. To be effective, we needed some of the major players directly at the table.) Where would we stand on groups primarily funded by government, such as the National Endowment for the Arts? (In many cases, we would need a close working relationship with such groups, but they should not be formal members.) The categories and tough decisions seemed to proliferate endlessly. We proposed that the organization should be "a membership association, and the formal members would be organizations with national interests and impact in philanthropy, voluntary action, or other independent activity relating to the educational, scientific, health, welfare, cultural, and religious life of the nation."

Among the reservations the committee had heard repeatedly was whether it was wise or even possible to construct an organization of both grant-making and grant-seeking entities. Many organizations that had to seek funds were understandably concerned that the new operation might be dominated by those who have the money, and many of those who made grants worried that their numerical minority would constantly put them at the mercy of an agenda controlled by the grant seekers. We concluded that the new organization was not that kind of enterprise. The mission and program were deliberately designed to reflect the mutual interests of these and many otherwise different and even competing groups. "All groups in and related to the sector have a stake in its future and they have to work together in some vehicle." We believed that the concept of the meeting ground provided that vehicle without infringing on the separate agendas of the many parts.

We also pointed out that CONVO and NCOP already were examples of cooperative efforts. From the start, CONVO had included both NCOP and the Council on Foundations, and NCOP included a great many representatives of public charities, including the Women's Action Alliance,

United Way, Nature Conservancy, and National Health Council. The Organizing Committee's own experience was a promising indication that when the focus is on the health and future of the sector as a whole, an otherwise very diverse group can discard labels and separate agendas.

We therefore recommended that the new organization should include the existing CONVO categories of members (national umbrella groups such as the National Association of Independent Colleges and Universities; nationwide organizations such as the National Urban League; and national organizations without nationwide affiliates, such as the Population Resources Center), and that it would also include foundations and corporations, such as those represented in NCOP, whose giving programs reflected national and international interests. Among the latter were regional and community foundations, statewide foundations, and major regional voluntary organizations that had national interests and impact. The organization was also to include national churches, unions, civic groups, cooperatives, and so on, as long as they were joining to participate in the agenda relating to philanthropy and voluntary action.

The emphasis on membership and on spreading the participation was carried over to decisions about governance. We concluded, for instance, that each member organization would have one vote, and that the voting membership body would have broader powers and involvement than usual. As another means of sharing participation and power, it was agreed that the organization should have a board of approximately forty-five persons, and further, to avoid concentrating power in a few people, that we should not have an executive committee. I was told repeatedly that such an arrangement could never work, but it did. It was particularly important that the members felt there was somebody at the table they could count on to represent their point of view.

Consistent with the spirit of involvement and spreading of leadership roles, it was agreed that even the chairperson would be limited to three one-year terms in that role. When the end of John Gardner's three years was approaching, the resolve of many of us was tested, but not John's. It was a wrenching change, but the right thing to do.

Some people still ask me—with appreciation or disdain—how we chose the title "chairperson." I explain that we left it entirely to the women who served on the committee. They caucused, decided, and that was it.

The rest of the work of the committee and its subsequent report dealt with essential issues such as size, budget, staffing, location, process and timetable for implementation, and much more. It also laid out the increasingly obvious stipulation, but one still very hard for many people to accept, that if the report was approved, both groups would be voting themselves out of existence. It was one thing to agree on most of the other issues, even dues maybe, but all the next steps were made more difficult by the reality and finality of the formal votes to dissolve.

The sensitivity of this situation was compounded, excruciatingly, by the fact that we couldn't reach agreement on the name of the new organization. It was awkward enough being asked to go out of business, but doubly hard to accept if one didn't know and was suspicious about what the successor organization would be called.

Long after we had achieved agreement on every other difficult, contentious, and divisive issue, and at a point when we wanted terribly to achieve closure before hard-won agreements unraveled, we couldn't get the two sides to agree on a name. Finally, in desperation, we agreed to reject any names, words, and connotations that each side said would be unacceptable. For example, CONVO did not want the term *philanthropy* used, and NCOP did not want the term *voluntary*. Each had concerns about what the message would be and did not want the other to appear the survivor. We agreed that we would submit the task to a professional firm, and the decision would then be made by Phil, Jim, John, and me.

The issue of the name went through one more roller-coaster loop before finally landing. We had been fortunate to enlist the firm of Ruder and Finn to provide expert study and advice, but after all their work, they recommended VOLUNTARY SECTOR, even with the awareness that the "V" word was at the top of NCOP's "no" list. Although the firm argued that its recommendation was sufficiently strong to be worth reopening negotiations with NCOP, they also agreed that INDEPENDENT SECTOR should be the backup choice. At that point, there was no way to retreat from our prior guarantees to NCOP and no sense taking the risk of reopening negotiations. Also, at a previous point, the Organizing Committee as a whole favored the name INDEPENDENT SECTOR.

At that point, we had been through four drafts of the committee's report, reflecting amendments negotiated with both organizations. We were also getting very close to NCOP's twenty-fifth anniversary conference, which was shaping up as a propitious occasion for cementing the deal. It had already become so much of a mutual enterprise that everyone thought of it as the launching of INDEPENDENT SECTOR. Thanks to the generous spirit of NCOP, CONVO was equally involved in the preparations, the program, and the possible celebration. The co-chairs were Ed Van Ness of the National Health Council and Pat Noonan of Nature Conservancy, each very much identified with both organizations. With the surge toward a new beginning, the theme for the conference "The Independent Sector: Reflections and Directions" fit the occasion perfectly.

With spirits high and most of the issues already resolved, the NCOP Board met the night before the conference and, with some caveats, approved what turned out to be the penultimate draft of the Organizing Committee report. The CONVO Board had already approved in principle a similar draft, also with some caveats, and there was a distinct likelihood that the remaining differences would be resolved at the final CONVO Board and Membership meetings in December. Although it wasn't over, and anything could happen to set us back, the Denver Conference was decidedly upbeat.

Finally, on December 12, 1979, the formalities were concluded—still without a name! The two organizations prepared to phase out, and we all turned to the formalities necessary to bring the new entity into being. With clear awareness that the future was still full of uncertainties and difficulties, I couldn't imagine that anything would ever again be as crazy, chaotic, and utterly exhausting as those eighteen months of three simultaneous full-time jobs.

Later in December, with all the votes final and with a little time to reflect and breathe, I went on one of my occasional solitary retreats which involved walking the deserted Rehoboth Beach for hours to try to clear my head and put the past and future in perspective. For at least the first day, I found myself so preoccupied with the chaos of the past that I went round and round with a rehashing of events. It wasn't until the evening of the second day, on a very cold but moonlit evening, when I had walked perhaps three miles down the beach, all the way from Rehoboth to Dewey, that somehow the thought and words popped into my mind: "The marathon dash is over." I stopped and found myself saying it over and over again, louder and louder, "The marathon dash is over," until I settled on a dune and cried with the amazement and relief of it.

« 7 »

Early Victories and Lessons

Independent Sector
1980–1985

John Gardner and I immediately appointed a nominating committee, which had the almost impossible assignment of ensuring that every possible representation was included. Just about every person had to be at least a "three-fer" in their affiliations. As we came down to the last opening we had to find a person who had at least five identifications: arts, female, Midwest, volunteer, and donor. It would have been easy to throw up our hands and pick someone from our impressive backup list, but I wanted to give it a try. I went to Chicago and talked to a few people who might possibly identify such a multifaceted candidate and actually came back with three names. John called what looked like the best of them and she accepted. Later a couple of members of the nominating committee chided me that they should have made the job *really* hard by requiring that she also be an Asian American who spoke Arabic.

Before the charter meeting, recruitment of members and fund raising went into high gear, with exhilarating progress on both fronts. To our relief and delight, a great many leadership organizations wanted to be registered as charter members. It also added to our stature that Bob Harlan, who was just finishing up many years as national head of the YMCA, had agreed to become executive vice president of Independent Sector.

Because there were many carryover program activities from the two originating organizations, and the organizing committee had already spelled out future programming directions, it was not necessary to come forward right away with new recommendations.

It couldn't have been better timing that shortly before the charter meeting, on March 5, 1980, the Supreme Court ruled in our favor, in *Village of Schaumburg v. Citizens for a Better Environment et al.*, that a community may not impose a flat percentage limit on the fund-raising costs of organizations raising money in its territory. The case was particularly significant because it reaffirmed that charitable solicitation is an activity that enjoys Constitutional protection as an element of free speech. In the case at hand, the Village of Schaumburg had denied a solicitation permit to a scrappy and highly credible environmental group called Citizens for a Better Environment, which was raising cain with the village leaders for their intolerable handling of environmental matters. The Citizens for a Better Environment would probably not have had much of a chance if we had not rallied a wide range of prestigious organizations to the case. The lower courts had realized that something more was involved than just a small local scrap. We were also enormously fortunate that the case was argued by the legal scholar Adam Yarmolinsky, a member of our new board. John Gardner had talked much earlier about the importance of early victories to help give the organization visibility, credibility, and excitement, but neither of us expected anything this big this soon.

With Schaumburg at hand the charter meeting started with a bang, but with a small problem literally and figuratively. We never dreamed we'd have so many charter members and others wanting to witness what this new undertaking was all about, and within a few weeks before the meeting we knew that the hall couldn't hold half of them. It was an acceptable crisis to have to change locations, but we had to be awfully sure that not one of the new members or prospects lost faith in us because they arrived at the wrong place.

John Gardner in his inaugural remarks and Senator Moynihan in his address on "Pluralism in the Independent Sector" added greatly to the spirit and significance of the day. John said in part: "Everyone likes beginnings. But few of us in our lifetimes are lucky enough to be in on a beginning that may prove important for the future of American life. . . . We want to preserve a great tradition in America. We want to ensure the vitality of a precious part of our society. But we intend to be honest about ourselves, and we intend to proceed with a regard for the good of the whole society. Not to benefit ourselves at the expense of others, not to pursue a course of self-aggrandizement, not to concentrate on the purposes of a few powerful elements in the sector but to serve all: These are principles we intend to honor."

Moynihan added this perspective: "I congratulate all of you on your act of creation. If anything exhibits the energy of the private sector over the past short year and a half, it's that a common sense of purpose and condition has emerged from the most disparate enterprises, from the American Theater Association to the Audubon Society all in one room, all for one purpose. . . . I think many of you will remember reading Joseph Schumpeter's last great book in which he said how this wonderfully creative civilization which we have produced in North America and Western Europe is going to come to an end—not in some great apocalyptic Armageddon in which one class takes over another class and destroys all classes. It will come to an end through the slow but steady conquest of the private sector by the public sector. There is nowhere that this is more in evidence and more advanced than with respect to the non-government enterprises of public concern which you represent. Little by little, you are being squeezed out of existence or slowly absorbed. . . . Your job is to assert that something of the most profound concern to American society is at issue, and that is our tradition of a plural, democratic society."

Our next major milestone was the first meeting of the new board. There was an initial fright when I looked up and realized that we had seated Faye Wattleton, head of Planned Parenthood, next to Monsignor Lawrence Corcoran, director of Catholic Charities. I was afraid we had blown ourselves out of the water. Fortunately, they seemed to get along and thereafter gave every indication of cordial relations. You won't find it surprising that I considered my selection as IS president a highlight of the meeting. Appropriately, there had been a formal selection committee, and at one point, I was told that an impressive and well-connected individual had made known his interest. I can remember thinking that this could be one of those situations where someone works his heart out to bring an organization to a major threshold, only to find that another person is selected to take it from there. Fortunately, the executive session lasted only a minute and I was approved.

Speaking of executive sessions and presidential matters, a few years later, when the board was discussing my performance and compensation, the group seemed stymied by wanting to express considerable appreciation without having to extend considerable compensation. They were concerned, as was I, that the financial remuneration not become a problem for our members, particularly those where salaries were far less than mine. As I understand it, the board searched for a way to express appreciation, but not *too* tangibly. Father Corcoran said the board could resolve the matter the same way his institution does by making me a monsignor. When I came back into the room, I was baffled by being addressed as "Monsignor," but when I learned the story I loved it, and for a long time afterward some routinely referred to me by that honorary title.

The board also had a chance to discuss program activities already underway and to begin to think about future efforts. It was a freewheeling session, with a good deal of opportunity for people to ask anything they wanted about any facet of our operation. For the most part, that relaxed approach seemed well received, but we could also tell that it was going to lead to some adjustment. For example, at the breaks and at almost every other board meeting for a few years, I would be approached by some directors, generally from cause-oriented voluntary groups, who expressed concern that there wasn't enough time to adequately involve the board in full debates and decisions. I would then be approached by others, usually from the business side, who expressed concern that we were talking the issues to death and should be more action oriented. Over the years, it was the corporate people who had to adjust the most, but that didn't mean they got over venting their frustration that I did not simply tell the board what I thought should be done. It took a great many meetings before our unique culture began to take hold, and even then it had a lot of room for differences and differentness.

The meeting was considerably more civil and cordial than the first meeting of the Organizing Committee, but the two did have in common an obvious wariness and uncertainty about how much common and uncommon ground the participants were now plunked down on. What saved the meeting was the inherent goodness of all the people at the table, however different and uncomfortable they felt, and the fact that most of the ideas and issues discussed were of common interest. An important part of the commonality was their respect for the person in the chair, John Gardner, so even if they found part of the experience foreign or awkward, they figured he must know what he was doing, and they'd hang in.

Fortunately, we had several fairly relaxed meetings before one session when very different viewpoints about our roles and priorities almost tore us apart. The disagreement related to our responsibility for dealing with proposed federal budget cuts and to the use of our supposed influence to reorder the funding priorities of foundations, federated fund-raising groups such as United Way, and corporate philanthropy. Shortly after newly elected President Reagan had announced his major budget reductions, which represented massive cuts for many voluntary organizations and the people they served, our board meeting was thrown into chaos with angry demands by several directors that IS turn almost all its attention and energy toward defeating the proposals in general and to restoring allocations for specific fields such as health and the arts.

At subsequent meetings, the demands for our intervention escalated, including an expectation and insistence that we cause our funder members to provide financial relief for threatened agencies and people. Although the majority of directors recognized that it was not within our intended mission and capacity to represent each part of the sector to government or to cause our members, whether grant makers or grant seekers, to reorder their priorities, it was still extremely difficult to make clear our limitations to those who were injured by the cuts. Our more general roles in government relations and the strengthening of philanthropy seemed pallid in comparison with the help that many people needed right away.

After several clashes and debates, it was generally accepted that we could not fulfill the roles expected or demanded of us without destroying our fragile togetherness. However, it was also agreed that we could and had to play a role in explaining to government and the public the consequences of such massive budget adjustments and the reality that private philanthropy and voluntary organizations could not "fill the gap." On an emergency basis, we commissioned Lester Salamon, then of the Urban Institute, to prepare a report on the issues—resulting in the remarkably illuminating and persuasive "The Federal Budget and the Nonprofit Sector," which IS published along with related data in a report called "Analysis of the Economic Recovery Programs' Direct Significance for Philanthropic and Voluntary Organizations and the People They Serve." We also hosted scores of sessions for various IS members to learn from these reports and from one another about what could be done to reverse or pare the cuts and how to increase private support.

Those were scary times for a barely born alliance struggling to hold and attract members and trying to serve as a bridge between donors and donees. We lost some important members and were a long time getting over some ill feeling between some directors. Fortunately for the long run, we survived this much too early crisis and, in the course of the struggle, gradually achieved a clearer understanding and at least some acceptance of what this confederation could and could not do.

Even during this tumultuous period, there were enough indications of the usefulness and even the impressiveness of the new organization that a general atmosphere of positiveness and spirit was building. For example, as word spread of the significance of the Supreme Court's ruling in the Schaumburg case, there was a clearer grasp of how important it was to the achievement of that ruling that the sector had been able to speak collectively and forcefully.

Despite all sorts of Congressional opposition, the Coalition of National Voluntary Organizations (CONVO) charitable contributions legislation, which would make the charitable deduction available to people who did not otherwise itemize their tax deductions, continued to grow in sponsorship and popularity, including becoming the only one of forty amendments accepted for the Senate Finance Committee's tax bill. The testimony we organized involved a wide variety of influential figures, including leaders of foundations, grass-roots organizations, environmental groups, universities, civil rights groups, youth-serving agencies, and many others who had probably never collaborated even around issues of common purpose.

The sector rallied to the defense of the U.S. Olympic Committee, whose charitable status had been threatened because it was unwilling to publicly support President Carter's boycott of the Moscow Olympics.

As plans developed for the 1980 National Conference on Philanthropy, a carryover of the National Council on Philanthropy, (NCOP) annual conferences, it was clear that people who previously had never thought about their affinity with so many different types of organizations were eager to explore common needs and to share thoughts about research on the sector, government relations, standards, board development, and much more.

What we began to hear was that people felt it was high time for various parts of the sector to be working together; that they liked what they saw in INDEPENDENT SECTOR in terms of process, participation, and representation and were impressed with early results. It certainly was evidence of interest and growing respect that recruitment of members was far ahead of projections, and that well within our timetable, we exceeded the grant support goal we had set for the three start up years.

It's fair to say that by the end of our first year, our successes had increased and our reputation had risen dramatically. Obviously, that was to the good, but it was also clear that expectations were rising even faster. Within just a year, we had an almost impossible reputation to live up to, a still very fragile coalition and board, and the certainty of inevitable disappointments. We may have looked awfully good, but I knew very well that critics and mistakes could combine to make us look like a flash in the pan.

We were beginning to learn how essential it was to be impressive with what we did tackle, to do everything possible to recognize what we couldn't take on, and to accept the reality that the more impressive we became, the more critics we would attract, particularly among those who didn't understand or wouldn't accept what we couldn't do.

It was also helpful that the members and directors found, usually to their surprise, that there was a common view of what IS should emphasize. In a major survey of the members and directors to secure thoughts about program priorities, there was striking agreement on the most important things to be done. For example, a distinct majority of both groups rated education of policymakers, the media, and the public the most important area for concentration. A summary of the survey results expressed it: "The most important goal for IS is to raise public, government, and total community understanding of the impact and necessity of the independent sector to American life."

The Organizing Committee had identified external and internal goals for the proposed information and education program. Under external, they emphasized "to improve public understanding of the sector's role and function in giving people alternatives, greater opportunities for participation, and for creating a more caring and effective society."

From the day the announcement of our formation appeared prominently in the *New York Times* and wire services, we were up to our necks getting the message out. In a remarkably short period, we became a respected source for reporters, editors, feature writers, and others who were trying to produce stories about aspects of voluntary effort. To sustain the coverage depended on our ability to keep the information flowing and to find new ways to tell the stories. We were able to create a steady stream of regular and special features drawing on our various reports, such as those on giving and volunteering, the relationship of religion and generosity, and the motivations of the generous. We also provided up-to-date information about contributions and tax policy, trends and levels of giving, and on and on.

Within a year of our founding, we were able to tell parts of the story on major TV shows such as *Today* and the *MacNeil/Lehrer News Hour*. The Associated Press found our releases of regular interest and used us as an active resource for wire service stories. Kathleen Teltsch of the *New York Times* began to place enough stories on the sector to be assigned to it as a full-time beat and, by her own account, began to look to us as her principal source of ideas and contacts. We were assisted greatly by the growth of electronic databases, which enabled any reporter, editor, or feature writer to locate us and to draw on stories that we had already filed or in which we were quoted. At the same time, we were feeding our members every compelling fact and story we could find, and increasingly these showed up in their own publications to help spread the word.

The primary stimulus for media coverage was our "Giving and Volunteering" reports. These biennial studies and releases usually led to major wire service stories and appearances on such shows as *Good Morning America*. We were fortunate that the attention was not limited to the few weeks surrounding the release of our biennial reports. With each feature and story, the word spread and the interest grew. Later, we scheduled news conferences and interviews on various parts of the reports, such as support for the arts, volunteering by Blacks, and the growing philanthropy of women.

The Public Information and Education Committee and staff began planning for a major film that would present visually and dramatically what the sector is and does to be used by our members to help millions of participants understand the context of their contributions of time and money. We hoped this would both reinforce the habits of participation and extend them to even more people. The film would also be appropriate for service clubs, other civic groups, classrooms and the broader media beginning with public television. The board quickly picked up the excitement and priority of it. Our only problem was that to do it well would cost a minimum of $300,000.

From prior discussions with the Gannett Foundation I thought the foundation might be willing to consider a major contribution to the film's production and was encouraged that Gene Dorsey, its president, was at least open to my coming to Rochester, New York, to talk about it. The journey there was filled with traumas well beyond those relating to a major request.

The only time we could all get together was an early morning about three weeks after my call. Unfortunately, I had an unbreakable commitment to give an after-dinner presentation in Hartford, Connecticut, the night before. After examining every possible transportation option, I concluded that the only way to do both was to charter a plane for a late-night flight. Obviously, it couldn't be anything fancy, but even at that, I wondered how it would look to the board and our members if it ever became known that I was flying around in chartered planes!

If they could have seen the plane and experienced the night, their largest worry would have been about my sanity. The plane was about as old as the pilot, which was not reassuring. It was also tiny, which the pilot said would allow me to sit in the copilot's seat with a good view of things, which turned out to be a bad scene. The flight was to take about an hour and a half, but because of head winds that seemed to be pushing us backward and detours that drew us away from our destination, it took closer to three hours—a nightmare of precipitous drops, mountainous bumps, and gyrating instrument dials (and passenger). During this ordeal, my pilot's efforts at reassurance never got better than "Don't worry, I do this all the time." Double jeopardy was never more poignant. I had little doubt that I was going to die, and it would be all over the papers that it happened in a chartered plane!

The good news is that the appointment went wonderfully. The foundation took a keen interest in the project and subsequently invested more than $300,000 in the film's production, promotion, and distribution. In early 1983, we released *To Care: America's Voluntary Spirit*, with premiers in thirteen metropolitan areas and extensive initial promotion to our members. The promotion quickly broadened to emphasize schools, service clubs, and television.

To Care was and still is used in orientation of volunteer leaders, in schools, and for special TV features about the sector. It was the most important and tangible step we took toward providing a common articulation of the sector's roles and impact. We were also becoming better at providing our members and media with specific information about the sector, and at advising members on how they could put such information to use to increase their income and effectiveness.

From the mid-1980s, there was increasing media attention on problems in the sector, particularly regular reports of fund-raising scams, high fund-raising costs, and gross mismanagement. INDEPENDENT SECTOR had already been deeply involved in efforts to promote openness, accountability, and effectiveness, but we were faced with the prospect that the public could lose faith in voluntary organizations. With materials already at hand, such as a values and ethics report and a companion report on performance and accountability, we were at least somewhat equipped to help communicate to media representatives, and through them the public, that the overwhelming majority of voluntary organizations performed remarkably well. Most of the problems being exposed involved fraudulent behavior, which was already against the law and should be exposed and prosecuted; and the media could help in informing donors, volunteers, and board members of existing guidelines about board responsibility, standards, ethics, and compliance with the law.

Initially, there were many sessions with skeptical or cynical reporters who thought we were trying to defend the sector, including the scoundrels. Later, most would be won over by evidence that we had been striving since our beginning to make clear what kind of behavior was expected of voluntary organizations and what was totally unacceptable.

Our communications achievements were often the envy of our members—even very large organizations with appealing causes and substantial public relations staffs. But with each success, most people just expected more. If we could get on the *CBS Evening News,* why didn't we make it onto NBC? Or if we got an op-ed piece in the *New York Times,* why couldn't we use those pages regularly for other worthy messages?

Through it all, our accomplishments were given high ratings by our members in their regular evaluations of our performance, which made it easier to live with the inevitable expectation that we should be able to turn on a media blitz at will.

Almost in a tie with public information and education, the membership rated relationships with government as our second highest priority. The Organizing Committee had the advantage of CONVO's prior activities, and we benefited greatly from the active participation of Congressmen Barber Conable and Joseph Fisher on the Organizing Committee and its government subcommittee. With those advantages, the committee proposed the following role for IS in its relationships with government: "to deal with the infinite interconnections between the two sectors, but particularly to ensure the healthy independence and continued viability of nonprofit organizations. This may include efforts to influence public policy where the welfare of the entire independent sector is concerned."

The Organizing Committee pointed out that excessive control by government was the greatest threat to the independence of nonprofit institutions, and that it was the emerging or unpopular organizations that were particularly at the mercy of all this regulation. The committee elaborated, "there is no greater danger to the preservation of our liberty than giving the powers that be any great control over what their own reformers might do." For those reasons, we moved quickly when we saw the advocacy rights of voluntary organizations threatened.

The first excruciating test came out of the Reagan White House in January 1982, wrapped in the Washington jargon "Amendments to OMB Circular A-122," often described as "defund the left." Whatever the source or purpose, I characterized it as "an egregious end run around freedom," but the task of restraining it and eventually rolling it back took nearly two years.

The Office of Management and Budget (OMB) Circular A-122 governs federal grants and contracts with nonprofit organizations. Without consultation, OMB proposed drastic changes in the treatment of advocacy activities, which eventually would have forced all voluntary organizations that accepted any government funds to forego their right to try to influence legislation or even communicate with government officials. For example, Catholic Charities, which helps to carry out government child care programs and is reimbursed for doing so, would have been prohibited from expressing itself on ways to improve those services. An organization that received only a tiny proportion of its total budget to help evaluate a federal program would have been disenfranchised. And all this was to go into effect in sixty days.

After verifying the accuracy of the scary rumors about the OMB actions, I called one of its top officials, who first denied that any such changes were in the making, then minimized their significance, then acknowledged and editorialized that they would indeed stop voluntary organizations from mucking up (not quite his term) the workings of the administration, and finally told me that if I thought anyone in the White House was going to change one G.D. word, I had manure (a euphemism) for brains. It was by far the most outrageously dishonest, threatening, and profane conversation I ever had with a public official. Not surprisingly, it ended with his obvious eagerness to be sure I understood that if I didn't like what he was telling me, I could go screw myself (or some such word).

Because the network of INDEPENDENT SECTOR was by then in place, we were able to create a firestorm of protest, including many examples of specific and horrendous implications for people and causes in almost every congressional district. There was also extensive media coverage.

For two months, OMB and the White House held firm, but their resolve was being challenged by high-level congressional interventions prompted largely by the local affiliates of our members. For example, Congressman Conable personally called James Baker, White House Chief of Staff, to voice his concerns, and followed up with formal letters to the President and Baker. There was heavy criticism from the media—for example, a *New York Times* editorial headed "OMB Bomb Throwers," written as a result of our meeting with a member of the editorial board.[2]

Our OMB task force, including 250 representatives of prominent organizations, many generally favorable to the Reagan administration, kept building the nationwide outcry. With all of that, David Stockman, director of OMB, finally announced withdrawal of the regulations. That was a relief and an important battle won, but it soon became obvious that we had only won the first stage of a protracted struggle. OMB treated the event as a temporary setback, figured that our outcry would die out, and that they could come back with more of the same and stick it in our ear. (My OMB contact would have put it differently.)

In November, eight months later, OMB's second draft was released. We had used the long interim to provide fuller evidence of the negative impact of their original proposal, but obviously we had not made a sufficient dent. There were improvements, but really only to try to satisfy some secondary concerns expressed by members of Congress about Congress's own responsibility for defining such controls. Fortunately, our new opening was provided by this emphasis on relationships with Congress, because both Houses called for hearings on the overall changes. Those hearings gave us the best possible opportunity to articulate our concerns and make our recommendations to the committees and to every influential member of Congress. Also, our formal testimony gave us a document to use in restimulating the grass roots.

In testimony before the House Government Affairs Committee, I emphasized that the new recommendations still represented serious infringements on the advocacy rights and responsibilities of voluntary organizations, and I urged that if there was a need to redefine lobbying, the definitions should be consistent with those contained in the Tax Code governing tax-exempt status.

With pressure mounting, OMB again extended the public comment period as we had recommended, and seemed to take more seriously the need for much greater amendment. In part, that was the result of enormous criticism expressed by the House Committee, especially its influential chairman, Jack Brooks, and by the fact that in the Senate, David Durenberger, a Republican, introduced legislation that would have overridden the authority and the actions of OMB. We had worked extensively with both legislators, largely through leaders of organizations in their constituencies.

Finally, in late April 1984, OMB issued a much revised recommendation that went a very long way to respond to our concerns. Also, although the comment period had ended, Congressman Brooks invited our participation in presenting requests for clarification "as to the allowability of the practices described," and our requests were sent to the president by Brooks and the ranking Republican on the Government Affairs Committee, Frank Horton. They and we were assured that our concerns would be accommodated.

After enough time had passed to be assured that our victory would hold, I began describing that long, harrowing struggle in ways that helped our members realize the significance of it—not just to take pride in the victory, but to achieve greater resolve and confidence in what we could achieve together. I wrote:

> During the past two years, we have led an all out struggle to force OMB to withdraw and almost totally revise the requirements of voluntary organizations in relation to their advocacy activities. Five years ago, we would have been powerless to protest, and those regulations would now be choking off the sector's most significant public service.

As far back as the spring of 1981, when against everyone's prediction and all odds we succeeded in getting the Senate Finance Committee to include the charitable deduction for all taxpayers in its tax bill, Senator Bob Packwood, a cosponsor of our legislation and a high-ranking member of the Finance Committee, told our board: "INDEPENDENT SECTOR has proved to be one of the most organized, efficient and knowledgeable networks I have had the pleasure to work with. I place major responsibility for the success of this bill on the efforts of your organization in getting the support of so many people and organizations from all over the United States. It is one of the few times that I have seen a bill lobbied so well."

When the charitable contributions legislation (CCL) was enacted four months later, I issued a congratulatory memo to IS members in which I said:

> Ours was a people's bill. Nobody took it seriously except you and your constituents—the people. *You* generated the outpouring that Senator Robert

Dole, Chairman of the Senate Finance Committee reported "couldn't be stopped." It's a beautiful demonstration of the responsiveness of elected officials to their constituents. Along the way there have been discouraging obstacles and setbacks but these have been more than matched with tenacity and organization. The result is glorious. It's a special occasion.

In my "Highlights for 1985," I described several successes in government relations activities, and to explain how and why we had prevailed in several uphill struggles, I stated: "In the past, the organizations of the sector have only been able to express themselves on such issues in disorganized fashion. We are now able to focus the passion, provide the facts, and organize ourselves in the congressional districts. That combination of passion, facts, and organization has achieved far greater results than anyone ever thought possible."

There were many crucial events in our relations with government, but the principal message was that we had developed the courage and capacity both to *fight* government when that was necessary and to *cooperate* with government when that was called for. Both approaches were necessary to the constructive pursuit of our mission. With each uphill victory we gained three advantages for future progress: the victories themselves; the inspiration we gained from the evidence that we could win; and greater respect from government, including greater reluctance to take us on. We knew they would all be needed to counter future ill-advised efforts to limit our roles.

Our research responsibilities and activities climbed rapidly to become one of our most visible and significant functions. The Organizing Committee had been fairly crisp and definite about research. The purpose of the program is "to provide a body of knowledge about the independent sector and about how to make it most useful to society." The IS research committee and the board added clarifications, so the charge became, "To develop an identifiable and growing research effort that produces the body of knowledge necessary to accurately define, describe, chart and understand the sector and the ways it can be of greater service to society."

A particularly important crossroads was faced as far back as 1979, when the CONVO research committee discussed our first Gallup survey of the public's attitudes toward giving and volunteering. A prominent fund raiser foresaw that many of the questions could elicit negative comments that might be better left unreported. He wanted assurances that the CONVO reports would be presented in such a way that the public would think even more positively about giving time and money to voluntary organizations. He even wanted mechanisms established to be sure that negative findings in the survey would not be leaked. It was a defining moment. He was not alone, but fortunately the majority expressed the firm position that if our research projects were tainted by subjectivity, bias, or propaganda, we would contradict and defeat our purposes right from the beginning.

With such important early decisions and with the benefit of prior work by CONVO and others, we were ready for rapid development of IS's research program beginning in early 1982. Five factors contributed to the next giant steps. First, a plan was in place. Second, we realized at almost every turn how much more we needed to know if we were to understand the sector and make the case for it. Third, income from memberships and a special solicitation gave us enough funds to support a research director and the first three years of programming. The fourth factor was that we were able to recruit Virginia Hodgkinson as our vice-president for research from a similar role with the National Association of Independent Colleges and Universities. And finally, Bob Payton, head of the Exxon Education Foundation, became head of the research committee and quickly helped to pull together an extraordinary group.

A major vehicle for the growth of our direct and indirect impacts was the research forums that we began to convene. They were designed with a number of purposes in mind: to reveal who was already studying what; to provide an outlet for those researchers and build a network among them; to provide a bridge between scholars and practitioners; to encourage academics and their disciplines and institutions to recognize the attractiveness and legitimacy of this field of research; to suggest ideas for research, including dissertations; to build interest among publishers; and to prompt funding sources to recognize the importance of such research. For our first research forum in 1983, we scoured the country for people with an interest in our subjects, and by 1995 there were several separate organizations of researchers encouraged and assisted by IS, including the International Society for Third-Sector Research.

From the beginning, these purposes were remarkably well served. For years, people would indicate that it was at a particular forum that they found a supportive network, met a future collaborator, got the idea for an academic course, learned about funding sources, identified possible publishers, learned about databases, and a great deal more. Later the books published annually by Jossey-Bass with the best of the papers from each forum helped build the foundations of future scholarship. All of our hopes for what might be possible in a full-blown research effort came together in those forums. Each was special, but it was the series as a whole that built the networks and generated the attention, confidence, support, and stimulation. In an unbelievably short time, a new, identifiable, and legitimate field of research had been created.

Another important decision about research priorities involved religion. It was not an area where many on our research committee and board wanted us to go. There was a fairly pervasive view that religious institutions were different from the rest of the sector and therefore not really appropriate for us to pay much attention to. This didn't include religiously affiliated services such as hospitals and schools.

It had been my own experience as a community organizer that religious congregations play an enormous role in motivating and guiding people to serve, providing social services, and raising the conscience of communities. Fortunately, Bob Payton and Virginia Hodgkinson joined with me as a stubborn core, and it was determined that religion, including religious congregations, would be prominent in any definition of our research interests.

Virginia and the research committee also turned their energies to stimulating the interest of various academic disciplines. We knew from the start that our greatest impact would be achieved by encouraging existing disciplines to recognize the validity and attractiveness of research relating to our sector.

Our initial foray in this direction almost came a cropper. With great pushing and pulling, we were able to organize a full day's seminar on philanthropy with a prominent group of social philosophers. For the first part of the day, four of us—Bob Payton, Michael Novak, Peter Dobkin Hall, and myself—attempted to present information and viewpoints designed to generate interest among these distinguished philosophers, but the reception was just barely polite. I think it's fair to say that they couldn't figure out what in the world we were saying that would hold the slightest interest for them. Finally, but without design, one of us pointed up the sector's role in advancing pluralism in a democratic society, and suddenly the philosophers took over what became an enormously animated discussion. Philanthropy was an impossible sell, but pluralism was easy, and the related discussion of current and prospective research was wonderfully rich. What had started as an absolute dud of a session even produced a book: *Philanthropy: Four Views*, published by Transaction Books and the Social Philosophy and Policy Center of Bowling Green State University.

Many research efforts came within the scope of the National Center for Charitable Statistics (NCCS), which initially was a joint project of the Council on Foundations, United Way, the American Association of Fund-Raising Counsel, and IS. In 1983 the other participants asked us to take full responsibility, and although enthusiastic about the work of NCCS, we saw severe obstacles to taking it on, including expectations of great expansion in the center's programming, and our research committee's worry that these immediate responsibilities would take us away from longer term investments in building the larger field of research.

In the end, our other NCCS partners accepted a less ambitious effort if we would agree to take it over. Our research committee continued to be wary but agreed that many of the functions were absolutely necessary—for example, producing the kind of statistics essential to building the larger research capacity—and that no one else seemed to be equipped to move readily and effectively into the breach. We worked out an arrangement by which the research committee would continue to focus almost exclusively on the longer range and broader goals, leaving NCCS as a separate committee.

There was another lesson that related to NCCS. A number of our funders who were eager to see us take it on assured us that they would continue to provide separate annual support for NCCS. On the basis of past experience, I predicted that it wouldn't be long before they, or more likely their successors in those jobs, questioned why they were making two grants to the same organization, but I was assured that the commitments were long term. Even while the merger was still in its early phase, many of those funders withdrew on the grounds that they were already providing support to IS.

Another possibly useful aside about funding is that many people assumed we could raise a great deal more money than we really could. There was also a fairly pervasive assumption that once IS had proved itself, many related functions could be put under our umbrella. I even had a call one day from one of our board members telling me that an organization he chaired had been given the good news that a major foundation was willing to approve a $2 million program-related investment for them if IS would become a partner and accept responsibility for repayment of the loan. No one had ever bothered to ask us if we might be willing. My board member was furious when I said I'd have to recommend against it, and his organization subsequently dropped membership in IS.

I've come away from this and so many other funding experiences with an absolute conviction about the necessity to stay one's own course without letting even friends and funders dictate what my organization should take on.

As I look back on the roles and impact of the research program, including our National Center for Charitable Statistics, I'm convinced the program was absolutely central in giving this previously invisible and diffused collection of agencies, crusades, and institutions a sense of common identity, acceptance as major players in the ways this country performs its public business, and the facts so necessary to the sector's growth in size and effectiveness. Statistics, classifications systems, inclusion in the U.S. Census, and other essential breakthroughs may not have seemed dramatic, but they told us who we are, what we do, and why it matters.

There was never any doubt within the Organizing Committee that effective sector leadership was essential to pursue. The committee summarized the responsibility: "Encouragement of effective operation and management of philanthropic and voluntary organizations to maximize their capacity to serve individuals and society as a whole."

As early as the second meeting of the IS board, several short-term projects were recommended, including meetings of interested members on such topics as use of electronic data processing; marketing for nonprofit organizations; planning; evaluation; board development; and, in light of the energy crisis of those years, energy conservation by IS members.

After successful efforts to secure start up funding for the program, Roger Heyns, head of the Hewlett Foundation, agreed to lead the initial Leadership and Management Committee, and Blenda Wilson joined the staff as vice president for leadership and management. Within a year, Brenda was lured away to the first of a succession of major leadership roles in her specialty field of higher education. She was replaced by Sandra Trice Gray, who provided her own good model of leadership for more than a dozen years. In those many years, Sandra and the organization were particularly helpful to the mission by constantly and aggressively seeking good examples of effectiveness and passing them along.

We were also fortunate to have at hand one of the country's most effective leaders, who was able to devote a good part of the next seven years to this side of our program. Shortly after John Gardner stepped out of the chair, he undertook a Studies in Leadership project with us.

It was John's plan to devote a good deal of attention to reflection and writing about the leadership lessons he had learned in many different settings. I learned indirectly that he didn't feel right about raising money for his own projects and therefore planned to work almost full-time for at least three years without remuneration or reimbursement. Even though he was ready to make these sacrifices, I felt that this towering public servant deserved better. The point I made to him flat out was that he was one of the nation's greatest assets, and that if he intended to remain active in public service, many funders would be eager to encourage and support that work. I was adamant, and he was stubborn. I told him he was no longer the chairperson, and I was going to raise the money anyway. After more words, he backed up halfway, but tried to compromise by stipulating that he would accept specially raised funds as long as they were to cover direct expenses and no salary or fee. I fudged and told him I would report that compromise to prospective funders but would abide by the conditions of their grants. It was the easiest fund raising I ever undertook, even with John's additional condition that he didn't want any one funder to be asked for more than a modest amount. It took only about ten visits to gain ten commitments, which all just happened to include conditions that compensation be paid for the work involved. Even then, what John would accept was woefully short of any reasonable estimate of his worth, but that was as far as he could be pushed. With the enthusiastic approval of the board, John's work became a project of IS, and we had the additional advantage of having him in our midst several more years.

In the next two years, John produced twelve "leadership papers," which are still in circulation and have been distributed in numbers well exceeding a quarter million. Examples include "The Nature of Leadership," "The Tasks of Leadership," "Leadership and Power," "The Moral Aspect of Leadership," and "Constituents and Followers."

On reading the very first paper, I told him, "Reads like the first chapter!" He scowled and said he had no intention of producing a book and certainly didn't want to be tied to that goal, but with each issue I would at least hint that it sure looked like the makings of a book, and finally I dropped all pretenses and began to refer to later issues as "chapter eight" or "chapter nine."

With those and some other writings and with the pamphlet series completed, he finally headed toward a book that in 1990 became *On Leadership*, probably the most important book for which IS has played a part. I felt forgiven and rewarded for my badgering and pushing when I discovered he had dedicated the book to me.

Fortunately, the Leadership Studies program continued for many years, focusing later on community leadership and community building, and including several wonderfully insightful papers such as "Building Community" and "National Renewal."

One additional reference to him belongs here, and that involves the creation of the John W. Gardner Leadership Award, established by the board and membership in 1984 in recognition of his service as the founding chairperson. It honors outstanding Americans "who in their own way exemplify the leadership and the ideals of John W. Gardner."

An area of cross over efforts for both our research and leadership programs involved our role in helping to create and encourage academic centers for the study of volunteering, philanthropy, civil society, pluralism, and so much more, and for the teaching and training of students, practitioners, volunteer leaders, and so many more. One example might be particularly interesting and a perfect illustration of the principle that if you know where you want to go, you're likely to be ready when opportunity knocks.

Hank Zuker, a prominent professional in the field of Jewish philanthropy and an adviser to Cleveland's Mandel family and their Premier Industrial Corporation, visited me, among many others, to try to determine what might be particularly important directions for future philanthropy of the Mandels. At that point, they were considering a colossal jump in their already generous annual support levels. Hank mentioned various possibilities, including new targets and ventures in areas the family was already invested in, such as Jewish education and culture, Cleveland area social services, the Council of Jewish Federations, and assistance to Israel.

I had known that Mort Mandel, with the assistance of his brothers, had used an extraordinary management style to develop Premier into a major economic force. Putting that together with IS's desire to get significant funders interested in research and leadership relating to the sector, I brainstormed with Hank about ways of improving the effectiveness of voluntary organizations in general, including attracting and nurturing capable young staff who would serve the sector long term. We discussed the notion that because of the Mandels' wide-ranging philanthropic interests, they might be naturals for investing in the greater effectiveness of the sector as a whole.

Hank was sufficiently interested to ask me to summarize my thoughts in writing, and after further consideration, I wrote a long memo to Hank and Mort that became the skeletal plan for what evolved into the comprehensive Mandel Center for Nonprofit Organizations. Most of the thoughts were not original with me. They were the product of prior discussions with many individuals about what IS and others could do to further the sector's unique roles. There were also some existing models of academic centers, though nothing quite so comprehensive as I was proposing.

My memo led to further conversations with Hank, others involved in Premier and Mandel philanthropies, and then with a broader group of Cleveland institutions, including the Cleveland and George Gund foundations. These in turn led to exploratory discussions with the president, provost, selected deans, and others at Case Western University. Top leadership of the university was interested, but understandably had a hard time selling this as a new priority when so many other needs and hopes existed in almost every part of the institution.

Finally, after more than two years of discussion, consultation, and negotiation, all parties agreed to participate in the formation of the Mandel Center. The center was formally launched in 1985 as a joint activity of the schools of management, law, and applied social studies. It quickly became an enormous resource for the development of new and strengthened leadership for agencies in the region, and a major force for research and its application in the development of more effective nonprofit organizations, both nationally and internationally.

There were many players involved in the development of the center, but Hank and Mort recall, as I do, that the initial flicker of the idea and the beginning blueprint and negotiations grew out of a concept at the ready within IS.

There was a similar pattern in discussions with people at Lilly Endowment and later at Indiana University. The idea of a center was substantially carried by Charles Johnson at Lilly Endowment, who involved me in discussions with his top leadership and then in joint conversations with Indiana University (IU) officials. Tom Ehrlich, IU's president, and his wife Ellen had a keen interest in philanthropy and the independent sector in general. I attended a meeting that included the heads of eight or nine schools within the university, and I recall worrying whether the ambitions might have gotten out of hand. They hadn't, and the idea blossomed into the most comprehensive of the academic centers, with major initial funding from Lilly. A fellow conspirator, Bob Payton, who had been the first chairman of the IS Research Committee, was enticed to become the center's first director, which couldn't have been more fortuitous for everyone who wanted to see more across-the-board academic involvement with our issues.

It's also interesting that after fifteen years as IS's director of research, Virginia Hodgkinson became the founding director of a new but already strikingly impressive Center for the Study of Voluntary Organizations and Service at Georgetown University.

Our goal was not to try to achieve a center in every major institution but to have a sufficient number of centers with regional and national prominence to provide visibility for the sector and respect for an academic role in its study and development. Similarly, our aim was not to try to establish a new academic discipline but rather to create a credible and respected field of interest reaching into and crossing all academic disciplines.

In my "Highlights of 1987," I mentioned the informal and sometimes more direct encouragement we had given to a "number of academic institutions and academicians to begin to pay overdue attention to this sector as a legitimate and attractive area for research, education and training, and the establishment within IS of a 'meeting ground' for the centers." I added, "This almost invisible activity of IS may turn out to be our most important long-term contribution to building an understanding of the role of the sector and the ways by which it fulfills its public services."

From our earliest days, we worked closely with the Association of Governing Boards for Colleges and Universities (AGB) to translate its successful experience into similar results for other parts of the sector. In 1987, after a year's consideration, we jointly launched the National Center for Nonprofit Boards (NCNB), which later became an independent body active throughout the country and even internationally. NCNB is now known as BoardSource.

Throughout our first fifteen years, IS focused a good deal on efforts to make the organizations of the sector even more effective than they were. That included such essential matters as openness and accountability, but also a large sense of moral responsibility and stewardship.

Beyond our direct activities, we tried to operate in ways that might serve as a good example to the field. This goal applied to the way we communicated with members, our approach to planning and evaluation, the organization of our government relations network, and the quality of our publications, news releases, research surveys, and so on. On the evidence of their evaluations of us, our members seemed to feel that our goal was being fulfilled.

One of our most timely and consequential endeavors to provide leadership and guidance at a time of crisis was our study on values and ethics, headed by Ira Hirschfield, and the related book, *Ethics and the Nation's Voluntary and Philanthropic Community*. The project had two primary origins. A number of board members who had agreed entirely with our position in three Supreme Court cases that threatened arbitrary government regulation of voluntary organizations felt that we had equal responsibility to articulate what the sector and its individual organizations must stand for. The other impetus was several media exposés calling attention to deceitful and illegal behavior by some voluntary organizations.

Almost as soon as the report was completed, the United Way scandal screeched through the country, and we were fortunately ready with a message for boards of all voluntary organizations and all their contributors about the standards to which the sector and its organizations must be bound. We also made clear that we were more critical than anyone else of organizations that failed those standards.

The report of the Committee on Values and Ethics stated that "concerns about lapses in ethical conduct arise in every part of society, but that the public expected the highest values and ethics to be practiced habitually in the institutions of the charitable, nonprofit sector. Because these institutions, fundamentally, were dedicated to enhancing basic human values, expectations of them are particularly high."

The title of the report included the phrase "obedience to the unenforceable," quoted from England's Lord Justice of Appeal John Fletcher Moulton more than sixty-five years earlier. "The true test of greatness," said Moulton, "is the extent to which the individuals composing the nation can be trusted to obey self-imposed law." The committee added: "In the independent sector, public trust stems from our willingness to go beyond the law or even the spirit of the law. We act ethically because it is the right thing to do."

The committee made a particular point that "When our institutions do not reflect high standards of openness, honesty and public service, our contributors and clients are ill-served. This sector depends upon public goodwill and participation. If public support is eroded, so is our capacity for public service."

We went on to underscore certain ethical behaviors that nonprofit organizations should stand for, including *commitment beyond self,* which is at the core of a civil society; *obedience to the laws,* a fundamental responsibility of stewardship; *commitment beyond the law,* or "obedience to the unenforceable"; and *commitment to the public good,* which requires that those who presume to serve the public good assume a public trust.

One of the largest, and I think most successful, projects in our Leadership and Management program grew out of a desire to learn more about what was already working well and then pass that knowledge along to our members and far beyond. As with research, we were handicapped by limited literature even about what constitutes excellence in nonprofit endeavor.

One of the frustrations for businesspeople serving on voluntary boards is that it is so hard to define and measure success. Nonprofits just don't have the simple measure of bottom-line profits. Many individuals from the commercial sector so desperately want voluntary organizations to mirror the best practices of business that they are extremely impatient with their nonprofit counterparts. It became routine to hear such observations as "These do-gooders and bleeding hearts just don't know how to manage" or "If we could just get more management discipline into these cause-oriented organizations, they would be far more effective."

It's my observation that these perceptions are usually inaccurate and unfair. Voluntary organizations, like businesses and other human institutions, vary in their effectiveness. About one third are models of excellence—beautiful examples of caring, innovation, and efficiency—one third are good to fair, and one third are poorly managed and generally ineffective.

With publication of our four-year study *Profiles of Excellence: Achieving Success in the Nonprofit Sector,* we took our largest step toward clarifying the characteristics of successful voluntary operations. The efforts of our staff, Burt Knauft and Sandra Gray, and consultant Renee Berger, produced a remarkably useful combination of evidence, examples, guidelines, and references. Their book is a long-term contribution to a still sparse literature and an immediate help to conscientious board and staff leaders.

One of the most important parts of the study was the determination of certain "hallmarks of excellence" that characterize the best of nonprofit organizations. To determine these standards, we asked our members, community foundations, United Ways, and others to nominate models of effectiveness. We didn't try to stipulate what constituted excellence, because that would have produced a self-fulfilling prophecy. We just asked them to name two or three voluntary organizations that they considered stunningly good, with some indication of why each was chosen. Several hundred organizations were brought to our attention. We then reduced that list to a manageable number, making sure that it included arts, social welfare, environment, and so on. After securing a good deal of information from these groups, we made more eliminations and then arranged field visits to interview clients, funders, board members, staff, and others associated with each of the remaining organizations. We were trying to find out whether these organizations really did measure up to their billing, and if so, what seemed to be the characteristics that made them so special. *Profiles of Excellence* summarized the common denominators that were found; described each of the organizations in some depth; and summarized how other organizations might replicate their performance.

The four hallmarks of excellence that we identified were primacy of mission, effective leadership, a dynamic board, and strong development efforts.

Perhaps the best vehicle we had for raising up models of good leadership and management practices was our annual meetings, where those topics took up 50 to 60 percent of the program. Sandra would have made it 75 percent! In any case, the attention to effectiveness was evidence that we were true to the Organizing Committee's belief that any group dedicated to preserving and strengthening this unique side of America has to devote a considerable part of its effort to the "encouragement of effective leadership and management of philanthropic and voluntary organizations to maximize their capacity to serve society."

Although we never intended it, at least not directly, our greatest early victory was assembling IS in the first place, and our greatest continuing challenge was keeping it together.

« 8 »

POWERED BY COALITION

INDEPENDENT SECTOR
1985–1995

The depth and breadth of INDEPENDENT SECTOR's impact correlated with its membership. We knew we couldn't take the membership for granted and that we had to invest substantial resources to retain and add members. We also had to be sure that we were strong in all the sector's categories, such as arts, education, civil rights, foundations, and corporations.

All that was the task of the membership committee, headed during the critical early years by Ken Albrecht of Equitable Life, former chairman of NCOP and a key member of the Organizing Committee. We worked hard to separate the membership and fund-raising functions because in a combined operation fund-raising would have received the most attention, and our short- and long-range strength depended primarily on the outreach and participation of our members. For example, our regular fund-raising appeals and special campaigns for project support were generally oversubscribed, and in all of those appeals, it was the members' enthusiastic endorsement that made those campaigns so successful.

Even as we approached our tenth anniversary, when all kinds of fund-raising projects were proposed, I argued that what we should celebrate and build on was our membership. We set a goal of 250 new members and, with the leadership of Ted Taylor of the Kresge Foundation and the staffing of Jeanne Bohlen, the Tenth Anniversary Membership Drive was successful, not only in going beyond the goal but in the quality of leadership groups enlisted and the breadth of fields represented.

The diversity of our membership was captured in an unusual story. The day before our 1985 annual meeting in New Orleans, John Thomas met with Nan Perndes, a *Times-Picayune* reporter who was trying to get a handle on just what this convention was all about. To describe our unusual collection of members, John indicated that some were philanthropists who were generous donors, some were philanthropoids who were executives of foundations, and some were philanthropees who spent the money. The opening line in the reporter's story the next day was, "Today more than 750 pists, poids, and pees descend on our city." It was not a bad way of capturing the makeup of our membership and the unusual experience of bringing them together on what the Organizing Committee called "the meeting ground." The committee anticipated quite accurately that once these organizations were even loosely linked, there would be many useful interchanges and mutual pursuits well beyond the defined program concentrations, such as research and government relations. We had predicted the development of "a greater sense of community among the organizations of the sector."

The yearly get-togethers were even called the Annual Meeting *and* Assembly of Members, and although the business aspects provided the legal reasons for coming together, the larger attraction by far was the chance to swap ideas and information, expand one's networks, and gain encouragement and maybe even inspiration to take back to difficult tasks. We also tried to achieve those results in regional meetings and briefings, which helped to involve even greater numbers of our members.

Many of our members discovered, in some cases to their surprise and ours, that leaders and organizations could learn a good deal from unlikely sources. I recall a session on marketing where one of the resource people was a marketing professional at the Salvation Army. In advance, some attendees told me they couldn't imagine how museums or universities could learn much on that topic from the Army, but the colonel was the hit of the day, demonstrating a sophistication as useful as it was surprising.

At most of our meetings, we worked hard to get the participants to mix, and we even spent a good deal of time organizing round tables and small discussion groups with assigned seating so that there could be a much richer sharing of experiences and contacts. Whenever we saw a table or room that represented individuals from community foundations, corporate philanthropy, housing, women's issues, opera, preservation, and international understanding, we knew we could leave them absolutely to themselves and the session would be wonderfully rich. That was our "meeting ground."

Some of my most trying times involved dealing with people who insisted that government protect their freedom to do what they passionately believed was in the public interest but who wanted the same government to use its power to squelch those with whom they bitterly disagreed. At one point when this pattern became ludicrous bordering on frightening, I wrote a piece that the *Christian Science Monitor* published as "Don't Save Me from the Left or Right."

From two extremes, people who believe passionately in freedom are calling for increased regulations to restrict what their opposites can do.

With the growing influence of conservative evangelical churches, liberals are calling for revision of the laws that define what a religion is and what religions can't do. From their side, influential conservatives are promoting legal schemes to "defund the left," to limit the outreach of organizations like Planned Parenthood that deal with causes they consider dangerous to the country.

Liberals, who for fifty years have been listening to their Roman Catholic priests tell them how to vote, or who still hear their black preachers endorse candidates, or who encouraged their Lutheran ministers to march in Selma, want to clamp down on what can be done in the name of religion. Conservatives, who preach faith in people, minimal government, and clearer separation of church and state, want expansion of governmental control over what they define as unholy.

If both sides get their way, we'll have more laws to protect us from the right and the left—and less freedom for everyone.

Out of passion and bitterness, both sides are losing sight of the protection of the larger freedoms of speech and assembly, and of their wide-open opportunities to spread what they consider the truth. Any infringement of these freedoms and opportunities will sooner or later infringe both of them and all of us.

If some people believe that the rest of us must be protected from certain extreme ideas, or if they're frightened that we won't make the right decisions for ourselves, our families, and our communities, there is comfort in Thomas Jefferson's advice: "I know of no safe depository of the ultimate powers of society but the people themselves; and if we think them not enlightened enough to exercise their control with a wholesome discretion, the remedy is not to take it from them, but to inform their discretion by education."

Norman Lear started People for the American Way to warn people of the seductive media campaigns of the Moral Majority, and if Lear goes too far, someone else will come along to correct him. Along the way, the people learn and grow.

There are some causes in the land that I believe are downright dangerous, and there are situations where opposing crusades spend staggering amounts only to achieve a standoff. Our protection—and theirs—is in our right to disclose what we know, not foreclose what they do.

If some groups clearly trespass the law, the authority is already at hand to deal with them. Hopefully, though, the law will not be administered with a heavy hand. Democracy and I can survive my priest telling me how to vote on a candidate who supports federal appropriations for abortions, but we will not survive if he can be too easily silenced on public issues, or if true believers in any cause can legally stifle their doubters.[3]

Although there were many significant purposes served through our meetings and the many major projects that grew out of them, most of what we did within the general category of "meeting ground" could never be adequately described, and even if it could, it would not seem nearly as useful as was really the case. Because there was a network that spread even far beyond our members, IS developed what in today's lingo is described as a "switchboard" and ours was lit up all the time. There were calls, e-mails, faxes, letters, and personal approaches requesting information and guidance on our program concentrations and every possible tangent of them, as well as subjects having nothing to do with them. Because we were gaining visibility and credibility, our members and a great many others turned to us regularly for things that might relate remotely to our mission and often did not even meet that criterion.

This responsibility became such a large part of our life that we were constantly trying to figure out how to organize it. On several occasions, we sought to determine if it really was as a great a load as we estimated, and those analyses indicated that approximately 15 to 20 percent of total staff time was taken up in responding to inquiries beyond our five program concentrations. These included requests for credible contacts or consultants to help with organizational problems or development; speakers and speech material; staff searches (and sometimes searches for board members); advice on fund raising; sources of help on bylaws and policies; financial guidelines, such as recommended levels of reserves; briefings on compensation, including benefits; and examples of awards programs.

At times some strains would develop within the board when I would try to interpret that these almost invisible services should be counted in and respected for what we did, especially for the members. I would point out that there were very good organizations, including some large umbrella groups, that *only* did an annual conference and maybe one publication such as a journal or newsletter, and for which registrations and subscriptions covered all their organizational costs and their members expected nothing more of them. I wasn't proposing that for us but just trying to use it as evidence that some of the functions we were taking for granted and really didn't count as parts of our "program" were in fact the total program of other respected and successful coalitions. Sometimes I would think I had made my point, only to be faced with a rejoinder such as, "Those activities are important and good, Brian, but we've got to do more that is tangible." I would want to strangle them, but they were after all, board members.

Also contributing to our success in sustaining the coalition was our ability to document IS's increasing program impact. At an early point, I was able to say, "In 1980, INDEPENDENT SECTOR represented only great needs and high hopes. Now, the evidence is clear that by working together the organizations of the sector can have enormous impact on the health of the sector and its ability to be of public service."

Building all facets of IS, including the membership, depended on the makeup and functions of the board of directors. We spent a great deal of time on board development, including far more time than is usually taken to study gaps, needs, best bests, and much more. The board meetings themselves were carefully organized to make the most of the time and talents of this very high level of leaders. Although most of them were selected as representative of a given subsector, such as religion or the environment, and it was very useful that the subsector felt its interests were being watched out for, the directors almost always looked at the broader mission and responsibilities of IS. The organization and I were blessed throughout those years with absolutely marvelous boards. The intended turnover made it hard for me to keep adjusting to the loss of so many special people. The newcomers would be just as good and were likely to be even more currently in tune with their side of the sector, but it was hard, especially for me, to have to adjust and to say goodbye to proven stalwarts and friends.

Our farewell gift for them was a particularly attractive box for a desk or coffee table with the IS symbol on top and a personalized plaque on the inside cover expressing our appreciation. I still visit with a lot of those people and invariably find their box prominently displayed. They were proud to be part of building this unique organization and welcomed being reminded of their contributions.

It's an understatement in the extreme to say that we were fortunate in the succession of enormously able, active, and prestigious chairpersons. During my years, each one served the full three years. They were John W. Gardner, Richard W. Lyman, John H. Filer, Eugene C. Dorsey, and Raul Yzaguirre.

Despite my pride in our coalition, I never thought of it as a model, but almost from the beginning we received inquiries about coalition building and over the years the interest escalated. This was more than idle curiosity. It reflected a pervasive and growing need to figure out how to create collaborations, federations, and other partnerships necessary to deal with the increasing complexity of communities and human needs. More and more people were finding that their causes were linked to others, and that solutions were not possible without allies. School dropouts and failures are related to inadequate nutrition, teen pregnancy, illiteracy, gangs, drugs, and so much more. International harmony is linked to control of nuclear power, reduction of hunger and famine, youth exchange, language training, and many other factors. Leaders of single-issue causes, trying to improve schools, transportation systems, or access to health care, realized they had to join with others to have enough leverage to make a difference.

Alarmingly, this overwhelming need for collaboration was and still is up against inadequate experience in forming and maintaining intricate alliances. Because we seemed to be achieving impressive results in building our coalition, we were besieged for information about how we had done it and guidance on how they might do it.

Although John Gardner and I had considerable experience with complex human institutions, I don't believe either of us thought of ourselves as experts on the topic. We had proceeded not from any textbooks or checklists but more from a random collection of well-learned *musts* and *mustn'ts* when dealing with people who have to work together but don't know it or don't want to.

In many ways, the whole of my book *Powered by Coalition* is necessary to the explanation, but I know from experience that most people who are interested in IS will sooner or later want to know what I think really caused it to succeed—and they don't want a book-length or even a chapter-length answer!

Here are ten possible lessons growing out of the IS experience. The first four of them have already been addressed in chapter 7, so elaboration is not provided here.

1. The problems were very real and growing, and the consequences of not addressing them became harder for conscientious people to ignore.

2. We made good use of the head starts and lessons provided by such groups as CONVO and NCOP, the Filer Commission, Committee for the Third Sector, and Alliance for Volunteerism.

3. The plan was visible enough to catch people's attention, bold enough to stir their passions, and potentially powerful enough to really make a difference.

4. We went for and achieved major early successes and communicated them in ways that built momentum for membership and support, and for moving to even higher levels of achievement.

5. We stretched inclusiveness to the point of bewilderment, despite concerns about being too broad, diverse, and unmanageable. In responding to inquiries and doubts about broad-based coalitions, I would almost always fall back on one of John Gardner's many apt phrases, "wholeness that incorporates diversity." My listeners would nod at the sagacity but quickly fall into worries about having people with too much differentness in the circle.

   One of the hardest things to do is to reach out to those you actively dislike or with whom you've had prior battles. It's hard enough to be open to those you don't know, but when the challenge extends to those you do know and wish you didn't, it's easier to argue for a smaller or at least different group of partners.

   One of the lessons about inclusiveness involves enormous forbearance and a sustained effort to understand where people are coming from and why.

   Even within relatively civil alliances, there will be times when many of the partners become tired of hearing different voices and viewpoints. Most of the participants will be preoccupied with their own busy and stressful responsibilities, and it will require all their forbearance to sit around listening to a lot of people who see things differently. Another of John's apt admonitions was a help to us, and might be for others: "To survive and succeed requires an infinite regard for differences among good people."

6. We stayed with and made the most of the common ground where we belonged, and we resisted every fierce effort to move us onto ground and into battles where we didn't belong. In the case of the first few meetings of the National Committee on Patients' Rights described earlier, the only thing that made it possible to proceed was to stay within the tiny strip of common ground until enough trust was established to widen the path.

   One of the most discouraging realities of coalitions is that people find it hard to accept the limitations of the group, and the stronger the coalition, the more likely the frustration. This doesn't mean that people have to compromise at the absolutely lowest common denominator. The more successful the partnership, the more certain it is to be pushed awfully hard to overextend itself. For IS, this was always the greatest threat to stability—and sometimes to survival. Even after the harsh clashes and bitter disappointments of our first few years, we never went very long without having to deal, perhaps to the point of confrontation, with new participants who hadn't gone through the process of learning our limitations or with more seasoned members who knew the ground rules but felt that their crisis merited an exception.

Because the expectations of IS, even within the common denominator of our members' interests, were always so much greater than resources, we had to find ways to establish what we could and couldn't do. To make such distinctions stick, we had to involve the members in decision making. That required a time-consuming process, but it often made the difference in heading off all the inevitable "bright ideas" and extravagant expectations.

We studiously avoided trying to meddle in issues that were the clear province of existing partnerships such as the Arts Alliance or the National Assembly of Health and Social Welfare Organizations, and in one of the toughest tests of our resolve, we stood absolutely firm when several foundations proposed that we establish specialist IS councils on health, arts, environment, social welfare, and so on, which would absorb the organizations dedicated to those interests. It was understandable that funders would find it easier to support just one umbrella organization rather than several, but we wouldn't have survived if we had moved in on those territories, and we certainly never would have had the experience to deal knowledgeably with their subjects. I would often return to the thought that not being daring is sometimes the most daring thing you can do.

7. From the start, we invested heavily in identifying, enlisting, and utilizing the right leadership for the mission and for the signal such people's participation conveyed. Every human institution depends on good leadership, but coalitions and collaborations require particular investment. They are usually pretty fragile operations, and the leaders and other partners are often preoccupied with their primary obligations, which compounds the tenuousness. The ad hoc nature of the enterprise, and the urgency of it, may help hold things together in the short run, but a longer-term effort will almost certainly require realistic degrees of investment to hold the partners together and maintain their commitment.

It is particularly important in a collaborative enterprise that leadership reflect the strengths and diversity of the group. That was the case at IS, and was a major reason for the rapid rise in the number of people who were willing to be involved. From the start, people like Phil Bernstein, Ken Albrecht, Bayard Ewing, Jim Lipscomb, Homer Wadsworth, and many others represented steadiness and credibility with their peers, capacity to stay with the enterprise even during the storms, and so very much more. These qualities grew in importance as the cast of characters grew. The members needed to know that people they trusted were centrally involved and would keep them informed of both progress and problems. Such leaders are absolutely necessary to counter the inevitable destructive critics who may be on the fringe or closer, and who through their egos, backbiting, or rigid adherence to their own agendas undermine an organization's prospects and make success infinitely more difficult.

There was one aspect of criticism that I do recall discussing with John Gardner early and often, and that was the fact that it's a great deal easier to be a critic than a builder. We had far more than our fair share of both, but one builder is worth dozens of critics, so the odds were definitely with us.

8. There was absolute commitment to process, including openness, team building, and infinite regard for differences of opinion among good people. Beginning with our earliest discussions with members of the CONVO and NCOP boards, continuing through the struggles of the Organizing Committee and into the first years of IS, we had to work awfully hard to build trust, step by step, until people knew that they could rely on us to do what we said we would do—or to explain openly and completely why we couldn't. People gradually accepted that there would be no surprises, no hidden agendas, and no back-room meetings when their interests were at stake.

As the networks grew, we continued building a shared leadership, so that when people beyond our reach expressed curiosity, concerns, doubt, or upset, there was someone to whom they could turn who would be able to say, "Don't worry, Mary is in the thick of it, and you know you can trust her." It was equally important that those who wanted the organization to do their bidding learned from people they respected that we would not bow to demands and pressure, no matter the source. That helped build trust, especially among those who feared we would be subject to control by United Way, the Ford Foundation, or other major institutions or groups of them.

One aspect of process that turned out to be an absolute lifesaver involved the identification of different levels of commitment we could assign to approved projects. As described in each of our five-year program plans, a committee of reference or the board, and in some cases the staff, could determine the level of commitment IS would provide. Those levels were: a letter of encouragement for an activity carried out entirely by others; agreement to let our members know about someone else's activity or about a request for their optional participation in it; written encouragement to IS members to consider participating in an ad hoc session or similar activity to be called and handled by the originating organization; agreement that IS would call an ad hoc session for interested members on a subject suggested by one or more members and likely to be of interest to others; agreement to organize and chair an ad hoc group exploring a somewhat complex subject or activity that needed sustained examination and that could result in a proposal for continuing or special IS attention; adoption of a position statement or other formal expression of organizational support for a particular bill, program, or initiative; agreement to pursue a topic or project through an existing IS function—for example, making it a topic at the Annual Meeting and Assembly of Members; assignment to an existing committee, or establishment of an ad hoc committee; an all-out effort, including possible utilization of our congressional network; and the securing of funding for special projects, including those requiring significant extra staffing.

9. A very real part of our success was attributable to our original and ongoing commitment to building the membership and other sources of financial support. In my eventual swan song to IS I said, "In putting it together, everything was the membership. We knew from the start it had to be an independent organization. In fact, we knew that this organization had to be truly independent if we were going to be anything like a model of the independent sector. Everything we've been able to accomplish relates to the quality, the conviction, and the participation of the membership."

10. Luck. I mentioned earlier in the book that I acknowledge the role that luck has played in my career. That certainly applies to IS. We benefited a great deal from the kind of luck that occurs when you are prepared for it, and we experienced the kind of luck when great things happen that you couldn't possibly have anticipated. We had our share of every kind, and must never be so smug as to think we did it all ourselves.

To figure out INDEPENDENT SECTOR, it may also be helpful to report on the session John Gardner and I had in the summer of 1995, seventeen years to the month after our first discussion about the need for some greater connectedness within the sprawling third sector. John and I stole away for two days to share thoughts and recollections about what had occurred in the blur of those intervening years. This too is explored substantially in *Powered By Coalition*.

My immediate task in the session was to gain the benefit of John's advice on the book I had been asked to write on INDEPENDENT SECTOR's beginnings and early years. I had even prepared an agenda. I wanted his thoughts about the book's scope, tone, and thrust, and his recollections of facts, events, and people.

Eventually, those purposes were well served, but before we could make headway on any of them, it became clear that each of us needed to get down to such basic wonderments as why we had taken on the challenge, why we had gambled so much on such a long shot, and why it had succeeded after all. It wasn't part of our plan for the time together, but we couldn't seem to look back without probing those bedrock considerations, and that started with a lot of brutally candid "Why in the world did we . . . ?" and "How did it ever . . . ?" It wasn't that we hadn't known what we were getting into. It was more that we knew and still went ahead. And our candor was not just in admitting our doubts but also in admitting a confidence in ourselves that in retrospect appears audacious.

At times in that conversation we asked each other genuinely and uncertainly whether we had been gamblers or visionaries, foolhardy or courageous, reckless or calculated. We let it all hang out—two battle-scarred survivors admitting to fear, and to bravery. In the end, we admitted we had thought we could win, that the cause was worth the gamble, and that the time and climate seemed right. But we also admitted that in fact we had been audacious, reckless, and foolhardy, tempered with at least some doses of courage, confidence, and vision. We acknowledged that we had been risk takers, but that we had not blindly followed an impulse. We had thrown caution to the wind not for the daring but because something unusual seemed to be in the air.

Looking back, the origins are terribly complex, but the essential dilemma was startlingly clear: Something had to be done to preserve and strengthen America's independent sector, but nothing was likely to succeed. The obstacles and the problems, presented to us with intensity and in growing litany, had dogged all previous efforts at creating an umbrella: a sector so broad that it defied commonality; antipathies and worse between many of the players; the disdain of university officials for grass-roots organizers and vice versa; the determination of funders to keep their distance from grant seekers; fear of the very size of a coalition large enough to span the sector; lack of confidence that such a group could really do anything about the sector's problems; reluctance to pay for still another layer of representation and structure; and on and on.

Perhaps the only thing that kept us at it in those early days was that although almost everyone assured us that every solution was foreclosed, they were equally determined that something had to be done. The contradiction helped make us at least curious about what, if anything, might be done to ease resistance, and that in turn led to further exploration. Gradually, we moved to a consideration of whether the unnamed somebody who ought to do something might be us. Then it was even more urgent to look at whether there really were signs in the wind to make this attempt any more promising than all the others.

Essentially what gnawed at us and nudged us toward commitment were six key observations. First, we found widespread conviction that the sector occupied an important place in American society and that it deserved to be further nurtured and developed. Second, it was clear that the problems facing the sector were threatening and pervasive and constituted a potential rallying point for common endeavor. Third, a growing roster of impressive allies was ready to sign on if we did. Fourth, other key figures, despite being pessimistic, seemed willing to at least keep an open mind. The fifth salient fact was that the National Council on Philanthropy and the Coalition of National Voluntary Organizations were in a position to provide some institutional underpinning. And finally, although various prior efforts might have failed to achieve ambitious goals to unite the sector, what they had accomplished and what had been learned from them could be built on.

Beyond those positive signs, there were less tangible factors that helped tip the scales. Although we didn't actually say it to each other until seventeen years later, John and I had felt that each of us would come to the task better prepared than those who had preceded us, or at least with unique experience behind us. Further, the two of us seemed to represent many of the varied assets and balances necessary to the teamwork that the next stages would require.

We also agreed that the time and circumstances would probably never be better for such a project, and finally a feeling grew in both of us that it was simply the right thing to do. So after much more testing, lining up of allies, and persuasion of other important figures to keep an open mind, we finally threw our hearts over the fence and took off on what turned out to be one hell of a ride.

Years later, after we had survived excruciating complications and crushing work schedules to see the confederation achieve impressive im-

pact and stature, I would hear people describe the organization's founding and development as so natural that it had just fallen into place. At
those moments, I didn't know whether to weep, scream, or kill. The better outlet was to tell a story.

A farmer had taken over a long-neglected property. The fields were
barely distinguishable, covered with weeds and trees. The barn had pretty
much collapsed, with much of the wood deteriorating or lost to theft. The
house leaned so badly, it seemed beyond renovation.

After years of struggle, the farmer finally brought the place to the point
where he wanted to show it off to his parson. With great pride, he took
the reverend to the fields now laden with produce, and the parson pro-
claimed, "The Lord doth provide." The farmer took the reverend to the
barn, wonderfully renewed and full of bellowing livestock, and the parson declared, "Praise the Lord." Finally, the minister was taken to the
house, now safe and cozy, and he intoned, "The Lord works in wondrous
ways." With some exasperation, the farmer responded, "Meaning no dis-
respect to you, Reverend, or the Almighty, but I just wish you could have
seen this place when God had it to Himself."

It won't surprise you that my book about IS begins, "Let me tell you
the way I remember it."

It was wonderfully gratifying that in 2000 a distinguished panel, chosen
to identify the ten events of the twentieth century that most heavily influenced the development of philanthropy and the nonprofit sector, included
the formation of INDEPENDENT SECTOR as one of the ten. The citation read:

> Independent Sector is formed
> Transformation of the nonprofit world from one of charities to an effective,
> professional part of the American economy was marked by creation of a
> primary voice in Washington, Independent Sector. Nonprofit groups took
> shape as more than mere exceptions to the tax code, but rather as a force
> that complemented business and government and added a sophisticated
> voice in policy making.[4]

That ranking, alongside Carnegie's philanthropies, Kennedy's Peace
Corps, and the NAACP's early and powerful voice for minorities, was
tangible recognition for what we and so many others gambled on and
struggled for beginning in 1978.

It was appropriate that I headed the book about our efforts and successes, *Powered by Coalition.*

« 9 »

WHAT'S A COMMUNITY ORGANIZER DOING GLOBALLY?

International Assignments
1985–2005

For a long time my different road stopped at the U.S. borders, and that was fine with me. Trying to get on top of national problems and opportunities had me stretched as far as I could manage.

I might have been tempted by some international connections and issues in the mental health field, but I couldn't have done them justice. In addition, my predecessor had been drawn to international assignments and this had been viewed negatively by people who thought he should be giving all his attention to problems at home. I got the message and, having little to contribute overseas, stayed clear. I assigned someone else as liaison to the World Federation for Mental Health and other international obligations that came along. My only personal exposure involved the consultation I mentioned earlier, when my counterpart in Britain insisted I not say a word about successes in pressing our government to expand research and services.

In my early years with INDEPENDENT SECTOR there were a few exposures but they didn't take me over the water. For example, I was approached by a management consultant who was under contract with a government in the Middle East that needed to establish a new community far into the desert. Oil had been struck, requiring a great many people to extract it, which meant that workers and their families had to be persuaded to move to a rather desolate spot. Someone got the notion that if the government could offer the attractions of a community complete with all imaginable support systems and amenities, the task might be doable.

What the consultant wanted me to do was to describe the support systems and amenities of an ideal American community and then advise them on how to set these up with everything paid for and sustained by the government. I explained that a very real part of the attraction of such entities in the United States is that the people really own and feel responsible for these associations and systems and want a good deal to say about how they are operated. I indicated that if all these community activities and organizations were owned and controlled by the government, they would not have the qualities the government was seeking. It took only a short time for the message to come back that the government would not tolerate such independent people and institutions and that therefore they would have to find a different way to accomplish their purposes.

While that experience borders on absurd, it nevertheless sticks in my mind as symbolic of how in so many places in the world, even in the United States, there is a great desire to have active citizens as long as people and their organizations don't make waves.

Another brief exposure that didn't involve travel but was useful to my broader orientation involved one of INDEPENDENT SECTOR's research forums, on the subject "The Nonprofit Sector in the Global Community: Voices from Many Nations." The forum and related book explored the roles and functions of the nonprofit sector in many nations and cultures and offered a rich agenda for further study by political scientists, historians, economists, sociologists, cultural anthropologists, and students of comparative government. It also provided examples of collaborative international programs in research and training, and ways to foster international coalitions.

At the urging of a few board members, I did attend a conference in Bonn of the International Standing Conference on Philanthropy (Interphil), which involved mostly Western Europeans, Americans, and a smattering of others. I remember not being impressed by the content but was fascinated by some of the individuals, many with whom I'm still in touch.

I also attended a meeting in Britain organized by the Ditchley Foundation that had an ambitious title, such as "the Future of philanthropy in the Western World," which helped to provide some important comparisons among our countries. For example, it became clear that for all our countries the total amount of money represented by voluntary organizations was minuscule compared to what our governments spent in the same categories. For instance, in Britain, the total voluntary sector was about 2 percent the size of government, compared with our 10 percent, and foundation and corporate grants were an almost invisible fraction of

1 percent. Even at that, representatives from those other countries argued that however small the percentage and even the money amounts were, they provided absolutely vital elements of flexibility, innovation, creativity, and capacity for criticism and reform and therefore must be preserved.

One of the issues discussed at that meeting was whether philanthropic monies should be used to supplement government expenditures, particularly at a time of government cutbacks. At that time, both Prime Minister Thatcher and President Reagan were urging private philanthropy to make up for some government retrenchment. Many U.S. mayors were also urging foundations and corporations to help government keep schools, libraries, and parks open and to maintain other public services. Our discussions made it clear that although philanthropy has a responsibility to deal with emergency matters, particularly those involving human suffering, in the long run the small amounts that philanthropy contributes must be reserved for *extra* purposes. If not, philanthropic expenditures will not represent anything unique and therefore might not be worth preserving.

Another interesting assignment that led to some follow-up activities began when Mort Mandel, who had been so very much involved in the establishment of the Mandel Center at Case Western, asked if I would be willing to go to Israel under the auspices of the Joint Distribution Committee, known fondly and admiringly as "The Joint." It took awhile for me to get used to the term. I had heard of "The Joint" but did not realize how important it was in funneling contributions to Israel that had been raised in the United States by both the United Jewish Appeal and Jewish Welfare Federation—thus the nickname. They wanted me to consult with Israeli leaders to study why more aspects of civil society, including a strong independent sector, had not developed there. I agreed to participate, in part because I was fascinated that what we generally describe as the Judeo-Christian influence on our civil society seemed to be weak in the Jewish homeland.

I wasn't far into my review when I realized that in its first fifty years, Israel and its people were necessarily preoccupied with building the governmental systems of defense, roads, education, housing, and much more. These had to be the focus. However, fifty years later they were surprised to realize that Israel of all places had a limited independent sector. They did have a great many quasi-governmental institutions, but these were really part of the way the government fulfilled its public business and were too dependent on government to be considered independent. Also at that stage, most of the contributed money came from sources outside the country. Today, Israel is far more aggressive in attending to the development of a truly *independent* voluntary structure, including the establishment of an organization along the lines of our INDEPENDENT SECTOR.

That experience has always stood out as a warning that even people committed to voluntary action can neglect this central aspect of a free society.

Another assignment that contributed to my international perspective involved organizing and chairing a 1989 Salzburg Seminar on "The Role of Non-Profit Organizations: Comparisons of Functions, Operations, and Trends," which included about fifty seminar fellows and faculty members from twenty countries. That group has also provided a number of ongoing contacts and friendships.

In 1992 I accepted an invitation to serve as a Yoshida Foundation Visiting Fellow in Japan. Every other year the Yoshida Foundation, in cooperation with the Asia Foundation, of the United States, invited an individual to spend three weeks in Japan, meeting with leaders and organizations on a topic of mutual interest. In my case the subject was the development of private philanthropy and the voluntary sector in our two countries. The foundation had been started to honor Shigeru Yoshida, the country's first Japanese Prime Minister after the U.S. occupation.

In advance of the trip I prepared a good many resource materials and had them translated into Japanese. Fortunately I tested the translations with a native speaker, who at first marveled at the size of our giving and volunteering but then became downright disbelieving. It turned out that my initial translator had turned millions into billions, so when I intended to say that we had one hundred *million* volunteers, the translation read one hundred *billion* and so on for all of my statistics. Had we not caught that colossal error, this so-called expert would have been sent back to the States in a rowboat.

Also in advance, I talked with a number of people familiar with Japanese philanthropy and nonprofit organizations and was provided a good many names of people I should try to visit. Two consistent bits of advice I received were, not to let them so seriously overschedule me professionally and socially that I would be totally worn down, and to be sure that in addition to Tokyo I spent time in other parts of the country. With all that preparation and advice, Ann and I were off for our first visit to Japan or any part of Asia.

Our largest initial surprise and surely something we were not at all prepared for was how regally a Yoshida Fellow and spouse are treated. I had hoped for business class air travel but hadn't requested it—and we got first class. I had hoped for an interpreter for at least key appointments and talks—and was greeted at the airport by an interpreter/guide with car and driver who would be with us throughout the trip. I had particularly hoped they would leave us some space for being just plain tourists—and they had booked us into all sorts of special places and events to make the most of our touring—at their expense. It was unreal and embarrassing, but when I protested and tried to pay our share I was advised that it was all part of the arrangement.

Most days were filled with appointments and presentations, and many evenings involved social/working dinners. The contacts represented a broad mix of people, very much high level, including government, academic, philanthropy, international relations, business, trade associations, media, and larger voluntary associations usually involved with international pursuits. Most spoke English, which eased the translation load for Yumi Hirobi, who insisted on using the free time to go off with Ann for extra sightseeing.

There were three large gatherings involving a talk and discussion. In most of these, as well as with many smaller groups and individual appointments, the people seemed only mildly interested in knowing about the U.S. philanthropic/voluntary sector or talking about theirs. They were certainly polite but not really connected, except when it came to United States–Japan relationships. The people enlisted for my sessions were for the most part not keenly interested in my topics, especially the advocacy roles of philanthropic and voluntary organizations. As I began to sort it out, I realized that most of the people I was seeing respected their government's close supervision and substantial funding of officially approved nongovernmental organizations, were interested in the international education side of voluntary endeavor, and did not seem to feel that what we call grass-roots associations played a very significant role in Japan.

In my advance reading and in some of the early appointments I personally arranged (which I later learned were described as "unauthorized"), I was gaining the impression that there was a significant movement developing among citizens concerned about such issues as the environment, health care, the elderly, rehabilitation, immigration, and more generally the exercise of freedom of speech and right of association. One of my pre-trip contacts in the United States, Jerry Yoshitomi, head of the Japanese/American Cultural and Community Center in Los Angeles and a member of the IS board, had urged me to meet with leaders of organizations that he described as "the counter cultural movement dealing for example with the most vulnerable," and he provided names and introductions.

There was even a book review in a Tokyo paper midway in our stay that reported on such developments. The book was titled *Japanese Working for a Better World*. The review began, "Even if you only read the introduction to this book your time will be well spent. This access guide to citizens' groups begins with an unadorned indictment against the legal and social obstacles that shackle grass roots activities in Japan. After you realize what the nonprofit (NPO) and nongovernmental organizations (NGO) in Japan are up against, you will inevitably have a much greater respect for the efforts of the forty seven activists profiled in the book."

I secured a copy, and the reading reinforced my sense that something significant was developing. However, when I probed the issue with my hosts I was advised to leave it alone. By then I had already met with enough of these groups to satisfy myself that they represented important causes and healthy aspirations. However, the tensions caused by these unauthorized visits became so intense that I was in jeopardy of embarrassing and offending my sponsors. At my final presentation to summarize impressions of the visit I did include a short reference to the possible value of such activists, but even that brought an uncharacteristic public rebuke from one of my friends and hosts.

For Ann, Japan was the trip of a lifetime. For me it was also a special experience, diminished somewhat by the rigid control over who I could see and what I could say. I dare say my sponsors were at least equally disappointed in me.

As interesting and helpful as these brief international experiences were, they didn't prepare me for what was to come. It started as a request to co-chair one meeting and ended up as one of the largest and longest running volunteer projects I ever undertook. And if I thought I was out of my element when I entered the mental health field, it was nothing compared to trying to operate at the international level. Fortunately, that MHA experience had taught me never to try to operate as an expert when I was out of my element. Despite that resolve, many true internationalists wondered who in the world I was to mess with their territory.

In early 1991, Jim Joseph, who was then head of the Council on Foundations, and I, as president of INDEPENDENT SECTOR, were asked to determine how and if foundations and others in the United States might respond to burgeoning requests for assistance from outside the country. In 1990 discussions had been held in Europe and the United States about the possible need for an international network to help strengthen philanthropy and voluntary initiative in various regions of the world and possibly globally. From all around the world, U.S. funders and others were being asked to help develop nongovernmental organizations and other forms of private initiative for public purposes. Similarly, the European Foundation Centre (EFC) was examining the same situation for its members. In both places there was a strong inclination not to try to rejuvenate the International Standing Conference for Philanthropy (Interphil) because it was considered too limited in scope, program, and finances.

After meetings and discussions with many interested organizations in the United States and with leaders of the EFC, there seemed to be consensus that much more examination was needed to define what the needs and possibilities were and what vehicles might be identified to carry forward a process of communication and cooperation. Jim and I were asked to establish what came to be called the "Exploratory Committee," which was to be as representative as possible of people, organizations, and countries, and constituted to provide credibility among all interested parties.

To satisfy those criteria, our selection required about six months for a great deal of outreach and checking. Fortunately, we had been able to assign Teri Siegl of the Council on Foundations and Sandra Gray of IS to assist in the process; and several funders from both continents provided support for the committee's work. By early fall of 1991 the Exploratory Committee was ready to assemble to "determine the need, if any, for international networking mechanisms among the global independent sector." The countries represented were:

Australia	Germany	Mexico	South Africa
Canada	Hungary	Russia	Trinidad and Tobago
Egypt	Japan	Saudi Arabia	United States
France	Kenya	Senegal	Venezuela

At our very first meeting, the process almost came totally apart. In our terribly disparate group, there were entirely different interpretations and reactions to such words and practices as philanthropy, voluntarism, civic and civil society, pluralism, nonprofit or nongovernmental organizations, advocacy, empowerment, participatory government, and on and on. At a point when we might have concluded that people who couldn't figure out what they had in common had little chance to decide what to do about it, one of our members, Miklós Marschall, then deputy mayor of Budapest and a leader of the so-called "informals" of predemocratic Hungary, observed that it was unlikely we could ever agree on terms that meant such different things in our various languages and cultures, but that what he was hearing around the table suggested that we all seemed to agree that effective societies exist in direct proportion to their degree of citizen participation and influence. With that articulation, our divided, quarrelsome, and wary group suddenly found common ground. Almost a year later, the group concluded: "Agreeing that there is a need to bring together private donors and nongovernmental organizations to strengthen citizen action and influence, we recommend the establishment of an international Alliance." We ended the report: "Most of us had not met when we became involved in this consideration and most of us were skeptical at the very least that anything could be accomplished. We have moved from the condition of unallied doubters to a unified body embracing a shared vision. Despite all our differences and differentness, we are agreed that something very significant may be unfolding in the world and that the moment should be seized."[5]

In this too sketchy review of the Exploratory Committee's work, it likely appears that all was orderly and preordained. In fact, it was messy, controversial, and often likely of failure. Fortunately we also had some special things working for us. It's important to provide the reader with a sense of both, starting with the positive factors and forces:

> *The credibility of the members* of the committee, particularly within their own countries and regions. Part of the advantage was that the group was enormously diverse, not just in terms of such important factors as race, gender and geography, but also of communities, cultures and roles. Despite the differences, there turned out to be a common commitment to a larger place for nongovernmental participation and influence in our own settings and throughout the regions and the world.

> *The structure of meetings* of the Exploratory and later the Organizing Committee provided substantial opportunities for the members to learn from each other's experiences. With both groups, these information exchanges were the most satisfying and maybe the most important parts of the gatherings. We were thrilled to find one another, to learn that others were making progress under excruciating circumstances, and to learn that there was evidence of a global movement toward empowerment. We drained each other of information and examples as mundane as how to build a membership, or as inspiring as breakthroughs in rights of women. Later we realized that what we might be building toward was an ever-enlarging circle for greater sharing and encouragement.

> *Once we were all satisfied* with such factors as transparency and respect for differences, we developed a comfort with the process.

> *We had sufficient financial support* that all of us were on equal footing. It was not just another gathering of those who could afford to be at the table.

These positive features helped us overcome the limitations that at times seemed likely to do us in, such as:

> *Awareness, which initially bordered on hostility,* of a process that had many typical trappings of control by the North.

Although diversity turned out to be an advantage, the widely disparate roles of the participants—grass roots organizers, academicians, association executives, funders, and more—made it extremely difficult to find common ground.

Some funders of the process who said they would let the project find its own way regularly contradicted that arrangement. From the start, some tried to tell us who must be on the committee or that the decisions reached were not acceptable. As a community organizer, I would respond that the group had struggled mightily to achieve consensus, or at least compromise, but I was often criticized—even scolded that I should never have let this or that happen.

There was a natural but constant obstacle represented by the fact that many if not most of the members used their countries or regions as the priority focus and were impatient and unsupportive when discussions shifted to other regions and to global considerations.

The determination from the start to have the alliance characterized as "minimal" was constantly contradicted by an escalation of the overall group's expectations and aspirations for what the central operation must do.

Many of these favorable and difficult features were carried over to the work of the Organizing Committee and into the early years of what became CIVICUS: World Alliance for Citizen Participation. It was never easy and always fragile, but a lot of good people struggled to have it succeed.[6]

To implement the Exploratory Committee's decisions, an Organizing Committee was appointed from among the group and I was asked to lead it. That committee met in October 1992 and January 1993 to try to work through many tough decisions about program priorities, dues, fund-raising responsibilities, staffing and much more. None of the agenda items was easy. This is not to suggest overwhelming dissent, but just that every topic called up different experiences and points of view that took a great deal of time to resolve or advance. Some we could only postpone. We agreed to focus initially on "capturing and portraying the almost invisible but dramatic development of citizen involvement and influence in the recent past and to use this information to accelerate the pace globally, regionally, nationally and locally." To address this goal, we decided on a three-part project to be undertaken immediately:

A Report on the State of Citizen Participation and Influence to include the progress that has been made even in the face of overwhelming impediments; enumeration of the obstacles that still exist; and plans for overcoming those obstacles based on advances already achieved in various parts of the world. The intent was not another study or survey but an action-oriented summary and process to inspire and guide those in the vineyards and to establish global, moral and political legitimacy and support for them.

A World Assembly in 1995 at which the report would be presented, along with examples of efforts that are succeeding and action strategies for accelerating the process.

A follow-up strategy to marshal resources and cooperation to move aggressively between the first World Assembly in 1995 and a second in 1997.

The Organizing Committee called for a founding board meeting in Barcelona in May 1993.

In the course of the work of the Organizing Committee, there were a few other developments that may help interpret the process, decisions, and difficulties. For example, when some participants began to realize that the organization would not give primary attention to their own specific causes, such as child health, refugees, women's rights, hunger, or illiteracy, it was hard to maintain their support. Some women participants were disbelieving to the point of rage that we would not put women's issues at the forefront of our mission. We pointed out that even if CIVICUS committed all its meager resources to women's causes around the world, we would make little or no difference and would leave out everything else on the urgent agenda. This argument didn't win us friends among the many dedicated advocates of myriad causes, but it did at least convince the majority that although we must speak out against all suffering, oppression and inequality, we could not take on each specific crusade as our own.

A different kind of crisis occurred after our report was written and when the Organizing Committee's work was essentially done. At that stage some funders, including two members of the committee, decided we would be better off at the beginning and perhaps indefinitely if CIVICUS limited its membership to funders. When I didn't respond supportively, they reacted that I was rigid and unreasonable. I wanted to strangle them. After all the thousands of hours trying to facilitate hundreds of agreements among very different people and views, I was suddenly chastised because I wouldn't chuck it all to satisfy the very different course preferred by a few funders. It was a bad moment for me. Had I even agreed to convey their recommendations to the Organizing Committee, it would have been the end of the beginning.

Another concern, and one that dogged the beginning and early years of CIVICUS, involved whether persons of stature and name recognition should be in the forefront. Two related factors drove the consideration for high-profile individuals. The first involved the desire for instant credibility, especially for fund raising. The second related to a perceived need for persons who were "acceptable," which translated as assuringly non-radical, which further translated as nonthreatening to the status quo.

At all levels these quandaries were real. We were brand spanking new and needed ways of gaining attention and startup grants. We were, at least in the significant minority, made up of people whose credibility was based on having helped force change in our own settings, and achievement of our goals required upsetting the status quo in many ways and places. The symbols often clashed as to what constituted credibility.

Two situations may help illustrate the quandary. Through the earnest involvement of our consultant Bill Dietel, former president of the Rockefeller Brothers Fund, we had the possibility of early and substantial support from David Rockefeller. Several on the committee saw this as a way of gaining essential recognition and support, but an equal number were alarmed that this symbol of wealth would convince people that we were under the control of those with economic power. Later, our attempt to resolve some of these conflicting realities took the form of the World Circle of Friends.

The other even more difficult situation is important to recall. We were trying to determine specific activities the new organization would emphasize, such as influence with the United Nations, international conferences, newsletters, and research, when one of our members burst out that we were totally missing the mark. This was Farida Allaghi, an exile from Libya working out of Saudi Arabia and trying to establish women's rights in the Middle East. Farida had faithfully attended all our meetings but was frequently disparaging of attention to organizational detail. Now she demanded that we not bother her or ourselves with silly talk of conferences or newsletters because, as she reproached us, "the only issue is courage."

From the chair, I wanted terribly to respond to the obvious depth of her feelings, but I was dumbfounded, as I could tell others were, about what she was trying to convey. Within that awkward moment, Farida, trembling with frustration and anger, grabbed her papers and started to leave. Several rose to stop her, and I tried to speak for all of us in an earnest plea for her to help us understand what it was that upset her so.

Still standing, and somewhere between disconsolate and furious, Farida explained that she came to these gatherings only because she found other persons who were also struggling against almost impossible odds to address human rights and survive oppressive governments, and that with every indication of progress she picked up from the group, she was able to return to her awful circumstances with a little more courage. "Please," she pleaded, "don't ever let us get so preoccupied with the details that we forget what this is all about, which is giving a little more hope and courage to people who spend a lot of their time wondering if they can possibly go on." That's an essential lesson for CIVICUS forevermore.

In advance of the founding board meeting of CIVICUS in Barcelona in May 1993, the organizing and nominating committees decided to have five co-chairpersons, one from each international region. I was asked to be one of the five and to serve in the role of chairperson of the Executive Committee and thereby coordinate the work of the five and supervise the staff director. It wasn't long before we realized that having five coequal chairpersons might be good for symbolism but it wasn't good for governance and management. I therefore functioned as the chairperson, and we prepared to change the bylaws to establish that position as the chief volunteer officer. We were particularly fortunate that Miklós Marschall had agreed to become our first executive director and was on the job early enough to help lead us once the organization was officially established.

The founding board meeting was celebratory and for the most part harmonious and productive. The World Report was developing well and the first World Assembly in Mexico City was looking very good. Generally it was an atmosphere of high anticipation. We felt keenly that we were in on the beginning of something terribly important.

Not far in the background of those early meetings, however, there were three issues that remained unresolved and caused increasing contention. The first involved the dues structure and payment of dues. Although the membership committee and board had agreed on a plan, it was being observed far more in the breach. On the other hand, there continued to be agreement that the core budget of CIVICUS should be covered by the membership. The second involved division of income between the central secretariat and the regions. Several regions felt that a higher amount and proportion of the organization's income should be assigned to the regions. This matter of division of funds caused the most serious difference within the board. The third involved fund raising. The board had agreed that although the majority of the initial money might come from the United States the majority of the number of grants should come from other regions. U.S. funders continued to press on this second point, to the considerable upset of some board members. None of these problems would be unexpected in a global organization, but the fact that they were all occurring simultaneously and so intensely made it hard to build unity and trust. For the whole of the first year the problems grew, but so did the delight with what was unfolding for Mexico City.

If one stops to compare the original dream and plan for CIVICUS with what transpired in Mexico City in January 1995, the success of that first assembly, so soon after the organization was founded, turned out as an absolutely glorious accomplishment. To watch those 500 people from more than fifty different countries find and spark one another had to be among the high points for all of us who dreamed of such a meeting ground. We acknowledged repeatedly that once those folks realized who they were and what they had in common, we could have just walked away and left them to their conversations and our purposes for the assembly would have been fulfilled.

Many factors made for that success, but certainly high among them were the focus on building a worldwide network of people who shared the essential dream of empowerment; the efforts to identify and attract people who were important to have in Mexico City; funding to provide support for about half of those who attended so that the participation was truly diverse, including those usually left out of such conversations but most important to reach; a World Report on Citizen Participation that formed the basis for prior reading, so that all who came had at least some grasp about what the state of civil society was worldwide and could move that understanding forward in the assembly and after returning home; a host committee that made the experience prestigious and fun; a program that acknowledged and took advantage of the vast diversity, while at the same time focusing on what we had in common; staff work that served as a model of organization effectiveness coupled with thoughtfulness and kindness; and an expectation accepted by most that this was only a beginning and that each of us was responsible to build on it, both for our own regions and for the meeting ground of CIVICUS.

It was a high note on which to leave my leadership roles. I had previously advised the Nominating Committee that I was not available for reelection to office or the board. At that point I was retiring from INDEPENDENT SECTOR and felt it was essential that someone else be on the board to continue IS's institutional backing of CIVICUS. I also indicated that "there is a need to spread the leadership among the board and regions. By 1995 it will be more than three years that I have carried principal responsibility which is both long enough for me and probably too long for the good of an organization whose principles call for shared and dispersed leadership."

In my swan song I pointed out that despite constant strains, the enterprise had moved forward with impressive, indeed amazing impact, and that the challenge was to grow the performance without a corresponding growth in the cracks.

I have remained a member of CIVICUS and am proud to have been elected to its World Circle of Friends. In 2000, at the request of CIVICUS, I prepared a summary of the early years under the heading "First Lights: Recollections of the Beginnings and First Years of CIVICUS: World Alliance for Citizenship Participation."

Internationalists can relax that I got out of their purview after my task was completed and that I was not foolish enough to seek a higher calling in international relations. On the other hand, I like to believe that at that stage an organizer was what CIVICUS needed, and despite the difficulties and duration of the assignment, I'm glad I took it on.

I didn't altogether forget the world, but retreated to ad hoc assignments where I could help without exaggerating my experience. For example, there was a consultation with leaders of Hong Kong's civil service shortly before the Chinese "takeover." I had become involved because some leaders of Hong Kong's NGO sector and some conscientious civil service leaders were concerned that there was little mention of nongovernmental activity in China's laws and that therefore, after June 30, 1997, those organizations would be particularly vulnerable to arbitrary rulings on what they could and could not do and even their right to exist.

In preparation for my visit, I did what checking was possible and found clear signs that Beijing and even the new Hong Kong government would emphasize responsibilities over rights and that groups critical of the government would be disbanded or muted. When I had an opportunity to ask a key person in the Hong Kong government whether provision would be made for the legal status and protection of nonprofit groups, he rushed to report that agreement had just been reached to allow such groups to register and that the conditions of approval were being worked out. Before he could move on, I asked him with whom the voluntary organizations would register and he readily replied that it would be the police.

Despite every indication that he was through with me and my line of questioning, I asked further if the police might too easily bar groups that criticize government policy. He said that they could and should because those groups would be trying to foment trouble if not rebellion. I interjected that I was not talking about groups advocating the overthrow of the government but about groups concerned with public policies or programs dealing with the environment or crippled children. The official cut me off by saying that such groups should seek more orderly ways to communicate with government.

Before he turned away altogether, I asked if the groups that were allowed to register would be allowed to hold public meetings, and he replied perhaps, if they got prior approval. "I suppose," I asked, "it would be the police who would make that decision?" "Of course," he said with finality. Within a week, the announcement was made that the new government would curb a range of civil rights, including placing limits on public demonstrations and having a requirement that all voluntary organizations register with the police.

The experience with Hong Kong underscored what I'd learned repeatedly in my work with CIVICUS: that there can be little hope for citizen participation and influence or even protection of such fundamental rights as free speech, assembly, and association if the laws don't stipulate these rights and the courts don't protect them.

Most of the international activities in which I was asked to engage supposed a contribution I could make. In every case, I came away learning much more than I contributed, and the most important learning by far was how important voluntary action, philanthropy, pluralism, and civil society are in the United States and how much more clearly our blessings are understood outside the country than within. I also was reminded of how fragile these rights are even in democracies and how essential it is that we not take them for granted.

« 10 »

BRIDGING THE WORLDS
OF ACTION AND WRITING

Fourteen Books, From the Practitioner's View
1975–2005

It wasn't my intention to become a writer. Perhaps like others I thought there might be a book in me someday, but like the rest I couldn't find the time or will to do it.

What probably turned me around was growing frustration that I was learning a great deal about community building but opportunities to spread the messages were limited. I would be part of training sessions and pass along what I'd learned about board building, fund raising, or advocacy and know from reactions that I was helping them, but the number of people I was able to reach was tiny. I did my best with pamphlets and occasional visual aids, but there was scant literature to help these determined souls know what to do and how to do it.

That gnawing contradiction stayed with me all the way through the Heart Association years and well into the Mental Health Association ones. The urgency came to the fore at one of the first meetings of thirteen executive directors of the major national health and welfare associations, convened by United Way of America in 1973. Very quickly, we identified a mutual concern about the quality of our training assistance to volunteer and staff leaders in the field. In a side conversation with Bob Harlan, national executive of the YMCA, he mentioned that they had gone so far as to create what was called Association Press to encourage, publish, and promote quality orientation and training materials for their organization and others. Bob indicated that they were having a hard time finding or developing book-length manuscripts that provided broader guidance to association leaders, and he asked if I would give it a try. I responded automatically that with my workload and travel schedule it was out of the question, but he asked me to think about it.

Although I tried to shake the idea, it stuck with me. I kept going back and forth—there was no way to fit it in, but in unintended moments I'd think about what I might try to cover. Then I tried stealing bits of time to consider content and how I might possibly manage it. A year passed with little progress and at the next gathering of the executives Bob brought up the proposal again, this time in full session, resulting in a mutual request for me to do it. I agreed to give it a try.

By then I really wanted to do it, but still couldn't see how. I had given the prospect enough thought to realize that in addition to time constraints, I had doubts whether I really knew enough about the many subjects that would need to be covered to constitute a credible book. I decided to find a week when I could break loose and hide away to identify essential topics and test whether I could do them justice.

It was for six very long and solitary days in the spring of 1974 that I hid out at a motel by Rehoboth Beach and walked, thought, and wrote to test if I had such a book in me and if so what it would take to get it out. I kept picturing myself talking to a typical group of eager voluntary organization leaders about each of the topics they needed to understand to do their jobs well. In the end, I felt I did have sufficient experience as a practitioner to write a practical book for others less experienced.

I had already planned that if that were so, I would take a second week in the summer to do a detailed outline and then a third week in the fall to draft the narratives. At each stage I imagined I was talking to my intended audience and trying to anticipate their likely questions. Between those weeks I did what I could to fill in the many blanks and weak spots, all with the help of my already overworked assistant. I did keep family and staff informed and they were all wonderfully understanding and even encouraging, but some I'm sure couldn't help wonder whether this was really priority.

After many more months of sporadic efforts to smooth and improve the gradually emerging manuscript, Association Press accepted the draft with enthusiasm and in my naiveté I figured it was pretty much a free ride from there. I wasn't yet familiar with the process of editing, which in this case was by no means limited to my many slips in grammar, but went so far as to combine chapters, omit others, and substitute a scholarly tone for my conversational one. They were far more experienced than I, which made it all the harder for a fair fight, but I learned that if I was intractable on my absolutes I could win some of the battles. Their ultimate revenge—

at least as Ann and I experienced it—was that when my baby was finally delivered, it had an absolutely vile pink cover. My protests were in vain because, as I learned, the publisher has final say about the cover. I do need to indicate that later experiences with editors have been far more positive, contributing not only to better books but to pleasant friendships. At least I liked the title, which was *Effective Leadership in Voluntary Organizations,* and the subtitle, *How to Make the Greatest Use of Citizen Service and Influence,* which reflected accurately my lifelong pursuit.

I was also pleased with the book's reception. One of the senior members of our group of seventeen agency leaders, George Elsey, president of the American Red Cross, described it as the "finest manual yet written for the volunteer who wants to get things done. The touch is light, the purpose is serious, the combination is stunning." Another, Vernon Jordan of the National Urban League, wrote, "A perceptive treatment of a major national issue by a pre-eminent leader in the field."

The book remained in print for about ten years, and after Association Press went out of business, a second edition (with a different cover!) was published by Walker & Company and lasted another ten years. I was delighted with the book's popularity, for it meant the lessons were really spreading. I confess it also felt good to be an author.

Subsequently, when it became apparent that *Effective Leadership* was seen and used primarily for staff training, a much revised version was prepared for volunteer leaders. Deliberately titled *The Board Member's Book,* it turned out to be even more popular and is now in its third printing and twentieth year.

To provide a lighter touch within *The Board Member's Book,* I slipped in something called "Minutes of the Last Meeting," a spoof on the idiosyncrasies and foibles of voluntary organizations. That part became so popular that several years later, realizing that some people learn more when humor is involved, I expanded that one episode to eight and the results were published as *Our Organization,* later revised and expanded under the title *Board Overboard: Laughs and Lessons for All But the Perfect Nonprofit.*

Recently, I sent both *The Board Member's Book* and *Board Overboard* to a new chairman of a board I sit on, and after reading both, he replied, "Now I have a book that tells me what to do and another that tells me what not to do. One way or the other you're determined to get me educated!"

My early books focused on improving the performance of nonprofit leaders and organizations, and with their publication, I assumed that such writing was happily behind me. While I liked being an author, I didn't appreciate the endless tedium of producing an actual book. By the time

I'd get to Chapter 7, I was contradicting everything said in Chapter 3, and by the time I submitted the whole manuscript to a publisher, it would get to an editor who would point out all the weaknesses I should have spotted long before. It's nice to be an author only when a book is finished and the cover, title, reviews, and sales are all okay.

A different need to help build the literature began to surface during the days of putting INDEPENDENT SECTOR together. From my earliest work with the National Council on Philanthropy and the Coalition of National Voluntary Organizations, I had been trying to communicate the role and impact of philanthropy and voluntary action in America. When INDE-PENDENT SECTOR was formed, I found that responsibility accentuated. One of our basic functions was to help the American people understand and take pride in our country's traditions of participation and generosity so that they are reinforced and passed along. One of my immediate diffi-culties was that the case was hard to document. People within the sector felt passionately about its impact but rarely could cite substantiating lit-erature. During a discussion of this dilemma at an early IS board meeting, Nancy Hanks, director of the National Endowment for the Arts, Rocke-feller family adviser, and volunteer leader extraordinaire, lamented that the only authority ever quoted was de Tocqueville. In deference to the person in the chair, someone countered that we now had John Gardner to quote, but Nancy topped that by noting, "John just quotes Tocqueville all the time."

John acknowledged there wasn't much else to quote. He often pointed out that there were whole libraries devoted to government and business but, as he put it, "You could carry in a Boy Scout's knapsack all that is written about the independent sector."

The absolutely essential need to get the sector's story out was such a major matter that John and I found ourselves concentrating on it at one of our early retreat-like sessions. I told him that out of desperate need for persuasive testimony, briefings, and interviews, I had gradually been pulling together some of the best literature I could find that set forth the philosophy and usefulness of pluralism, voluntarism, philanthropy, and citizen participation. I said I was doing this to create a resource for my-self and to build credibility for my arguments, but had begun to think it might be worthwhile to pull such writings together in a book. I expressed doubts whether I was the right person to do that job or would have time for it, but John was adamant that I should take it on—and to get with it.

With extraordinary assistance of Ann O'Connell, we located close to one thousand possibilities, but with almost every one, additional leads surfaced. The project could have been endless, but fully acknowledging that we had not turned over every stone, we finally went ahead with forty-five selections, under the title *America's Voluntary Spirit: A Book of Readings*.

I wanted the volume as a whole to provide a good overview of what the sector means to the American experience and to be a valuable resource for speakers and writers. I was particularly determined that the book represent a balanced view. If it turned out to be too glowing or self-congratulatory, it wouldn't be accurate or useful. At the same time, I wanted it to be a manageable volume rather than an all-inclusive tome.

Examples of chapter titles and their authors might help convey the scope of the book. Representative of earlier periods are such pieces as: "Man the Reformer," Ralph Waldo Emerson; "Of the Use Which the Americans Make of Public Associations in Civil Life," Alexis de Tocqueville; "The Gospel of Wealth," Andrew Carnegie; "The Difficult Art of Giving," John D. Rockefeller; and "Principles of Public Giving," Julius Rosenwald.

From more recent times there are: "Altruism: Self-Sacrifice for Others" Lewis Thomas; "Private Initiative for the Public Good," John W. Gardner; "The Third Sector," John D. Rockefeller 3rd; "The Third Sector: Keystone of a Caring Society," Waldemar Nielsen; "The Social Goals of a Corporation," John H. Filer; "We Cannot Live for Ourselves Alone,"Vernon E. Jordan, Jr.; and "Our Religious Heritage," Brian O'Connell.

To make the book more valuable to scholars and others looking for additional documentation and literature, the bibliography that Ann prepared covered more than 600 references.

To my surprise, *America's Voluntary Spirit* turned out to be far more popular than imagined, and more than twenty years later it's still in print and selling, particularly to researchers and organizers new to the field who welcome having so much of the best relevant literature at hand. Much of it still seems to interpret what the sector means to the kind of society we are. For one example, here's a treasure from *McGuffey's Reader* of 1844! It is still one of the best descriptions why people must care about their neighbors and others.

Entitled "True and False Philanthropy," it starts with a Mr. Fantom talking about global designs for doing good while a Mr. Goodman tries to get Fantom to focus on some needs closer to home. For two pages, Goodman brings up a great many immediate needs of society, but Fantom disparages the attention each would take away from his sweeping solutions to society's problems.

Mr. Goodman says, "But one must begin to love somewhere and I think it is as natural to love one's own family, and to do good in one's own neighborhood, as to anybody else. And if every man in every family, village, and country did the same, why then all the schemes would be met, and the end of one village or town where I was doing good, would be the beginning of another village where somebody else was doing good; so my schemes would jut into my neighbor's; his projects would unite with those of some other local reformer; and all would fit with a sort of dovetail exactness."

Mr. Fantom snorts, "Sir, a man of large views will be on the watch for great occasions to prove his benevolence."

And Mr. Goodman concludes, "Yes, sir; but if they are so distant that he cannot reach them, or so vast that he cannot grasp them, he may let a thousand little, snug, kind, good actions slip through his fingers in the meanwhile; and so, between the great things that he cannot do, and the little ones that he will not do, life passes, and nothing will be done."[7]

I can't resist one more, which in this case points out that beyond the urgent causes and crusades, the independent sector simply provides people with a chance to do their own thing—to be different—to be unique. In an Occasional Paper, "The Third Sector: Keystone of a Caring Society," published by INDEPENDENT SECTOR, Waldemar Nielsen, drawing in part from his book *The Endangered Sector,* summarized the variety of interests that Americans freely pursue through their voluntary organizations:

> If your interest is people, you can help the elderly by a contribution to the Grey Panthers; or teenagers through the Jean Teen Scene of Chicago; or young children through your local nursery school; or everyone by giving to the Rock of all Ages in Philadelphia.
>
> If your interest is animals, there is the ASPCA and Adopt-A-Pet; if fishes, the Isaac Walton League; if birds, the American Homing Pigeon Institute or the Easter Bird Banding Association.
>
> If you are a WASP, there is the English Speaking Union and the Mayflower Descendants Association; if you have a still older association with the country, there is the Redcliff Chippewa Fund or the Museum of the American Indian.
>
> If your vision is local, there is the Cook County Special Bail Project and Clean Up the Ghetto in Philadelphia; if national, there is America the Beautiful; if global, there is the United Nations Association; if celestial, there are the Sidewalk Astronomers of San Francisco.
>
> If you are interested in tradition and social continuity, there is the Society for the Preservation of Historic Landmarks and the Portland Friends of

Cast Iron Architecture; if social change is your passion, there is Common
Cause; and, if that seems too sober for you, there is the Union of Radical
Political Revolutionary Satire in New York.

If your pleasure is music, there is a supermarket of choices—from Vocal
Jazz to the Philharmonic Society to the American Guild of English Hand
Bellringers.

If you don't know quite what you want, there is Get Your Head Together, Inc. of Glen Ridge, New Jersey. If your interests are contradictory,
there is the Great Silence Broadcasting Foundation of California. If they are
ambiguous, there is the Tombstone Health Service of Arizona.[8]

My *Philanthropy in Action* book grew out of a similar need to draw
on history, but in this case, to achieve a ready grasp of many grants that
had achieved remarkable results. I was always on the lookout for good
examples of gifts that made a remarkable difference. It was frustrating
how often even leaders in the field would respond with something like,
"Well, there's Carnegie's libraries and Rockefeller's yellow fever discov-
ery and hundreds if not thousands of others but they don't come to mind
at the moment."

For *Philanthropy in Action,* an even fuller and much more difficult
search of the literature was necessary, but both books reinforced the conclusions of the Organizing Committee that created IS: "the voluntary sector is taken for granted, is seriously neglected in scholarship, and can be
successfully challenged by skeptics who are made all the more suspicious
by our generalizations."

Philanthropy has not been a topic of much contemporary interest.
Prior to the 1930s and particularly from about 1800 to 1930, there was
a great deal written about the subject. Our bibliography illustrates that
during that period, books and periodicals gave substantial attention to it.
Beginning with the Depression and the New Deal, observers of the contemporary scene were understandably more interested in the growing role
and functions of government. It was not until the 1960s that voluntary
initiative and the philanthropy that supports it began to get much exposure again, but interest in philanthropy is still far less than it was a hundred years ago.

Unfortunately, much of the best of early literature is lost or buried, and
we've only recently begun to resurrect it. Some of the best books are
exceedingly rare. Many others are hardly known to the leaders of philanthropy and from my observation are rarely in their collections. If, indeed, "what is past is prologue" and we want students and the public to
understand the role of philanthropy in our society, we need to be famil-

iar with our own literature. For this reason, we—again, largely Ann—compiled an extensive bibliography.

It was important to prepare the reader that *Philanthropy in Action* was not a definitive record of grant making, or, to borrow from Robert Bremner's introduction to his *American Philanthropy*, "is not an encyclopedia of good works." Our effort was just one attempt to pull together a few hundred random examples of successful grants that help tell the story of what philanthropy does and how.

I like to think that our examples helped make the point that philanthropy plays many different roles but its central value is the extra dimension it provides for seeing and doing things differently. Philanthropy doesn't take the place of government or other basic institutions, but it does provide additional ways to address our problems and aspirations and to keep our basic institutions responsive and effective. Paul Ylvisaker, who served on the boards of several foundations and as a consultant to the Council on Foundations, said, "Philanthropy is America's passing gear."

Philanthropy operates in thousands of different ways, many inspirational, some silly, and a few downright dangerous. Contrast the Rockefeller Foundation's "Green Revolution," which increased food supply for millions, with the Emma A. Robinson Christmas Dinner Trust Fund for Horses, or Garrett Smith's funding of John Brown's raid on Harpers Ferry, and you have some feel for the scope. It is unreasonable to expect that all philanthropic organizations will be on the cutting edge. While much of the good that philanthropy does is accomplished out there, many funders find themselves encouraging organizations toward excellence, intervening where human misery is greatest, or nourishing the human spirit.

I tried to identify several of the different although admittedly overlapping roles that philanthropy plays and ended up with nine. At times in this exercise there were four or five and at other times seventeen or eighteen, so clearly there is nothing rigid in the delineation and enumeration of roles. More important than the general outline are the illustrations that help show philanthropy in action. My nine roles are: discover new frontiers of knowledge; support and encourage excellence; enable people to exercise their potential; relieve human misery; preserve and enhance democratic government and institutions; make communities a better place to live; nourish the spirit; create tolerance, understanding, and peace among people; remember the dead. The latter may not seem to be a separate role—more a motivation—but in our research it shows up as such a pervasive factor that I chose to give it separate consideration.

I might have settled for just two roles—to relieve human misery, and to maximize human potential—but the extended list allows a closer examination of the various ways that philanthropy makes a difference. If I were really pressed and had to reduce it all the way back to just one role, it would be "to serve as America's extra dimension." A few examples might provide a better sense of philanthropy in action.

When I was growing up in Worcester, Massachusetts, we had a neighbor who was considered odd because he kept trying to put rockets in the air. Almost nobody thought he could do it and the few who did worried that he could cause perpetual rain, bring the sky falling in or shoot an angel.

Robert H. Goddard was known derisively as "the moon man." In 1920 he made the laughable prediction that a rocket could go to the moon. For years the only money he had for research came from his own pocket. His first grant came in 1917, a five-thousand-dollar gift from the Hodgkins Fund of the Smithsonian Institution for "constructing and launching a high altitude rocket." Nine years later his modest attempt to fulfill the terms of that grant rose 41 feet and flew for 2.5 seconds—just far enough to encourage Goddard and just short enough to discourage funders.

In 1929 a larger model blasted off, literally and figuratively. The explosion did send his missile 100 feet up but started a fire several thousand feet wide. Most of the press attention focused on the fire, but a few stories marveled at the accomplishment; one of these articles was read by Mrs. Harry Guggenheim.

The history of Goddard's rocketry and the Guggenheims' support of it are nicely captured in Milton Lomask's *Seed Money: The Guggenheim Story*. Lomask reports that the culmination of Goddard's work was a rocket that became "the parent of all the 9,000 mile Adases and Redstones that will ever fly, all the Sputniks that will ever circle planet earth, all the Project Mercury, Saturn and Jupiter capsules that will ever soar to Venus, Moon and Mars."[9]

There don't seem to be figures on how much Goddard received from various sources for his lifetime of research, but it probably was a good deal less than a half million dollars. Matched against what his work has led to, it is appropriate that the Guggenheim story is told under the title *Seed Money*.

Perhaps the most universally applauded grants to America's communities were Andrew Carnegie's gifts of 1,680 libraries. Despite the obvious merit of those facilities and our awareness, a hundred years later, of their contributions to learning, the grants were often viewed with suspicion and hostility. Many community leaders said that they saw through his condition that if he paid for the building, they would have to buy the books and maintain the service. In place after place, the gifts were attacked on the grounds that ordinary people didn't need to read, would steal all the books anyway, or should be satisfied with their school books. In his book *Philanthropy's Role in Civilization,* Arnaud C. Marts reported that in one community, signs appeared that said this:

> Ratepayers!
> Resist this free library dodge and
> save yourself from the burden of $6,000
> of additional taxation.[10]

Marts also reported that for many years even the progressive state of Massachusetts prohibited any municipality from taxing people for the support of a library. He added "The son of a president of Harvard published a book in 1875 in which he endeavored to dissuade his fellow citizens against appropriations for libraries."[11]

The history of philanthropy is full of grants that we can't possibly imagine were controversial, but that in their time seemed radical and ill advised. Massachusetts was on the better side of the controversy involving kindergartens, but most other states saw that movement as sinister. Elizabeth Peabody of Boston, a sister of Horace Mann, donated her own funds and raised money from her friends to establish the first English-speaking kindergarten.

It is hard to fathom that kindergartens could have been threatening to anyone, but Peabody started a very long and bitter dispute. Her attackers said that children that age were too young to learn and belonged in the home anyway, that her idea undermined the family, transferred to the state a private responsibility, and would raise taxes that were already too high or were needed for "real" public services. The cries of bloated government and encouraging family dependence on government caused many states to enact laws prohibiting the use of public funds for children of kindergarten age. It took about fifty years for the program to gain acceptance.

A hundred years after Peabody's first kindergarten, Carnegie's foundation, the Carnegie Corporation of New York, tried to take the idea a step further by funding "Head Start," a program for disadvantaged children of prekindergarten age, and thirty years later the fur is still flying. Will day care be next?

And for the fun of it: If it's true that God loves a cheerful giver, he must also have a particularly warm spot for Dr. D. K. Pearsons, who gave everything away, and did it in good spirit. For example, when he sent the enormous sum of $50,000 to Montpelier Seminary in Vermont in 1912, Dr. Pearson appended this note:

> Fifty-thousand dollars farewell! You have been in my keeping for many years, and you have been a faithful servant . . . go into the keeping of young men and God's blessing go with you! Do your duty, and give the poor boys and girls of Vermont a fair chance.[12]

William G. Rogers in *Ladies Bountiful* commented on assistance given to James Joyce by Lady Gregory, for whom Joyce coined this limerick:

> There was a kind lady called Gregory
> Said "come to me, poets in beggary,"
> But found her imprudence
> When thousands of students
> Cried "all, we are in that category."[13]

Volunteers in Action came next and addressed the same need for examples of range and effectiveness. For this one, Ann, because she was a more experienced and active volunteer than I and shared so much of the work, became co-author. It was the third in the trilogy of books including *America's Voluntary Spirit* and *Philanthropy in Action,* all published by the Foundation Center and designed to help fulfill IS's efforts to provide more ready reference material about America's voluntary activity and to encourage further research and writing about it.

In some ways, *Volunteers in Action* is the most appealing of the three books. It deals, necessarily, with people—particularly people who are wonderfully special. To some extent their attractiveness was a worry, because we didn't want readers to feel that their own volunteering might not measure up to our examples. In Part III, "Becoming Part of the Action," and at several other points, we made the case that "it is the composite of the work of millions of volunteers that adds up to the compassion, spirit, and power that are the quintessential characteristics of voluntary action in America. Everyone can make a difference, and many people do."

We identified seven roles that volunteers and voluntary organizations represent, and for each role we provided examples of volunteers in action. The roles are obviously arbitrary and overlapping, but by listing seven we tried to illustrate more precisely the ways that volunteers make a difference: serving those most in need; lifting people toward self-reliance; advocating and empowering; cooperating in mutual dependence and assistance; exercising religious belief; and serving many other causes and places: from arts to zoos, and from schools to cemeteries.

Here is just a tiny sampling of the many hundreds of profiles.

When Pearl Williams was 106 years old, she decided it was time to add a new dimension to her volunteer activity. She was already a foster grand-parent in the Retired Senior Volunteers Program and was active in her church, but as reported in *Ebony* in December 1975, "she had recently completed an assignment with Pepperdine State Pre-School Children's Proj-ect which had required her to work four hours a day, five days a week, and she was beginning to look for something to fill the void." Mrs. Williams de-cided to go into training to work with abused children.[14]

In the state of Washington, there are more than 600 "Master Garden-ers" operating in 18 counties. There are also close to 200 "Master Food Preservers." The job of these volunteer "Masters" is to recruit and train other "Masters," who in turn will work with thousands of people to teach them to garden and to preserve their produce.[15]

The name Mother Jones hardly suggests hellfire and revolution, but fur-ther examination reveals a woman who was one of the fiercest advocates in American history. In the 10th anniversary issue of the magazine dedicated to and named after her, the editors note, "When Mary Harris Jones was in-troduced to a college audience as a 'great humanitarian,' she retorted, 'No! I'm a hell raiser!' And so she was. Mother Jones started unions, ran strikes, fought for prison reform, supported revolutions, and spent weeks at a time in jail!"[16]

Some people volunteer in ways that are designed just to help other people feel good. Clarence Chapman of Tamaroa, IL, and his son sit at a busy corner during rush hour and for at least two hours every day wave and shout greetings to every motorist passing by just to show they care. Charles Kuralt featured the Chapmans on his television program "On the Road," and you could see how much their gestures meant to the good spirits of people slowed in traffic.[17]

In the next chapter I refer to books written after leaving the action of IS, but this is probably a good time to address the very common curiosity about how I found time to bridge the worlds of action and writing and how I addressed such a very different activity.

As indicated earlier, the time issue started as insoluble until I decided it was just going to happen, and even though I was up against all odds and pressures I somehow squeezed some writing time in. I don't think I neglected essential or important responsibilities. I know I did learn lessons about what I didn't need to do, or do so much of, and that I could delegate things that people actually welcomed a chance to do. Even with that, I benefited enormously from the patience, forbearance, and help provided by coworkers.

As time passed and other books were published, the organizations I headed seemed to respect this different side of my contribution. Later still, I was provided by the IS Board with a month off each year to concentrate on the writing, which brings me toward the how.

I learned early that I couldn't make much headway by taking a morning off each week or any other halfway measures. I already worked most Saturdays, and any time off during the week just pushed the load into Sundays. Also I found that even if I took a full day off, I continued to think about what had transpired in the past couple of days or what was to come in the next few. It was not creative time.

For a while, I followed the schedule for the first book, *Effective Leadership,* taking three separate weeks off over the year, and that worked quite well, but I still found that a book-length project requires such immersion, at least for me, that I needed one longer stretch to think it through and get it together. Also, after being in the IS job for several years, I was ready for relief from stress and pressures, and that helped lead me to experiment with a full month away. I chose February because that was the least disruptive for the organization. The prior year would have been wrapped up and the new one well under way. It never failed, though, that by late January I would be convinced it was absolutely impossible to get away, but somehow I did. It's a side lesson on how much work can actually get done in a short period of time when the deadline is absolute and personally important.

So early each February 1, Ann and I would be on our way, the only two odd ones heading to Cape Cod for the month of February. We had a small cottage there, which made the arrangement financially possible. We have always enjoyed the Cape at all seasons and found the winter isolation to be a plus for our purposes. By then, Ann was my research assistant and would have developed much of the material with which we would be working. She was also my primary sounding board, reader, and advisor from start to finish. Her role deserves additional comment.

For a while when I first attempted books I depended on various staff persons to fill in as very part-time research assistants who welcomed the experience and a small stipend but who were quite mobile and susceptible to opportunities elsewhere. At one critical stage, I learned that a particularly good aide was marrying and moving, and I came home so frustrated and off balance that I told Ann I was thinking of giving up this unrealistic writing business. As usual, she was sympathetic and helpful in thinking it through. At one stage, she asked me to be more specific about what my expectations were for the job and exactly what the individual did. After I covered it, she stunned me by saying that those sounded like things that she could do and might enjoy. All kinds of warning bells went off. All I could think of was that we might open ourselves to more togetherness and stress than even our good marriage could survive. On the other hand, I had always enjoyed her participation in such projects.

After much further discussion, we agreed to a trial run. I had worked enough with other assistants to know how important it was to impose my "three no's rule," which meant that the first time we disagreed I would listen carefully, but if I said "no" that was the decision. However, she could come back a second time and argue the point and I would promise to listen even more carefully but if I again said "no" that really was it. If she thought it so absolutely important to come back a third time, I would again reconsider but if I said "no" that time, it was the end, kaput, done, decided, finished, dead.

Ann turned out to be the most extraordinary research assistant I ever had, and yet she insisted on doing it all for far below minimum wage. She could go to the Library of Congress and in one day dig up more obscure and diverse references than anybody else, and she knew how to organize the materials, summarize them, do rewrites, and just about anything I needed to get a grasp of what we had and how it might fit in. In later stages of the writing, she was also effective in the editing, smoothing, and everything else that I needed help with. In addition, she was her usual pleasant companion and friend. Even the third "no" didn't spoil dinnertime! The additional dimension to our relationship strengthened and enriched it. Februarys were not only successful for the writing but were wonderfully special for the two of us.

What we would do in advance of the month, particularly toward the beginning of a book, was think enough about it to be pretty sure of the subject, purpose, audience, and the way the topic might break down into subunits or chapters. At that stage it was all enormously fluid, but the talks with Ann and others provided a pretty good feel for the eventual product. With that, the two of us, with help from others, would decide what resource materials we would need, from my own experience or things I was aware of and from what Ann would dig up at the library or other sources. This would all be done within the snippets of time I could devote to it leading up to a fairly rigorous agenda for February. The month would be devoted to possible structure, contents, detailed outlines, writing when we were far enough along, and identification of additional materials needed and where we might locate them. Through this process and timetable we were able to complete a book about every two years.

The first couple of Februarys I worked seven days a week, from 6 or 7 in the morning until about 1:30 P.M., when Ann would bang on the door until I stopped. At a late lunch, we would talk about where I was, what the problems were, and how she might help, all concluding by 2:30 P.M. After the first year I didn't attempt to go back at it for the afternoon, and after the second year I didn't work Sundays. It was overdoing it for my own good and for the project. So afternoons were free for walks, rides, movies, and antiquing. (At the end of February we would always buy one special thing for the house to celebrate the progress, reward ourselves, and make the place even more our own.)

I'll say just one more thing about the process, only because people find it interesting, bordering on baffling.

Once I have a detailed outline of a chapter at hand I will, just as I am doing this very moment, have a picture in my mind of the audience I want to talk to, and then I begin dictating as though we were having a conversation in which I want to communicate something that interests all of us and about which they want to know what I think. When I come across complex points, I usually stop to think and scribble before proceeding with the dictation. All this makes for some terribly ragged first drafts, but at least they are in conversational tone and the material is at hand for later editing. My purpose is to make the most of the time and to have my audience vividly in mind, including a tone that is collegial.

The material usually has to go through at least three drafts, and even at that, when the chapters are all put together, there have to be additional efforts to achieve flow and comprehension before testing the whole of it with at least a few readers who can be counted on to supply friendly candor. With adjustments for their critiques, the manuscript is ready to submit to a publisher and if accepted will be further strengthened by their advice and editing. Finally, out of all that necessary process a book finally emerges (on which I will have insisted on at least a veto on the cover and title!).

One last, last point, primarily for the fun of it.

When people hear that I write books, the most common question is, "What kind of computer do you use?" I explain that I don't use one, and the response is inevitably something like, "Oh, but you must!" I reply that I actually don't use a computer or even a word processor, and, shocked, they will reply, "But that's such a waste of time. You'd be able to do it so much better and quicker with a modern computer." I remain calm but indicate that "my old-fashioned way seems to work so I think I'll stay with it." But they will insist on knowing what other system there could possibly be. I apologetically indicate that I use the old lined pads, but, hoping to mollify them a little bit, I indicate that I no longer use the yellow pads because they don't reproduce well on the fax. This will usually elicit a sarcastic comment like, "Well, at least you use a fax!" As we near what I am determined will be the end of the conversation, my adversary (by then that's how I describe them) will say, "Well I don't know how you do it but I can only tell you that you would be so much better off with a computer." At that point I ask the crank (by then that's how I feel about them) how many books he or she has written, to which they will inevitably respond, "I've never written any books." And I will end it in feigned agitation: "I've written fourteen, so leave me alone."

So much for how I write books.

Another frequent reaction I get, but one more pleasant to deal with, involves those who want to talk about the rewards and satisfactions they assume that publishing books provides. They genuinely mean these as compliments and seem sincerely to envy a person who has actually produced a book. That part I like.

With many, though, it leads to their exaggerated notion and interest in how much money I make from this sideline, or how soon I will be on the *Oprah Winfrey Show.* It's fascinating that so many, and I would guess the majority of people, assume that writing books quite automatically means one is rich and famous. I even had one interviewer start off with, "So you write books, how come I've never heard of you?!" I'm afraid most people never have. I'm also sorry that the royalties don't go very far either. I had one book that paid me enough the first few years to take Ann to New York for a weekend, but the last time I got a check from them it wouldn't buy breakfast at Dunkin' Donuts.

I've had a few books that sold more than 25,000 copies and one that went over 50,000, which may be best-sellers in my league but hardly what my conversationalists expect to hear. I've never dared try to average out what I make per hour from writing books because I guess it would come out somewhere between five and ten cents.

I've also found a new standard for ambivalence, quite common among authors at my level. It's when a person approaches you and says something like, "Your chapter (or even your whole book) on voluntary action is so good I've Xeroxed it a hundred times." I'm tempted sometimes (actually most of the time) to ask if they've ever thought of buying a hundred copies, but I stifle it and take satisfaction that at least the message is getting out.

It's a pretty common reaction that people think that writing books must be great fun. They really don't believe it's tedious, bordering on painful. Having experienced a lot of both, I have to say that on balance the satisfactions, stimulation, and diversions from the everyday make it a decidedly positive experience. Also, I've found that writing in one's field increases your visibility and credibility, giving a boost to having more influence—not a ton, but some.

Because writing books was such a different experience for me, I've tended to emphasize them here, but I know firsthand that most of us get our messages across and contribute to public awareness and education through pamphlets, articles, op-ed pieces, occasional papers, speeches, testimonies, interviews, news releases, and all the greatly expanding opportunities of electronic media. So we're all really writers, but I have the slight advantage that my grandkids, who haven't the slightest notion of what I ever did or do, are at least not stumped to describe me. They just say, "He writes books," and as long as no one asks "What about?" they've covered the subject to their satisfaction—and to mine too.

IMPROBABLE PROFESSOR

University College of Citizenship
and Public Service, Tufts University
1995–2005

After fifteen years as president of INDEPENDENT SECTOR (IS) plus the two years of its founding, and approaching my sixty-fourth birthday, I was asked by the leadership if I would stay beyond sixty-five. If not, they felt they should begin succession planning.

It was hard to face leaving, but surprisingly clear that it was the right thing to do. It had been an enormously demanding assignment on top of twenty-seven taxing years in the earlier jobs. Also, I'd had a couple of bouts with cancer, and although surgery and radiation seemed to solve the problem, the experience changes one's outlook in important ways. Fortunately, the organization and I were in very good shape, so it was a sensible time for transition for both of us. I advised the board—and the celebration began (with my always hoping it reflected appreciation and not delight!).

I knew I wanted to remain active but without running anything ever again. I also couldn't imagine not doing anything and that was underscored when a friend of mine said that to adjust to retirement one had to learn to spread things out. For example, he said, "You never want to get a haircut and mail your letters the same day." I also knew that many individuals assume that when they retire, the world will beat a path to their door offering interesting and remunerative things to do, but for most people the phone never rings.

As I was pondering and exploring how to establish more promising prospects, I was approached by Emmett Carson, then of the Ford Foundation, who wanted to know if I planned to continue to be active in areas of mutual interest. I assured him I did and indicated some particular things I very much wanted to pursue. Emmett encouraged me to describe those interests in a way he could share with the foundation's leaders. He also asked me to think about exempt organizations with which I might affiliate to which Ford could make a grant.

That gloriously encouraging conversation led me to be much more specific about my concentrations. Above all, I wanted to continue to strengthen the capacity of the independent sector here and abroad for greatest possible service to society. Second, I hoped to improve understanding and appreciation of the roles and values of the sector among policymakers and the public. Third, I intended to increase my efforts to promote active citizenship and community service and to help establish a clear understanding of the fundamental relationship between such participation and the effectiveness of communities and societies. And finally, I wanted to help achieve a clearer understanding of the relative public service roles of the government and independent sectors and to build bridges between leaders of both for greater cooperation and coordination.

I looked for possible affiliations that would be compatible with those goals and would allow me to concentrate on them without other heavy responsibilities. The organization that best fit that bill turned out to be the Lincoln Filene Center for Citizenship and Public Affairs at Tufts University. After extended three-way discussions and clarifications, there was agreement that we all wanted to advance work in the areas I'd chosen, and that Emmett and the Ford leadership would recommend three years of support to Tufts, with the possibility of two additional years. Subsequently, the application was approved, and I was appointed Professor of Citizenship and Public Service.

The degree of concentration and the horizons of my work were extended when the Kellogg Foundation matched Ford as a primary sponsor and the Mott and Hearst foundations added their encouragement and support for specific projects. When the five years were up, Atlantic Philanthropies provided major support for another five years and several others helped with project grants. And thus it turned out that there was indeed life after IS and age sixty-five.

For all of the ten years, I've used every opportunity to acknowledge that I am not posing or functioning as an academic or scholar. I'm not quite a rogue professor but I'm certainly an improbable one. My lecturing, writing, and advising are always from the practitioner's point of view. Indeed, when I received the learned title of professor, my two brothers, who are *real* professors, feigned absolute horror that the professoriate was severely undercut by my appointment. I didn't get away with trying to take credit for my honorary degrees. They reminded me that only earned doctorates count. When the give and take calmed down, I put some of the blame on them for at least getting me involved in the writing. I had even dedicated the *Civil Society* book: "To my brothers Thomas E. and Jeffrey O'Connell, both academicians and authors, who convinced me long ago that practitioners too have an obligation to be writers."

I was particularly fortunate that Tufts accepted my request that I not have a regular teaching load or administrative responsibilities. I knew I'd be out of my element as a classroom leader and wanted to be free to do whatever I thought would contribute most to the agreed areas of concentration. I was lucky also that the center and its director, Rob Hollister, valued having a practitioner around to help reflect ground-level experience.

Although I've emphasized how welcome it was to be relatively unencumbered, that's always comparative. Just by staying in harness and remaining active means one can't escape the steady stream of visitors, calls, and correspondence requesting some form of assistance, usually participation, and no one who cares about the field can say no to all of it. My guess is that at least half of my time relates to such requests. I also guess that though I'm supposed to be half-time, I average forty to fifty hours a week, but having worked so many years at double time, forty hours seems delightfully relaxed.

One of the first things I had to work on was getting better at saying no. Although I had worked at that over the years, it was still my nature to say yes to far more things than I should. The only way I finally came closer to solving it was to change my conditioned response from yes to no. Previously someone would call to request time in some form and, wanting to help, I'd be too likely to agree. Much of the time, I realized later, especially as the day of the speech or trip or first meeting came close, that it was something I shouldn't have accepted. Now I almost routinely respond to every request by saying that I'm already committed for that time or am badly overcommitted for that period. Even if I think I want to do it, the most I say is that I'll check to see if there's any chance the schedule might be switched or eased. In nine out of ten cases, I know within a day that I shouldn't do it. For the one in ten I still want to do after twenty-four hours, I accept and look forward to it.

One of the beauties of my new situation is that I'm free to do what I want to do, able to decline most of what I don't, and conditioned to say no most of the time. I sometimes reflect on and recall the old Bavarian saying: "Ve get too soon oldt und too late shmart."

Almost before the first year began, I started to get enormous pressure to get into the fray involving House Speaker Newt Gingrich's proposals for massive shifts of government responsibilities to philanthropic and voluntary organizations. I resisted most of the expectations of a leadership role but felt it necessary to try to provide information and guidance to help achieve a more informed approach to all of the issues involved, including things described as devolution, privatization, and reinventing government. Initially, I did a series of pieces for IS, including sample op-ed pieces, letters to the editor, editorials, and briefing memos. That led to an extensive discussion draft of a paper for an IS Government Relations Forum, which I keynoted, and for a Filene Center Occasional Paper, "Re-examining the Roles and Relationships of Voluntary Organizations and Government."

One of the largest assignments of that period was an article, "A Major Transfer of Government Responsibilities to Voluntary Organizations? Proceed with Caution," published by *Public Administration Review* (PAR) in early 1996. This was a follow-up to an article I had done for them in 1989 headed, "What Voluntary Organizations Can and Cannot Do for America." The core theme of the new piece was, "We make a terrible mistake if we exaggerate what voluntary organizations can do, particularly if it allows us to exaggerate what government need not do."

I continue to be involved in three issues that relate to misunderstandings of the roles and capacities of the independent sector and a consequent undermining of voluntary and philanthropic organizations: the relative roles of the government and independent sectors, including who should do what in fulfilling public responsibilities; how the public business should be paid for, including financial relationships and responsibilities when government expects voluntary organizations to provide legislatively mandated services; and preserving the preeminent roles and rights of voluntary organizations to engage in advocacy and empowerment.

The difference between my tasks during the INDEPENDENT SECTOR years and later was that I was no longer an activist and organizer, largely because that requires rallying the troops, which is IS's role. My new role was to try to share the lessons and views from all my organizing years in order to inform and prepare current and future leaders in both sectors for their contributions to participatory democracy. For those who think that sounds like more fun, I can report from being on both sides that being an activist is much more fun and provides far more tangible rewards. The advantage I do have is that my new part is easier—not easy, but at least easier.

Other carryover obligations I brought with me involved service on some boards. I had not served on many while at IS because it would have been impossible to decide among so many member organizations and I didn't have the time anyway. Exceptions I made involved boards with which I had prior connections or represented central liaisons for IS. The first category included my alma mater, Tufts, CIVICUS, the Hogg Foundation (for mental health), and the National Academy of Public Administration (NAPA).

I remained chair of CIVICUS through our first international assembly in 1995 and then stepped off the board in favor of Sara Meléndez, my successor at IS. The Hogg Foundation provided a link to my long investment and interest in the field of mental health/mental illness and was based in Texas, which gave me helpful and fuller exposure to the Southwest. (Incidentally, and just for amusement, very often when I mention the Hogg Foundation, people ask me if it's really true there was a woman involved whose name was Ima Hogg. I assure them it was so and that she was a grand and able leader of the cause. They would then go on to comment that therefore it must also be true that there was a brother called Ura Hogg, but I have to tell them that part was pure fabrication. Ima had to struggle through on her own.)

In the category of organizations where it was useful to IS for me to serve on a board, a good example was the Points of Light Foundation, where I had been asked by the first President Bush to help organize the foundation. Many of our members were pleased I was involved, but some who felt that the President was not sufficiently supportive of their issues or of voluntary organizations in general were upset that I was so identified with him. My view and our board's was that it was helpful to be as close as possible to a project that had chances to produce results important to our cause.

The National Academy of Public Administration (NAPA) represented both a personal interest and a natural liaison for IS. I had been elected a Fellow of the Academy in 1985, which had significance because I was perhaps the only person to be elected who had never served in government. I'd had various advisory posts but never been an elected or appointed official or civil servant. My election was a reflection of NAPA's fairly new and healthy interest in nongovernmental organizations, developed in part because their studies revealed that approximately one-third of graduates of schools of public administration were employed by voluntary organizations. From our side, we were eager to work with them in achieving a definition of public service that was broader than government.

After leaving IS, it was even more important to stay involved with NAPA to pursue the part of my agenda relating to achieving a clearer understanding of the relative public service roles of the government and independent sectors and to build bridges between leaders of both sectors for greater cooperation. Therefore, I spent considerable time working

with NAPA, including two terms on the board, and with related organizations such as the National Association of Schools of Public Policy and
Administration and the American Society of Public Administration. It
served as a tangible indication of the usefulness of such collaborations
that NAPA's 1999 annual meeting and forum, which I chaired, were devoted entirely to "Citizenship and Governance."

Earlier at a NAPA meeting I had given one of the principal speeches,
"It's Time to Make a Mesh of Things," which later became an Occasional
Paper of the Lincoln Filene Center. The title was taken from an expression often used by my dean at the Maxwell School, Paul Appleby, who
told us that "the role of a public administrator is to make a mesh of
things." As I said in the speech and paper, "They didn't teach us how, and
still don't, but if we are committed to decentralized and dispersed systems
that must also be effective, manageable, and accountable, we had better
learn now."

Another new board for me and everyone else involved is Bridgespan.
It began when Tom Tierney, then the current world wide head of Bain &
Company, an enormously successful management consulting firm, began
exploring how the company might become even more charitably involved
and in what ways it might represent a different contribution to public
causes. After many conversations with his Bain partners, Tom realized
that the members felt that they had been blessed with financial success
and they were eager to find the best possible ways to pay back. Like other
management consulting groups, they had done a good deal of pro bono
work with voluntary institutions and organizations, but that didn't seem to
achieve the kind of impact they wanted. The firm's hallmark of success was
in helping clients achieve breakthroughs to much higher levels of achievement. Tom wondered whether that model could be applied to our sector.

I responded with a combination of encouragement and caution. I was
absolutely delighted with their genuine desire to make such a difference,
but based on prior experience with management firms I worried that they
would treat this side of their efforts as second fiddle, resulting in second-
class service. In most prior efforts by business corporations there was almost a demeaning notion that if these consultations could result in any
form of more businesslike behavior, the engagement could be considered
a success. They rarely understood the nature of voluntary enterprise or
acknowledged the very real differences between the two types of organizations, particularly relating to the roles of volunteer leaders and boards.

From all of Tom's explorations, he and his partners decided the best
approach was to establish a separate 501(c)(3) organization devoted exclusively to nonprofit organizations with all the usual services but with
lower fees, and all of it drawing very much on Bain's experience. Startup

funding was provided by Bain and several foundations all interested in supporting this bold experiment at capacity building. The object was to undertake with the client organizations a thorough analysis of the organization's mission, governance, staffing, finances, performance, and potential and to develop together a plan to focus those assets in ways that could achieve breakthrough results. The engagement was not to achieve a strategy to get around a pesky stream of difficulty but how to build larger bridges to greater horizons. All this is still an experiment but the results are decidedly encouraging with a sufficient breadth of organizations in terms of mission and size to suggest that the lessons can have quite broad application.

From the start, and with increasing emphasis, Bridgespan has developed a capacity to apply whatever lessons are learned to a far broader number and range of organizations than are represented in the consulting engagements. This includes publishing reports, newsletters, and other material to share what is being learned. The effort on this side of the enterprise is to be on the lookout for the characteristics of nonprofit organizations most likely to lead to superior performance and what the underlying factors are that produce those characteristics.

A still newer experiment of Bridgespan is a division called Bridgestar, which is attempting to find ways to build bridges between organizations that can profit from more experienced people in such fields as management, finance, and marketing and to link those organizations with individuals who may be interested in a transfer to the nonprofit side.

It's still too early to be sure Bridgespan and its Bridgestar program can fulfill our goals and dreams, but the signs are good. There was an early breakthrough that provided particular excitement and encouragement. A client, almost desperately trying to expand to respond to pressing and growing needs, realized it had to do something very unusual to meet the tests and was willing to go through Bridgespan's process to see if it would help. At the end of the engagement the client was able to present its new plan to a previously doubting foundation, which this time around awarded a whopping $6 million to put the plan to work. Subsequently, three other foundations bet another $4 million on the business plan. The organization and the funders acknowledge that such grants could never have come about without significantly revised plans and operations. We don't expect all breakthroughs will be that dramatic, but it was a wonderfully positive sign and morale builder for all concerned.

My newest board involves The Cape Cod Foundation, which I joined to be involved closer to home. I've always been a great promoter of the community foundation movement and welcome the chance to help this impressive local one develop even further.

When I first came to Tufts, I had commitments to produce two books as quickly as possible. The first might be described as a labor of love because it involved a volume of my own writings. Several people and organizations involved with INDEPENDENT SECTOR, including The Foundation Center, agreed to produce such a book if I would put it together. At first I found the notion a bit vain and the merits rather reaching. I gradually realized that if these published pieces still had value, additional exposure could be useful.

The task appeared reasonably easy. All I had to do was assemble a lot of speeches, chapters, testimonies, op-ed pieces, and the like; select the best; put them in some order; and ship them off. How naive I was! The actual experience was the latest of many hard lessons this practitioner had to learn about the world of writing and publishing. The pieces obviously didn't fit, they were repetitious or contradictory, and they revealed very different styles and efforts to meet the expectations of varied audiences.

After far more time than I ever thought the project would take, the overall result was still uneven, but I'm reconciled, or perhaps I've rationalized, that a book of writings covering disparate subjects, purposes, and outlets isn't very likely to be smooth. Even with the shortcomings, what I still wanted to say seemed to come through, at least well enough to go ahead. Also, it seemed useful to have in one place certain reference pieces that various people over the years had found instructive, encouraging, or constructively provocative. The Foundation Center thought so, and I'm grateful for their interest in publishing *People Power: Service, Advocacy, Empowerment,* in 1995.

The second book I had agreed to do took even more digging and time because it involved what the proposers described as a history of INDEPENDENT SECTOR. At times both my office and home study were literally stuffed with boxes of accumulated records, including materials from predecessor organizations such as the Filer and Peterson commissions. People also assumed that this assignment could be turned around fairly quickly. All I had to do was record what I remembered and send it off. It deserved and needed so much more, because I was probably the only person who possessed so much information representing a significant part of the history of the sector over as much as seventy-five or a hundred years. After two years of the struggle, *Powered by Coalition: The Story of* INDEPENDENT SECTOR was published by Jossey-Bass in 1997.

About three years into my professorship, I began working on first one and then two books, which took up a good part of my time for the next few years.

The first one related to a project I had undertaken some years before but that turned into an absolute flop. I had tried to put together a popularized presentation of the good news about giving and volunteering, including guidelines for people who would like to get involved or more involved. By then I had done hundreds of presentations to general audiences, which revealed that Americans want to know more about volunteers and volunteering. At the same time, I'd never seen anything approaching an authoritative but popular presentation of the enormous difference made by givers and volunteers and of the ways that individuals can become involved. Although I couldn't be objective, I had also talked to enough reporters and general audiences to know that if the topics of giving and volunteering are packaged popularly, the interest is extraordinary.

That's why I worked so hard on a draft of a book called *Making a Difference,* which was rejected by several publishers of popular books. I was almost ready to give up when I was referred to an agent who showed great interest, although he thought my draft would be improved by the participation of a writer in whom he had confidence. It wasn't surprising that the writer would need to be paid but it was surprising how much he wanted to be paid, yet having already invested so much time and some money, I went ahead. Based on the kind of questions the writer asked and additional materials requested, I began to be concerned about his approach, and after many delays and supplemental payments, when he and the agent submitted their masterpiece, I was appalled. Not only was it insultingly simplistic but grossly overpromising, such as "follow these steps and you'll find yourself in the headlines!" It was also frighteningly inaccurate, without any regard to the factual information I had provided. My data and examples weren't sensational enough, so the writer made up his own. I was so disgusted I choked down the loss of time and money and withdrew from the project in every way.

Much, much later I described my dilemma to Lynn Luckow, head of Jossey-Bass Publishers. He agreed that there was a need to get the message out but didn't think my approach was the answer. However, at that point he wasn't sure what might work but said he would think about it. To my surprise and delight, he came back with the idea that the message might best be communicated through the tales and pictures of volunteers in action, demonstrating what they do and how they do it, with their own words about what it means to them to be involved. Interspersed with their pictures and stories would be short interludes of narration conveying the broader story of giving and volunteering in America.

To check his own judgment, Lynn had discussed the project with Chronicle Books, one of the country's foremost producers of photographic journalism, and they not only liked the idea but wanted to be part of it. Lynn asked if I would be willing to come to San Francisco to talk to both groups, and I was practically on the plane the next day. Subsequently, their mutual enthusiasm for the effort reached the level that both agreed to take it on as a pro bono project to help reach an even larger number of Americans.

Voices from the Heart: In Celebration of America's Volunteers was published early in 2000, and was designed as a gift for volunteer leaders and organizations to present to special volunteers in their circles. More broadly, the book helps Americans realize how important volunteers and their organizations are to people, causes, and communities and to the very kind of nation we are. It's intended to lift up this compelling subject so that millions of people understand far better than they do now that volunteers help give this country its national character. Chronicle Books outdid itself in the extraordinary photography of twenty-five inspiring people, ranging in age from thirteen to eighty-six, who, in their own words, describe the experience of being involved far better than I or any other writer could ever do. My narratives simply use their stories as examples of what is multiplied millions of times over every day in every community throughout the country.

The other book I started was a bit more complex and aimed at a somewhat narrower audience, those "public intellectuals" who think, read, discuss, and act on the major issues of their communities and times. I wanted the book to help awaken such people to the reality that effective communities and societies depend on the degree they are involved.

At least this book didn't have a long time finding a publisher. The University Press of New England (UPNE) and Tufts, a long-standing member of UPNE, had decided to undertake a new series and had chosen "Civil Society" as their topic. The press learned of my writing on the subject and, after review of early drafts, asked if I would allow it to publish the book to initiate the series. I was tremendously complimented and encouraged that they would take the risk of having a practitioner in the lead of a series that most people assumed would be of scholarly character. Many such volumes followed, but the press thought it sent an important message to have me go first.

The only down side to the deal was that they wanted it finished soon, at least within the year. That was just about three months after agreeing with Chronicle and Jossey-Bass to produce *Voices,* also to be completed within a year. The last thing I wanted to face was two books with similar deadlines. However, both were on topics particularly important to me and neither was postponable. It was a crazy year but one of the most rewarding of my life. I did, however, resolve never, ever to do another book and said so very publicly, especially to well-meaning individuals who asked, "What's next?"

Thus, as I indicated in the introduction to this book, it surprised even me when I found myself thinking of still another one. I suppressed, denied, dismissed, and ignored it but it wouldn't go away. As I scribble and dictate this first draft, I'm not even sure it will see the light of day, but God and John Gardner seem to have ganged up on me to "tell the stories."

In the course of my working on the civil society topic, including the book, I became increasingly aware of and concerned about the growing contradiction between the willingness of Americans to be active volunteers, contrasted with the evidence that most Americans, including a majority of high school and college students, are not inclined to have much to do with government. I found myself raising the topic in speeches and briefings, and began reading everything I could find on it.

In a combination of speeches in Florida in the fall of 2001, I concentrated on those negative attitudes in meetings with groups involving public administrators, elected officials, citizen leaders, academicians, media, and others and was struck by their concerns about the state of their communities. The complexities of the problems that confronted them, the growing chasm between citizens and government, and how obvious it was that voluntary organizations couldn't take on the bulk of public responsibilities caused these leaders to be confused and discouraged. It turned out that one of these people was the current editor of the journal *Public Integrity*, who asked me if I would consider writing on the topic for them. As usual with such representatives, I explained that I was not a scholar, which I could tell represented an impediment, but he left it that he would like to see us try to work something out. Very soon, he called and asked if I would consider doing a Commentary, which he said would not need to be a scholarly paper but a synthesis of my experience and observations as a practitioner. On that basis, I was interested in pulling together my thoughts to try to explain the problems and offer up possible approaches.

Because of my schedule and the journal's, and because some of the people on that side were only used to scholarly submissions, it took an agonizingly long time to finish. Finally, in 2003 the journal published "Citizen Participation and Influence in America: Impressive Performance and Alarming Shortfalls."

Although much of my professorship is devoted to the interesting combination of reflective writing and interactive engagement, I also have the special opportunity to be among students who teach and inspire me far beyond what I may contribute to them. Whether we talk about careers, crusades that have shaped the country, the state of democracy, or how to root out nonprofit organizations that cheat in the name of charity, the students are inquisitive, sharp, challenging, articulate, caring, and determined. They're also funny and fun. To have these exposures and connections in my sixties and seventies and to feel that I have some influence on these special people is about as good as it gets.

I also have another advantage that other faculty find almost unbelievable. Because my arrangement, including external funding, leaves me free to do what I think is important for me to concentrate on, I don't actually teach any classes but lecture or co-teach in some and am available to students and faculty. What naturally bothers the real teachers is that I have all the fun and stimulation without having to organize the class, read the papers or grade the exams. That's a state of Nirvana requiring that I keep a very low profile in other circumstances. The only thing that saves me is that some of the genuine professors who hear me lecture in their classes no doubt report "No wonder they pay him not to teach."

One of the internal projects I've concentrated on while at Tufts has been the development of what is now our University College of Citizenship and Public Service (UCCPS). At its simplest, the mission is to be certain that in the future every graduate of Tufts, whether an English major, physician, philosopher, economist, engineer, artist, or foreign service officer, will have been oriented to and prepared for a lifetime of active citizenship and service to society.

It is a college without walls, for it fulfills its ambitions through the active involvement of every school and department of the university. The central job of UCCPS is to work with each unit of Tufts to be certain that creative ways are found to supplement the curriculum so that all students understand the relationship of their subject or subjects to inclusive democracy.

Although there will be some students who decide to pursue full-time careers in voluntary institutions, our basic emphasis is that a fundamental role of education is to prepare citizens as the primary office holders of government, a concept central to the formation of the country. Many national studies make clear how much we have neglected this function of education at all levels from kindergarten through university, and that there has been particular resistance particularly at the top, where there has been long-standing debate in higher education about whether universities should teach the philosophy and fundamentals of citizenship. Some don't think the subject scholarly enough. When that disturbing notion was surfacing in the 1980s, I was invited to give the keynote address at the American Association of Higher Education's national conference, and I took the opportunity to say:

> The United States is the longest-lived democracy in the history of the world. This democracy has provided almost all of us with greater freedom and opportunity than any nation of human beings has ever known. Among the crucial factors that foster and preserve that democracy and those freedoms are active citizenship and personal community service. No leader or leadership institution can presume that fostering active citizenship to prolong our democracy and to extend those glorious freedoms for those who come after us is someone else's business.[18]

I mentioned earlier that I was pleased that my *Civil Society* book led off the UPNE/Tufts book series. It's not a coincidence that my chapter on "Preserving and Strengthening Civil Society" begins with the recommendation: "Bring into every level of formal education a preparation for citizenship and an understanding of the essential role of civil society in preserving and strengthening a civil democracy." I am pleased and proud that my university has undertaken a significant leadership role in this direction. It began with an extended process, during which Tufts examined what a single institution might do to fulfill such a responsibility and perhaps do it in a way that might provide leadership to other colleges and to education in general. There had been a long history of citizen involvement at Tufts, including the fifty years of the Lincoln Filene Center.

Discussions were at first informal and pretty much limited to a few departments such as political science. The important spark came at the somewhat improbable level of the trustees at a board retreat not long after John DiBiaggio became president. The trustees were "blue-skying" about what significant changes might be considered that would represent major improvements in what we do for our students and what signature programs we could develop that would provide even greater distinctiveness and distinction for the university. I knew of DiBiaggio's interest in citizenship education. He and I had met around the subject when he was head of Michigan State, and we had talked some about it when I chaired the committee that brought him to Tufts. We had not, however, raised the subject at the retreat as part of any strategy, but it emerged as one of many possible ideas for the future. I realized later that it was not surprising that trustees would want to think about such prospects. They were, after all, involved in many other civic leadership roles, and therefore would grasp the importance of citizens being willing and prepared for public involvement.

Even with that orientation, it took about two years for the idea to take hold, but the first step was a major one. For the first time in about fifty years, the board amended the Tufts mission to include that the very definition of a Tufts education would include preparation for active citizenship. That was followed by another three years of committee work to figure out how that mission might be addressed and to try to win the support—or reduce the resistance—of a very broad spectrum, including faculty, who would quite naturally worry about another new emphasis that would compete for resources.

After several drafts and reviews, including board-level critiques, the concept of the University College was approved to "integrate the values and exercise of active citizenship across the curriculum." The toughest hurdle we had to surmount was the constant effort to have us settle for something that would be considered a center or institute. I had learned in working with many such units that over time a center is likely to get more and more isolated and less and less visible. It was the board that saw the wisdom and the need to underscore the broader intent including in the name itself.

Although students are the focus, the design and execution include emphasis on everything from alumni to research. We were enormously fortunate to receive a stunning $10 million grant from Pierre and Pamela Omidyar, both Tufts alumni, which they stipulated was not to be used for endowment but for building a solid framework to get University College up and running.

After many efforts to interpret what this very different and sweeping enterprise is all about, I know it takes specific examples for the listener or reader to grasp what is unfolding. For example, a professor of civil and environmental engineering whose specialty is soil now organizes classes into teams to work with communities on studies of soil contamination and remediation. The outcome includes a plan and strategy for correction, and students who have developed both technical and community skills.

An English professor was at first baffled and put off by the challenge to make her literature classes civics friendly until she realized that with only modest changes in the reading requirements, books could be included that combine great writing with social lessons, such as Dickens' *A Tale of Two Cities,* Frank McCourt's *Angela's Ashes,* and any of Langston Hughes's poetry volumes.

In a communication and media studies class, teams of students are given the challenge and experience of producing TV-ready documentaries created to educate and activate citizens on social issues the students believe are essential to address.

A professor of nutrition policy science has taken her course and students to schools and school districts to work with students, administrators, cafeteria personnel, and others to achieve a better understanding of the personal and societal consequences of obesity and how individuals, schools, and even neighborhood restaurants can combine forces to improve eating habits for students and their families. The Tufts students find the course particularly interesting and feel better prepared for practical experience.

A professor of Russian language had not found a way to bring his subject alive or even to get most students performing at acceptable levels. As he thought about how his courses could possibly relate to community, he hit on the experiment of assigning students to do oral histories of older Russian immigrants who are eager to talk about their backgrounds and struggles. Indirectly, this provides students with an understanding of immigrant conclaves in urban settings, while directly and dramatically improving their grades.

A senior mathematics professor whose specialty is calculus couldn't find a way to bridge his subject with the personal side of his life, which includes a high degree of community involvement. He initially described the two parts of his life as absolutely separate. After thinking it over, he decided that for starters he would regularly talk to his students about what he did in the community on his own time. Later he added a section to his web site providing information about the volunteer service he does and why. In this way he is not only teaching math but demonstrating that educated people should also be good at community building, and along the way they become more interesting individuals.

With each breakthrough in ways that classes, departments, and schools at Tufts adapt their teaching to include strengthening communities and democracy, there is awareness that core learnings are not sacrificed but enhanced, and that along the way we are creating a common and reinforcing commitment to society.

It has certainly helped in the stimulation of such creative approaches that the current president of Tufts, Lawrence S. Bacow, and the provost, Jamshed Bharucha, have been enthusiastically involved.

This wonderful period of my professional life—really a splendid topping off of my career—is beginning to wind down. I note that most of my remaining titles have "emeritus" appended to them, which is appreciated except that a Latin scholar friend of mine translates it as "E, you're out, and MERITUS, you deserve it." I remain affiliated with Tufts, do the occasional lecture and speech and provide advice here and there, but more and more it is my writing that has to speak for me. I'm increasingly attracted to Sean O'Casey's view, "I'd rather be inspired by idleness than bullied by busyness."

« 12 »

IF THE PAST IS PROLOGUE

For Those Going Forward
2005–2055

I've reached the stage of the book and my journey when I should lift up those learnings that are the most important to underscore for those going forward. As one attractively irreverent student put it after listening to one of my long litanies of what he and his classmates should know, "OK old man, what's *most* important to remember?" After many false starts that included far too many points, I decided to come at the task by telling you what five priorities I would emphasize if I had another fifty years. As I worked on that effort, I found myself consummately envious of your opportunities in the future. Not being able to be by your side is almost more than I can bear. God speed and good journey were never more heartfelt.

Each of my five most urgent messages has already been covered in the book. I considered just referring you to those particular pages but decided that this summary wouldn't then be as clear or persuasive as I mean it to be. Also, this chapter may sometimes serve as a stand-alone piece, which wouldn't work if the central arguments were not at hand.

With those caveats, here is what the old man thinks is most important for civic leaders and the staff who support them to know and do in your own lifelong efforts to achieve maximum citizen participation and influence.

ONE: *Help Americans to understand and take pride in the extraordinary degree of participation and generosity that already exists*

Most leaders of voluntary enterprises don't realize how positive the climate is for recruitment into their causes and therefore don't take advantage of the pervasive desire of people to be involved.

One hundred million citizens already volunteer. That's a staggering one out of every two of us over the age of thirteen. We give an average of four hours a week to the causes of our choice. The base of participation is spreading. There are more young people, more men, and more older people. Every economic group is involved. We are the only country in the world where volunteering is so wonderfully pervasive. What Alexis de Tocqueville described as "our habits of the heart" is still one of the nation's most distinguishing and distinguished features.

Research tells us that people who are involved, like being able to make a difference, feel good about themselves for doing it, gain new skills and confidence, meet and become friends with interesting people who are also making the effort, and feel that the experiences add new dimensions to their lives in many other rewarding ways.

Research also serves up other fascinating facts and opportunities, such as: The largest reason people volunteer (or give money) is that someone asks them; people who are not involved respect and envy those who are; and most people who are on the sidelines are not there because they don't believe in it. They wish they were involved in the service and satisfactions but are not sure they have anything to offer or haven't been invited to give it a try.

I'm always surprised when I hear people say they want to get involved but the opportunities just don't seem to come along. My surprise doubles when I hear organization leaders express frustration that they can't find people to volunteer. Both the individuals and the causes are missing out.

Sometimes those who are not volunteering worry that they won't be dedicated enough or able to give the time necessary to make a dent. Nothing could be further from the truth. Indeed, it is the composite of all the volunteering that leads to the compassion, spirit, and power that are characteristics of voluntary action in America. The important thing is that a great many people are involved in all kinds of causes and they have many opportunities to influence their own lives and be of service to others. Today, anyone who cares and is prepared to do something about it can make a difference.

We who are supposed to be the communicators of how very much volunteers and voluntary organizations contribute to society don't seem to realize what we can do for our own organization and all causes if we accept greater responsibility to help people understand how much this independent sector contributes to the most urgent needs of our communities and times. In very recent years our organizations and institutions have achieved inspiring progress in causes dealing with hospice services for the dying; preservation and conservation of almost every natural asset ranging from clean air to endangered species; learning disabilities; civil rights; nuclear control; peace; AIDS; cancer control; conflict resolution; independent living for the elderly; teen pregnancy; and so very much more.

Whether one's interest is wildflowers or civil rights, arthritis, or clean air, oriental art or literacy, the dying or unborn, organizations are already at work, and if they don't suit our passion it's still a wonderful part of America that we can go out and start our own.

In doing the book *Voices From the Heart: In Celebration of America's Volunteers,* I tried to tell some of the stories through the real-life profiles of twenty-five very different people who volunteer in twenty-five very different roles. One of the purposes of the book is to provide voluntary organizations and leaders with a gift for special people in their circles. In the introduction I say, "So enter the celebration—look, read and enjoy. Listen to these voices from the heart. As Walt Whitman described it, "listen to America singing."[19]

TWO: *Invest in capacity building so that voluntary organizations have a greater chance to fulfill their essential missions.*

At a time when many in voluntary organizations criticize our counterparts in business for being so fixated on "quarterly results" that they can't see the future, we overlook the fact that our own long-term scopes are often rusted in place on "today." The nonprofit sector is the most labor-intensive of the three sectors but invests by far the least in its future, and it recoils from spending more for fear of being criticized for high overhead. We worry about the effectiveness of our organizations, agree on the need to attract more bright young people, shudder at the implications of high staff turnover, talk endlessly about expanding the base of financial and volunteer support, and cringe at the paltry levels of investment available for planning and evaluation, but we turn our backs on all this common sense with the rationalization that we are too busy doing good and that no one will give us money to invest in these "extras" anyway.

At a meeting involving the metropolitan heads of one of the country's largest social service organizations, I talked about the alarming mismatch between what they expect of their volunteer and staff leaders and what they actually invest in them. To a person they agreed, but when I took it the next step and talked about greater investment they said I should know that they don't have funds for such luxuries. Before the conversation went stone cold, we calculated that the proportion of their million-dollar budgets going toward staff development was about 1 percent. My guess is that for the sector as a whole it's far less.

When I try to talk about how much businesses spend on human resource development (HRD) and research and development (R&D), leaders of voluntary organizations turn me off as though the comparisons were not fair. I generate some attention when I indicate how much money even small and medium-sized community governments spend on finding and nurturing young leaders, but the curiosity is mostly grounded in envy. Even volunteer leaders who come from business will only stay with me through the part of the conversation that relates to applying their own human investment practices, but their interest founders against immediate financial and service deficits.

Several years ago the Council of Jewish Federations (CJF) undertook an interesting study to try to determine why certain of their local units do so much better than average. They assumed that the explanation would relate to the number of Jews in those communities, their per-capita income, or the number of Jewish-owned businesses. However, the largest factor by far turned out to be quality of staff as measured by its capacity to effectively involve and provide assistance to an increasing number of volunteer leaders. As a result of that study, the CJF reoriented its national operations to emphasize staff development, including the establishment of the Philip Bernstein Training Center, named after its own able staff director.

Over the years, including times of economic downturn and government cutbacks in support for the programs and services of voluntary organizations, I've met with at least 200 board and staff delegations seeking advice on fund raising. I start with encouragement, but I follow up quickly with how much work is in store. I indicate that their organization must be prepared to devote at least 20 percent of its resources to fund raising and that the board and chief staff officer will have to devote closer to one third of their time for the next few years. Despite their apparent conviction, the response is rarely, "If that's what it's going to take, we'll do it!" In the majority of cases, the reaction is rejection, anger, and insult.

Often the chief staff officer is the most offended. Those physicians, social workers, historians, or former foreign service officers are upset that I should undercut their professional status by putting them in such a substantial fund-raising role. I always try to convey that fund raising is really a matter of the people who care about a cause and know it firsthand, telling the story with the same conviction that they tell it every day to colleagues, friends, and neighbors.

Most of these delegations leave shaking their heads, already thinking about finding more reasonable advice. Later, I hear that they have merged, reduced their focus substantially, closed, or are looking for a new executive director. I can predict that in the interim, they went into further deficit or secured a grant from a foundation or board member to hire a development director to whom they turned over the noxious assignment.

I know I'm being direct here, but it's deliberate. My primary message is to tell you how much you can do and to urge you to proceed with optimism. However, that would be irresponsible if I didn't couple it with the truest lessons I've ever learned in community organizing, all involving what it takes to launch and sustain a significant fund-raising effort.

Very often I find that organizations think of stewardship only as the prudent handling of funds, but it should also include building the greater capacity of the organization to fulfill its urgent purposes. I'm not calling for irresponsible high flyers but the careful planning and organizing of financial development.

Several years ago the new leadership of one of the nation's largest and most successful businesses asked me to advise them on how they could make the greatest possible difference through the company's philanthropy. I deliberately called my response, "The Growth Fund" with the subhead "An Investment Initiative for Nonprofit Enterprise." The following may give you a sense of it:

> The Growth Fund is a project to apply to nonprofit endeavor the capacity building strategies practiced routinely by successful businesses. By establishing The Growth Fund, the company would demonstrate that a realistic part of grantmaking, especially by corporations, should be directed to helping nonprofits learn what businesses know and do best, which involves investing in effectiveness and growth.
>
> The project would have four parts: to build into the sector's orientation and practice an awareness that investment in capacity building is an essential and seriously neglected responsibility of philanthropic and voluntary organizations; to assist the sector in identifying significant impediments to growth within the sector and strategies for dealing with them such as documenting the lack of investment in recruiting and nurturing public service-minded young people and creating pooled efforts for recruitment, traineeships, job placement, training, transfers, etc.; to provide matching funds to support competitively selected projects of voluntary organizations that have the greatest likelihood of demonstrating that investment in growth pays off; and to publicize examples of investment activities of philanthropic and voluntary organizations that are considered models of capacity building.[20]

Unfortunately, there was another change of leadership in the company and the new CEO didn't pursue the plan. Perhaps some day another company, foundation or group of grantmakers will establish something like The Growth Fund.

To illustrate how strongly I believe in investing for greater achievement, but at the same time exposing my failures to win the day, there was another proposal I thought and continue to think would make a substantial difference. It is for an Academy of Nonprofit Leaders, which would be the nonprofit sector's equivalent of the military's Command and General Staff College, where top staff and volunteer leaders would finally have a place to gather to consider the larger issues relating to the sector's role and future and where leadership responsibilities to deal with those issues would be emphasized.

At the time I was retiring from IS I was requested to do a piece for the twenty-fifth anniversary issue of *Fundraising Management*. Not surprisingly, I chose as my topic, "The Future Looks Good—For Those Who Invest In It," and I ended it, "for the organization that has a worthy cause, is open and accountable, and invests in its development, the outlook is very bright."[21]

THREE: *Preserve at all cost the necessary independence of voluntary organizations to be the vehicles through which citizens express their collective hopes and dreams and their criticisms and outrage.*

No individuals or institutions are entirely independent of government, but our democratic society depends substantially on the relative independence of philanthropic and voluntary institutions.

There are many challenges to that independence. Some of this is natural and healthy and some is built into the realities of concentration of power. Daniel Patrick Moynihan, speaking at the founding meeting of INDEPENDENT SECTOR, described the ultimate threat of government's domination of our sector.

> I think many of you will remember reading Joseph Schumpeter's last great book (*Capitalism, Socialism and Democracy;* 1942), in which he said how this wonderfully creative civilization that we have produced in North America and Western Europe is going to come to an end—not in some great apocalyptic Armageddon in which one class takes over another class and destroys all classes. No. It will come to an end through the slow but steady conquest of the private sector by the public sector.

The IS Organizing Committee identified a litany of concerns, including the degree of government funding for nonprofit organizations, but with rules and regulations that go far beyond any contractual obligations of voluntary organizations to perform specified services; challenges to advocacy rights and roles; reduction of the exemption from property taxes; proposed taxes on endowments; and limitations on deductions of contributions. The committee underscored that it is the emerging or unpopular organizations that are particularly at the mercy of all the regulation. It elaborated, "There is no greater danger to the preservation of our liberty than giving the powers that be any great control over what their own reformers might do." The Organizing Committee favored the name INDE-PENDENT SECTOR because the most important element this sector represents in American society is its relative independence.

In the book *People Power* I wrote, "The impacts of voluntary action can generally be categorized as service, advocacy and empowerment and although each is important, the relative worth to society is in inverse proportion to the dollars and encouragement provided. As important as direct services are, they are to my mind and experience decidedly secondary to the functions of advocacy and empowerment where the dollars and staff are comparatively tiny but where the contributions to democracy are immense."

Over the fifteen years of my active leadership of IS there were eleven very serious efforts to limit the advocacy rights of voluntary organizations; they came at us from many different directions. In 1993 alone, there were five serious legislative and regulatory proposals that would have dangerously limited the advocacy rights of voluntary organizations and their funders. Successful efforts to defeat those threats took every speck of effort by every part of the IS coalition, but in the end we were able to prevail.

As I look back, I find it terribly disheartening to see how many of the same battles we have to fight over and over again. For example, it's heartbreaking that so many people in government, in different administrations and parties, challenge the advocacy role and rights of our organizations. They just don't seem to understand that advocacy is often our best service. When they reflect on the great accomplishments of the sector, such as civil rights and child welfare, even they tend to cite the results of our advocacy activities. Perhaps the opposition is due to a belief that advocacy implies criticism. Whatever the cause, these negative attitudes are discouraging and persistent.

Frederick Douglass expressed it this way: "Those who profess to favor freedom, and yet deprecate agitation, are people who want crops without plowing the ground. They want the ocean without the awful roar of its many waters." Justice John Harlan interpreted it: "The constitutional right of free expression is powerful medicine in a society as diverse and populous as ours; that the air may at times seem filled with verbal cacophony is, in this sense, not a sign of weakness but of strength."

Very consistently we faired well in Supreme Court cases that reinforced the principle that voluntary organizations represent an extension of freedom of speech, but we can't assume that the courts will always be with us. As the great jurist Learned Hand expressed it: "I often wonder whether we do not rest our hopes too much upon constitutions, upon laws and courts. These are false hopes; believe me, these are false hopes. Liberty lies in the hearts of men; when it dies there, no constitution, no law, no court can save it."

In my experience with CIVICUS: World Alliance for Citizen Participation, I was constantly reminded of the common truth of our times, that the small, everyday freedoms and the liberty of societies depend on the degree to which citizens are allowed to have influence and do in fact exercise that power. Conversely, that experience made me all the more aware that to be denied or to lose those everyday rights is to be trapped in suffocating powerlessness. I also understood far better how much the rest of the world recognizes and envies our advanced state of what such people often describe as buffer zones between government and the individual. Far better than ourselves, they realize what we've got and how absolutely essential it is to liberation. They know, too, that although democracies are more likely to encourage and allow independent citizen initiative, achieving a democratic form of government does not by itself ensure support for such essentials as freedom of speech and right of association.

The key messages in the CIVICUS experience were how truly fortunate we are to have a participatory, independent, influential civil society; how much more clearly our blessings are understood outside the country than within; and how fragile these rights and opportunities are, even in democracies.

FOUR: *Recognize and address the alarming shortfalls of citizen participation in democratic government.*

Although Americans are impressively involved in volunteering, we are strangely and alarmingly not often involved with government.

It is a fundamental precept of American democracy that citizens are the primary office holders of government, and we are dangerously neglecting that quintessential responsibility. Any analysis of how this sorry state of civic involvement came to pass is complicated by a wide range of often firmly held opinions about the state of our society, the effectiveness of government, and whether anything can be done to turn the public around.

At its simplest, if we serve but don't vote, something is terribly wrong with our democracy. If in our voluntary organizations we are trying to deal with the most basic needs of our clients, communities, and country but don't feel it is our responsibility to make government more effective, we limit our ability to fulfill those responsibilities. And if we insist that government performance should be worthy of democracy but don't automatically encourage young people to run for office or serve in appointed or career positions, we establish a dangerous, self-fulfilling prophecy.

Some views and the publicity they seem to attract and spread make it particularly hard to be objective and hopeful. In his book titled *Malevolent Leaders: Popular Discontent in America,* Stephen C. Craig says, "We know for a fact that Americans have been mad as hell for quite a few years. What remains to be seen is whether they are prepared to let their leaders know that they refuse to take it anymore."[22]

Daniel Yankelovich begins a *Kettering Review* article, "The American public is in a foul mood. People are frustrated and angry. They are anxious and off balance. They are pessimistic about the future and cynical about all forms of leadership and government."[23]

The publisher of Georgie Anne Geyer's book *Americans No More: The Death of Citizenship* describes her message as, "Citizenship in the United States has changed drastically and for the worse."[24]

The Kennedy School of Government at Harvard has undertaken a multi year project, "Visions of Government for the Twenty-First Century," which began with an analysis called "Why People Don't Trust Government." In the introduction of the book of the same title, Joseph S. Nye, Jr., sets out some of the concerns the school uncovered: "Confidence in government has declined. In 1964, three-quarters of the American public said that they trusted the federal government to do the right thing most of the time. Today only a quarter of Americans admit to such trust. The numbers are only slightly better—35 percent—for state government. Some polls show even lower levels." The top reasons cited for distrusting government are that it is inefficient, wastes money, and spends on the wrong things.[25] From my experience, these generalizations may be firmly held but are not firmly documented.

Equally inaccurate and unfair are the generalized perceptions that most elected officials are not really interested in their constituents and that most people who work in government are lazy, not particularly competent, and could not make it in the private sector. For fifty years I have worked closely with elected and career officials at all levels of government and found the considerable majority to be dedicated, hard-working, and effective.

Publishers and the media certainly contribute to the negativism, for example, Geyer ends her book with a hopeful prospect and agenda, but the book's title and promotion concentrate on "the death of citizenship." Balance and hope are rarely captured in the sound bites about government.

Perhaps the most dangerous indicator of attitudes toward government is that young people don't want to get involved with it. A *New York Times* story by Adam Clymer reported that "students say they give their time to help the homeless, tutor children and clean up polluted streams but they tell poll takers that their interest in public service does not extend to voting or even talking about politics."[26]

Through all the real and perceived problems between government and citizens, there are indications of ways to sort through what is really wrong and, as important, what is really right about government. There are ways for communities and leaders to determine and address major needs without going round and round on the useless notion that the crises are so overwhelming and the government so inept that progress isn't possible.

For a good starting place, I go back to Nye and his co-authors, who begin with "why people don't trust government" but end with some revealing and encouraging findings. For example, Nye provides helpful balance to otherwise disturbing information about trust by indicating that "the public overwhelmingly thinks the United States is the best place to live [80 percent] and we like our democratic system of government [90 percent]," and then he observes, "something is steady."[27]

Although it seems obvious, I don't think most people who are struggling with the enormity and complexity of society's problems realize that underneath so much that seems so wrong, there is the firm bedrock of people's devotion to this country. Something is indeed steady.

The Kennedy School book also provides fascinating examples of how far off the mark some of our impressions and even some of our largest concerns about government turn out to be. Derek Bok recounts a series of extreme misperceptions, such as, "Most people estimate that more than 50 cents of every dollar in the Social Security program is eaten up in overhead. The true figure is less than two cents." He reports on more than seventy-five "specific objectives of importance to most Americans," such as the economy, housing, and percentage of people graduating from high school, and concludes that despite the public's assumptions to the contrary, "the United States has made definite progress over the past few decades in the vast majority of [the seventy-five] cases."[28] Bok acknowledges that some things are very wrong, such as our health care system, but by narrowing in on these we can make progress.

Even when we focus on some of our toughest problems and worries, it is helpful to be rational rather than hopeless or mean spirited. For example, the concerns of some and perhaps many of the people who are disillusioned, angry, and even frightened might be eased by gaining a better perspective on the issues.

Even the terror of crime, which surveys tell us is the gravest worry of the greatest number of people, yields to citizen outrage and action. People are taking back their neighborhoods and growing more aware that failure to confront crime and such attendant issues as drugs and poverty is no longer tolerable for anybody.

A great many Americans are also alarmed about the changing makeup of the U.S. population, particularly the new waves of refugees and immigrants. Although the problems are real, it is helpful to realize that most of us descend from people who were in the same circumstances, and that much of the strength of America stems from the values of immigrants, including hard work, belief in education, and the practice of religion. In "The Seeds of Urban Renewal," Michael Sviridoff wrote eloquently about the positive side of our current population mix: "Masses of new people arrive each day, uplifting forsaken neighborhoods in ways beyond the expectation of earlier and failed urban redevelopment. They demonstrate, as did the older migrations, that new people possessed of a sturdy work ethic and stable families matter more than buildings."[29]

Another example in which understanding may ease concern relates to the so-called common values that so many people seem to espouse. A hard look at the issue reveals that a great problem involves whose and what values the various proponents would have us embrace. Many of those who plead for and even insist on a return to common beliefs and behavior in worship, patriotism, and togetherness hold rigidly to their own often skewed perception of those values. In his book *One Nation, After All,* Alan Wolfe indicates that Americans still hold to the same basic values and accept that we all must be involved in achieving civility, including respecting differences in the way people look, speak, and worship.[30]

The central point is that the problems that frustrate, frighten, or distance citizens are the responsibility of citizens to address, and the evidence is increasingly clear that when citizens get aroused, involved, and organized, progress occurs.

Here are a series of positive building blocks that I think can provide hope and direction for leaders struggling against negativism and hopelessness:

How proud Americans are of our country and democracy. ("Something is steady.")

How active and effective we are as participants in our voluntary organizations.

How wrong we often are in our generalized perceptions of the ineffectiveness of government.

How effective people can be throughout their neighborhoods and communities when they get aroused, involved and organized.

I dwell on these positive building blocks because so many community and national leaders are bewildered and immobilized by the complex mix of all the problems that seem to overwhelm them. They don't know where to start or move. As complex and difficult as it all is, it begins with sorting out the facts, deciding what is most important to change, and mobilizing the forces around those priorities.

In the public arena, such a process has to begin with government leaders who are comfortable with citizens as partners and who have these characteristics:

A passionate belief in participatory democracy, including the multiplication of participants and the dispersion of power.

A capacity both to enlarge and to survive the democratic cacophony in order to hear the individual shrieks—and songs.

An ability to educate the public, including the single-issue players, so that we are all better informed of the relationship between our special interests and the larger society in which those interests must be pursued.

An ability to make decisions, and to say no—even to you and to me.

In *Civil Society: The Underpinnings of American Democracy,* I ended the book with a "Summing Up: Prospects for an Enduring Democracy," and because those conclusions relate so much to citizen participation and influence, I repeat some of it here.[31]

Through all my hopefulness I must still confront the awful question of whether this democracy will survive another century and maybe beyond. No other democracy has lasted as long as ours, so we cannot assume that ours will just keep rolling on. My sense is that the prospects should be reasonably good. The design of our government, including the power of citizens to shape it, is still essentially intact. Our problems in the last part of the twentieth century are not nearly as great as the traumas of the second half of the preceding one, and our progress in protecting and extending democracy for most Americans has been dramatic. We also have a fairly clear grasp of what we can do to preserve and strengthen civil society and therefore democracy. With common sense and some luck, we should be all right.

But despite my general optimism, I worry, and most of what I worry about is whether 250 years beyond our founding it is really practical to expect that people will realize that it could come apart and will do everything possible to keep that from happening. Although it seems eminently logical that rational people would never ever let such a democracy unravel, I've been around long enough and have read enough to know that people and history can be tragically irrational. I find myself worrying what the consequences would be if in the course of the new century we experience a worsening of such factors as selfishness, taking liberty for granted, governmental limits on citizen participation, denial of basic rights in the name of security, the influence of special interests on public officials, separation between the haves and have-nots, intolerance, and incivility. How much deterioration of our civil society would it take to weaken democracy irreparably?

Gibbon's observations on the decline of Athenian democracy keep ringing in my ears, so I include them here: "In the end, more than they wanted freedom, they wanted security. They wanted a comfortable life and they lost it all—security, comfort and freedom. When the Athenians finally wanted not to give to society but for society to give to them, when the freedom they wished for most was freedom from responsibility, then Athens ceased to be free."[32]

For fifty years, coinciding with the last half of the extraordinary twentieth century, I have been in the midst of citizen movements dealing with some of the most urgent causes of these times, and along the way have learned what it really means for people to be liberated and what is required to maintain our freedoms.

When I match the meaning of those lessons against what I consider to be the public's limited grasp of them and against my firsthand awareness of how easily our rights as empowered citizens are eroded, I feel I should go on and on with the writing and explaining and exclaiming. Far short of that, I have to accept that this message must serve as "my letter to the World,"[33] to borrow Emily Dickinson's apt description of a heartfelt message aimed at everyone out there. My letter to everyone is about the glory of our freedoms, coupled with our responsibility to pass them on to future generations.

The Indians who are quite literally the Native Americans believe in responsibility to the "seventh generation," meaning that every major act of communal life should be measured for its impact on the seventh successor generation. Although that might exceed the reach of most of us, it should convey our responsibility to be as certain as possible that our democracy will still provide liberating freedoms and opportunities for successive generations, including our great, great, great, great-grandchildren.

For those who would respond that it is not practical to plan so far ahead or who believe that we can't know what major events, even calamities, could change everything between now and then, it's useful to consider how much we owe to those we commonly call our founding fathers, of whom we are little more than their seventh generation. Consider, too, that the freedoms they fought for are not likely to be lost in an apocalypse but through our indifference or lack of will.

When such worries begin to make me grim, I realize that we at least have a choice of what kind of a nation we will be, and holding onto liberty is astronomically better than struggling to attain it in the first place. Our democracy can last but only if we accept and practice the enduring democratic covenant recently and cogently summarized by John W. Gardner:

Freedom and responsibility
Liberty and duty
That's the deal.[34]

I pray we will solemnly commit to that pledge and prepare our children and their children to pass it on.

FIVE: *Teach participatory democracy.*

If I had to reduce all of the messages and learnings to one, it would be to build into every level of education a preparation for active citizenship and community service for all Americans.

When the country was founded, there were grave doubts above giving the vote and the right to hold office to most people, particularly the under-educated. When the principle of "citizens as the primary office-holders of government" was put forward, the debate intensified and was only narrowly won by Thomas Jefferson's argument: "I know of no safe depository for the ultimate powers of society but the people themselves; and if we think them not enlightened enough to exercise their control with a wholesome discretion, the remedy is not to take it from them, but to inform their discretion by education."[35]

"The civic mission of American education" is the formal dedication of the book *Civitas: A Framework for Civic Education:* "We believe that education for citizenship is the primary reason for establishing universal education in the American republic; i.e. the purpose to develop among all students, whether in private or in public schools, the virtues, sentiments, knowledge, and skills of good citizenship."[36]

In his foreword to *Higher Education and the Practice of Democratic Politics: A Political Education Reader,* David Mathews, discussing the origins of his book, proposes this goal for all forms of participation:

> Over five years ago, a small informal group of faculty, administrators and students from a wide range of institutions began meeting to discuss a common concern with the way academia is educating young people for political responsibility, civic competence, and public leadership. . . .
>
> In the sum, if colleges and universities are responsible for the development of the minds of their students, then they are certainly responsible for those particular modes of rationality that are civic . . . [and] that responsibility requires a reconsideration of even our best efforts to prepare the next generation for public life.[37]

Even in the face of these resolves and lessons, the subject of civics was gradually dropped for everyone. Now we wring our hands at the consequences and even allow educators to rationalize that the subject was not important or popular enough to continue or scholarly enough to reinstate. Fortunately, there are clear signs that thoughtful people are again realizing that we can't exercise participatory democracy without educating and training people for their essential roles.

At the elementary and high school levels, a growing number of communities provide and encourage volunteer assignments and intellectual opportunities in the classroom to understand what all the participation means to the quality for society. Community Service Learning (CSL) is the umbrella concept that has come to describe the dual roles. It's described as "a method of teaching that promotes caring, contributing citizens; makes abstract knowledge relevant; engages the community in teaching efforts; and effects real community change."

More than one thousand colleges and universities are now part of Campus Compact, which requires demonstrated commitment on the part of the institutions and direct involvement of their presidents "to help students develop the values and skills of citizenship through participation in public and community service."

In addition to David Mathews's group there are other important studies, writings and action such as Thomas Ehrlich's book *Civic Responsibility in Higher Education,* done in conjunction with the American Council on Education, and the University College of Citizenship and Public Service at Tufts University through which every Tufts student will be prepared for a lifetime of active citizenship and service to society.

INDEPENDENT SECTOR and its former research director Virginia Hodgkinson have done studies that identify the factors most likely to assure that younger and future generations will accept the essential obligation of service to society, including the obligation to pass these attributes on to their successors. There are at least six primary factors that determine if a young person is likely to become an active participant as an adult. As summarized in INDEPENDENT SECTOR's *Care and Community in Modern Society: Passing On the Tradition of Service to Future Generations,* young people grow up to be active participants if they: had parents or other adult role models who volunteered; were involved in a youth group or other voluntary organization; were involved in a religious congregation where they were volunteers or were introduced to volunteer assignments outside the congregation; were exposed to volunteering as part of school activity; saw respected young peers volunteer; or were influenced by favorable media coverage of volunteering. If one or more of these factors are present, a young person is almost certain to become an active community figure. For example, if both parents volunteered, there is a 75 percent likelihood that their children will become volunteers. Sixty percent will be volunteers if only one parent volunteered.[38]

As a result of all the recent research and teaching practices, we now know a good deal about how to pass along the habits of participation and responsibility, and we must organize ourselves to make sure the knowledge is put to work. By spreading and strengthening the involvement of parents, schools, congregations, youth-serving organizations, and the media, we are likely to see the rewards for generations.

As you consider your approach to these five priorities and to so many other of your leadership opportunities and obligations, I take the liberty of suggesting an overarching concentration that has to do with the spirit you engender for those who look to you for meaning and guidance. In my Mental Health Association days, I partnered with our top volunteer officer, Geri Joseph, to develop a list of the primary characteristics of effective civic leaders. Although the listing covered many appealing and impressive behaviors, the highlight by far was the ability "to keep the dream alive."

Volunteer and staff leaders get so preoccupied with urgent tasks and with the obstacles that stand in the way of advancing the crucial mission and goals of the enterprise that we forget or neglect how absolutely essential it is to tend to morale and enthusiasm.

People who get involved with public causes open themselves to frustration and disappointment, but—through it all and after it all—those moments of making change happen for the better can be among our lasting joys. There's something wonderfully rewarding in being part of an effort that makes a difference. And there's something rewarding in being among other people when they're at their best too.

When we take inventory of the meaning of our lives, these special experiences have to be among the high points. Happiness is, in the end, a simple thing. Despite how complicated we try to make it or the entrapments we substitute for it, happiness is caring and being able to do something about it.

In the community sense, caring is public service in all its many forms. As far back as the twelfth century, the highest order and benefit of service were described by Maimonides in the Mishna Torah: "The highest degree, than which there is nothing higher, is to take hold of a Jew who has been crushed and to give him a gift or a loan or to enter into partnership with him or to find work for him, and then to put him on his feet so he will not be dependent on his fellow man."

In a world just sixty years removed from the slaughter of six million Jews, and still rampant with disease and other indignities of the vilest form and breadth, there is room for concern and caring. Indeed, in this still young democracy, there is total dependence on citizen determination to preserve the freedoms so recently declared and to extend them to all.

The problems of contemporary society are more complex, the solutions more involved, and the satisfactions more obscure, but the basic ingredients are still the caring and the resolve to make things better. From the simplicity of these have come today's exciting efforts on behalf of humanitarian causes, ranging from equality to environment and from health to peace.

In the course of these efforts, there is at work a silent cycle of cause and effect that I call the "genius of fulfillment"—that is, the harder people work for others and for the fulfillment of important social goals, the more fulfilled they are themselves. Confucius expressed it by saying, "Goodness is God," meaning that the more good we do, the happier we are, and the totality of it all is a supreme state of being. Thus, he said, God is not only a Supreme Being apart from us, but a supreme state of being within us.

A simpler way of looking at the meaning of service is a quotation from an epitaph:

> What I spent is gone
> What I kept is lost
> But what I gave to charity
> Will be mine forever.

How we express the meaning of service doesn't really matter. It can be charity or enlightened self-interest or simply humanity to other people. These are all ways of describing why we serve, why service provides some of our happiest moments, and why the good that we do lives after us.

Carry on.

Appendix
Chief Volunteer Officers with Whom I Served

As mentioned in the introduction, the early drafts of the book included lists of the top volunteer leaders in the organizations where I served as staff director; however, preliminary readers advised that these interfered with the flow and would be more appropriate to an appendix. I agreed only when I was satisfied that this wouldn't obscure a central point of the book, that staff leaders are usually effective to the extent they serve to multiply the participation and impact of the volunteer leaders with whom they work.

I wish it were possible to list the thousands of officers, board members, and committee heads who deserve the recognition and my personal thanks, but that would go on almost endlessly. I hope in listing at least the top officers that they might be representative of their legions of allies who made such a difference in important public causes.

In the American Heart Association–Maryland, 1956–1961, the volunteer presidents were Dulany Foster, Nelson Offutt, Nathan Needle, MD, Sidney Scherlis, MD, and Raeburn Parker.

For the American Heart Association–California, 1961–1966 the board chairmen were Elwood Ennis, Lloyd Graybiel, and Richard Dotts, and the presidents were Drs. John Sampson, Harney Cordua, William Thomas, Arthur Feinfield, and Eldon Ellis.

In the National Mental Health Association, 1966–1978, the presidents were Jeanette Rockefeller, Earl Warren, Jr., Geri Joseph, James Chapman, Irving Chase, Helen Wright, Linden Wheeler, Gerridee Wheeler, Thomas Watkins, Chasey Pell, and Arnold Barach.

For the National Council on Philanthropy, Kenneth Albrecht and James Lipscomb were the chairmen and for the Coalition of National Voluntary Organizations; Bayard Ewing and Philip Bernstein were the presidents.

At INDEPENDENT SECTOR the chairpersons were John W. Gardner, Richard W. Lyman, John H. Filer, Eugene C. Dorsey, and Raul Yzaguirre.

In pulling together those lists, memories flooded in reminding me all over again how crucial it is to our democracy that such citizen leaders are so involved and so remarkably effective. I certainly was blessed, and the country all the more so.

Notes

1. William W. Moore, *Fighting for Life: A History of the American Heart Association, 1911–1975* (Dallas, Texas: American Heart Association, 1983), iv.

2. "The OMB Bomb Throwers" *New York Times* [editorial] (March 15, 1983), A24.

3. Brian O'Connell, "Don't Save Me From the Left or Right," *Christian Science Monitor,* December 28, 1983.

4. "Back to the Future: How the Past Century Shaped Today's Nonprofit World," *Chronicle of Philanthropy,* January 11, 2001 49–51. (Based on a study "What Ten Events Most Heavily Influenced the Development of the Nonprofit World During the Past Century?" conducted by the Alford Group, Skokie, Ill.)

5. Brian O'Connell, "'First Lights': Recollections of the Beginnings and First Years of CIVICUS: World Alliance for Citizen Participation," prepared for CIVICUS, Washington, D.C., 2000), 3–6.

6. Ibid., 6–7.

7. Brian O'Connell, *America's Voluntary Spirit: A Book of Readings* (New York: The Foundation Center, 1983), 59–61. From "True and False Philanthropy," *McGuffey's Newly Revised Eclectic Reader* (1844).

8. Ibid., 284–85 (from Waldemar Nielson's Occasional Paper, "The Third Sector: Keystone for a Caring Society," INDEPENDENT SECTOR, Washington, D.C., 1980).

9. Brian O'Connell, *Philanthopy in Action* (New York: The Foundation Center, 1987), 13–14 (from Milton Lomask's *Seed Money: The Guggenheim Story* [New York: Farrar Straus and Co., 1964]).

10. Ibid., 51–52 (from Arnaud C. Marts' *Philanthropy's Role in Civilization: Its Contribution to Human Freedom* [New York: Harper & Bros., 1973]).

11. Ibid., 118.

12. Ibid., 118 (from *Literary Digest,* May 1912).

13. Ibid., 151–52 (from William G. Roger's *Ladies Bountiful,* [New York: Harcourt, Brace and World, 1968]).

14. Brian and Ann B. O'Connell, *Volunteers in Action,* 13 (New York: The Foundation Center, 1989 [from *Ebony,* December 1975]).

15. Ibid., 47 (from *Cooperative Extension Review,* Fall 1982).

16. Ibid., 92–93 (from *Mother Jones,* July/August, 1986).

17. Ibid., 239 (from *On the Road,* Charles Kuralt).

18. Brian O'Connell, keynote address to the National Conference on Higher

Education, Chicago (March 17, 1985), sponsored by American Association of Higher Education, Washington, D.C.

19. Brian O'Connell, *Voices from the Heart: In Celebration of America's Volunteers* (San Francisco: Chronicle Books and Jossey-Bass, 1999), 17.

20. Brian O'Connell, "Hopes Not Realized and Other Regrets," in *Powered By Coalition: The Story of* INDEPENDENT SECTOR (New York: The Foundation Center, 1997), 175–76.

21. Brian O'Connell, "The Future Looks Good—For Those Who Invest in It," *Fund Raising Management* (March 1994), 39–42.

22. Stephen C. Craig, *The Malevolent Leaders: Popular Discontent in America* (Boulder, Colo.: Westview Press, 1993), 184.

23. Daniel Yankelovich, *Kettering Review* (Fall 1995), 6.

24. Georgie Anne Geyer, *Americans No More: The Death of Citizenship* (New York: Atlantic Monthly Press, 1996), book jacket.

25. Joseph S. Nye, Jr., "Introduction: The Decline of Confidence in Government," in *Why People Don't Trust Government,* ed. Joseph S. Nye, Jr., Philip D. Zelikow, and David C. King (Cambridge, Mass.: Harvard University Press, 1997), 1.

26. Adam Clymer, "Students Not Drawn to Community Service," *New York Times* (January 12, 2000), 14.

27. Nye, 3.

28. Derek Bok, "Measuring the Performance of Government," in *Why People Don't Trust Government,* ed. Joseph S. Nye, Jr., Philip D. Zelikow, and David C. King (Cambridge, Mass.: Harvard University Press, 1997), 56.

29. Michael Sviridoff, "The Seeds of Urban Renewal," *The Public Interest* (Winter 1994), 401–406.

30. Alan Wolfe, *One Nation, After All* (New York: Viking, 1998), 154–55.

31. Brian O'Connell, "Summing Up," in *Civil Society: The Underpinnings of American Democracy* (Tufts University/University Press of New England, 1999), 124–26.

32. Ibid., 124 (from Edward Gibbon, 1788, cited in "The Moral Foundations of Society" by Margaret Thatcher, for the Web site "The Ultimate Truth," www.logicsouth.com [Seattle, Wash., 1995]).

33. Emily Dickinson, *The Complete Poems of Emily Dickinson,* ed. Thomas H. Johnson (Boston: Little, Brown, 1960), 211.

34. John W. Gardner, "Building Community" (Washington, D.C.: INDEPENDENT SECTOR, 1991), 10. (Gardner's statement has appeared in slightly different variations. In a letter to me in summer 1998, he indicated that he prefers it as quoted on page 199).

35. Thomas Jefferson, cited in *Civitas: A Framework for Civic Education,* ed. Charles F. Bahmueller, John H. Buchanan, Jr., and Charles N. Quigley, National Council for the Social Studies Bulletin no. 86 (Calabasas, Calif.: Center for Civic Education, 1991), 637.

36. Center for Civic Education, *Civitas: A Framework for Civic Education,* ed. Charles F. Bahmueller, John H. Buchanan, Jr., and Charles N. Quigley, Na-

tional Council for the Social Studies Bulletin no. 86 (Calabasas, Calif.: Center for Civic Education, 1991), 3.

37. David Mathews, "Foreword," in *Higher Education and the Practice of Democratic Politics: A Political Education Reader*, ed. Bernard Murchland (Dayton, Ohio: Kettering Foundation, 1991), xvi.

38. Virginia A. Hodgkinson, "Key Factors Influencing Caring, Involvement and Country," in *Care and Community in Modern Society: Passing on the Tradition of Service to Future Generations*, ed. Paul G. Schervish, Virginia A. Hodgkinson, Margaret Gates, and Associates (San Francisco: Jossey-Bass/Washington, D.C.: INDEPENDENT SECTOR, 1995), 21–49.

References

For the reader's easy reference, the following alphabetical listing of writings referred to in the book includes materials already covered in the notes.

Aldrin, Edwin E., Jr. *Return to Earth* (New York: Random House, 1973).

Beers, Clifford. *A Mind That Found Itself* (New York: Longmans, Green, 1908).

Bok, Derek. "Measuring the Performance of Government," in *Why People Don't Trust Government,* ed. Joseph S. Nye, Jr., Philip D. Zelikow, and David C. King (Cambridge, Mass: Harvard University Press, 1997), 56.

Bremner, Robert H. *American Philanthropy* (Chicago: University of Chicago Press, 1960).

Carter, Richard. *The Gentle Legions* (Garden City, N.Y.: Doubleday, 1961).

CIVICUS. "Citizens: Strengthening Global Civil Society" [Organization Committee report] (Washington, D.C.: CIVICUS World Alliance for Citizen Participation, 1993).

Clymer, Adam. "Students Not Drawn to Voting or Politics," *New York Times* (January 12, 2000), 14.

Commission on Foundations and Private Philanthropy. *Foundations, Private Giving, and Public Policy* (Chicago: University of Chicago Press, 1970).

Commission on Private Philanthropy and Public Needs. *Giving in America: Toward a Stronger Private Sector* (Washington, D.C.: Commission on Private Philanthropy and Public Needs, 1975).

Cornuelle, Richard C. *Reclaiming the American Dream* (New York: Random House, 1965).

Craig, Stephen C. *The Malevolent Leaders: Popular Discontent in America* (Boulder, Colo.: Westview Press, 1993).

Dickinson, Emily. *The Complete Poems of Emily Dickinson,* ed. Thomas H. Johnson (Boston: Little, Brown, 1960).

Donee Group. "Private Philanthropy; Vital and Innovative? Or Passive and Irrelevant?" (Washington, D.C.: National Committee for Responsive Philanthropy, 1975).

Eells, Richard, ed. *International Business Philanthropy* (Old Tappan, N.J.: National Council on Philanthropy/Macmillan, 1979).

Ehrlich, Thomas, ed., and the American Council on Education. *Civic Responsibility and Higher Education* (Phoenix, Ariz.: Oryx Press, 2000).

Frost, Robert. *The Complete Poetry of Robert Frost,* ed. Edward Connery Lathem (New York: Henry Holt, 1969).

Gardner, John W. "Building Community" (Washington, D.C.: INDEPENDENT SEC-
    TOR, 1991).
——. Inaugural remarks at the founding of INDEPENDENT SECTOR (March 5,
    1980).
——. "Leadership Papers Nos. 1–12." (Washington, D.C.: INDEPENDENT SEC-
    TOR, 1986).
——. "National Renewal" (Washington, D.C.: INDEPENDENT SECTOR, 1995).
——. *On Leadership* (New York: Free Press/Macmillan, 1990).
Gardner, John W., and Brian O'Connell. "To Preserve an Independent Sector"
    [Report of the Organizing Committee] (Washington, D.C: INDEPENDENT SEC-
    TOR, 1979).
Geyer, Georgie Anne. *Americans No More: The Death of Citizenship* (New York:
    Atlantic Monthly Press, 1996).
Gibbon, Edward. 1788. Cited in "The Moral Foundations of Society" by Mar-
    garet Thatcher, for the web site "The Ultimate Truth" www.logicsouth.com
    (Seattle, Wash.: Conservative Consensus, 1995).
Green, Hannah (a.k.a. Joanne Greenberg). *I Never Promised You a Rose Garden*
    (New York: Holt, Rinehart and Winston, 1964).
Hamlin, Robert. *Voluntary Health and Welfare Agencies in the United States*
    (New York: Schoolmasters' Press, 1961).
Hodgkinson, Virginia A., Margaret Gates, Paul G. Schervis, and Associates. *Care
    and Community in Modern Society: Passing on the Tradition of Service to Fu-
    ture Generations* [for INDEPENDENT SECTOR] (San Francisco: Jossey-Bass, 1995).
INDEPENDENT SECTOR. "Ethics and the Nation's Voluntary and Philanthropic Com-
    munity: Obedience to the Unenforceable" (Washington, D.C.: INDEPENDENT
    SECTOR, 1991).
INDEPENDENT SECTOR. Biannual Reports, "Giving and Volunteering in the United
    States," Virginia Hodgkinson, director and editor (Washington, D.C.: INDE-
    PENDENT SECTOR, 1980–98).
Jefferson, Thomas. 1785. Cited in *Civitas: A Framework for Civic Education,* ed.
    Charles F. Bahmueller, John H. Buchanan, Jr., and Charles N. Quigley, Na-
    tional Council for the Social Studies, Bulletin no. 86 (Calabasas, Calif.: Cen-
    ter for Civic Education, 1991).
Knauft, E. B., Renee A. Berger, and Sandra A. Gray. *Profiles of Excellence:
    Achieving Success in the Nonprofit Sector* [for INDEPENDENT SECTOR] (San
    Francisco: INDEPENDENT SECTOR/Jossey-Bass, 1991).
Lippincott, Earl, and Elling Aannestad. "How Can Businessmen Evaluate the
    Management of Voluntary Welfare Agencies?," *Harvard Business Review*
    (November–December, 1964, 42–46).
Lomask, Milton. *Seed Money: The Guggenheim Story* (New York: Farrar Straus,
    1964).
Marts, Arnaud. *Philanthropy's Role in Civilization: Its Contribution to Human
    Freedom* (New York: Harper & Bros., 1973).
Menninger, William C. "The Criteria for Emotional Maturity" (Topeka, Kans.:
    Menninger Foundation, 1960).

Minkin, Jacob S. *The World of Moses Maimonides* (New York: Thomas Yoseloff Press, 1957).

Moore, William W. *Fighting for Life: A History of the American Heart Association, 1911–1975* (Dallas, Tex.: American Heart Association, 1983).

Moynihan, Daniel Patrick. "Pluralism and the Independent Sector." Inaugural remarks at the founding of INDEPENDENT SECTOR, March 5, 1980 (Washington, D.C.: INDEPENDENT SECTOR, 1980).

Murchland, Bernard, ed. *Higher Education and the Practice of Democratic Politics: A Political Education Reader* (Dayton, Ohio: Kettering Foundation, 1991).

Ney, Joseph S., Jr. "Introduction: The Decline of Confidence in Government" in *Why People Don't Trust Government*, ed. Joseph S. Nye, Jr., Philip D. Zelikow, and David C. King (Cambridge, Mass.: Harvard University Press, 1997), 1.

Nielson, Waldemar A. *The Golden Donors* (New York: Truman Talley Books/ E. P. Dutton, 1985).

———. *The Endangered Sector* (New York: NAL/ Dutton, 1979).

———. "The Third Sector: Keystone of a Caring Society." An Occasional Paper for INDEPENDENT SECTOR (Washington, D.C.: INDEPENDENT SECTOR, 1982).

O'Connell, Brian. *America's Voluntary Spirit: A Book of Readings* (New York: The Foundation Center, 1983).

———. *The Board Members Book: Making a Difference in Voluntary Organizations* (New York: The Foundation Center, 1985).

———. *Board Overboard: Laughs and Lessons for All but the Perfect Nonprofit* (San Francisco: Jossey-Bass, 1996).

———. "Citizen Participation and Influence in America: Impressive Performance and Alarming Shortfalls." *Public Integrity* (Spring 2003), 159–169.

———. "Don't Save Me From the Left or Right." *Christian Science Monitor* (December 28, 1983), 21.

———. *Effective Leadership in Voluntary Organizations: How to Make the Greatest Use of Citizen Service and Influence* (New York: Walker and Company, 1976).

———. "Feasibility Study of Closer Collaboration Between the Coalition of National Voluntary Organizations (CONVO) and the National Council on Philanthropy (NCOP)" (Washington, D.C.: Coalition of National Organizations, 1978).

———. *Finding Values That Work: The Search for Fulfillment* (New York: Walker and Company, 1978).

———. "'First Lights,' Recollections of the Beginnings and First Years of CIVICUS: World Alliance for Citizen Participation" (Washington, D.C.: CIVICUS, 2000).

———. "The Future Looks Good for Those Who Invest In It," *Fundraising Management* (March 1994), 39–42.

———. "It's Time to Make a Mesh of Things," Occasional Paper for Lincoln Filene Center (Medford, Mass.: Tufts University, 1997).

———. "A Major Transfer of Government Responsibility to Voluntary Organizations? Proceed with Caution." *Public Administration Review* (May/June 1996), 222–225.

————. *Our Organization* (New York: Walker and Company, 1987).

————. *People Power: Service, Advocacy, Empowerment* (New York: The Foundation Center, 1994).

————. *Philanthropy in Action* (New York: The Foundation Center, 1987).

————. *Powered by Coalition: The Story of* INDEPENDENT SECTOR (San Francisco: Jossey-Bass, 1997).

————. "Reexamining the Roles and Relationships of Voluntary Organizations and Government," Occasional Paper for Lincoln Filene Center (Medford, Mass.: Tufts University, 1995).

————. "Summing Up: Prospects for an Enduring Democracy," in *Civil Society: The Underpinnings of American Democracy* (Hanover, N.H.: University Press of New England/Tufts University, 1999), chap. 8.

————. *Voices From the Heart: In Celebration of America's Volunteers* (San Francisco: Chronicle Books and Jossey-Bass, 1999).

————. "What Voluntary Activity Can and Cannot Do For America," *Public Administration Review* (September/October 1989), 486–491.

————. "What Colleges and Universities Must Do to Instill Civic Spirit in Young Adults." Keynote address to the National Conference on Higher Education (March 17, 1985), sponsored by the American Association of Higher Education, Washington, D.C.

O'Connell, Brian, and Ann Brown O'Connell. *Volunteers in Action* (New York: The Foundation Center, 1989).

Payton, Robert R., Michael Novak, Brian O'Connell, and Peter Dobkin Hall. *Philanthropy: Four Views* (New Brunswick, N.J.: Social Philosophy and Public Center and Transaction Books, 1988).

Saiki, Maggi Kinser, and Keigo Shibata. *Japanese Working for a Better World* (Tokyo, Japan: for Hannoki, Inc., 1992).

Salamon, Lester M., and Alan J. Abramson. "The Federal Budget and the Nonprofit Sector" (later referred to as "Analysis of the Economic Recovery Programs' Direct Significance for Philanthropic and Voluntary Organizations and the People They Serve") (Washington, D.C.: Urban Institute/INDEPENDENT SECTOR, 1982).

Schumpeter, Joseph R. "Capitalism, Socialism and Democracy" (New York: Harper and Brothers, 1942).

U. S. Treasury Department. "Report on Private Foundations" (Washington, D.C.: Author, 1965).

Yankelovitch, Daniel. "Three Destructive Trends" *Kettering Review* (Fall 1995), 6–15.

Selected Other Writings of Brian O'Connell

"Accepting Tax Dollars: Voluntary Agencies Must Ask: What Price Independence?," *Foundation News* (July/August 1976). Washington, D.C.: Council on Foundations.

"Already 1,000 Points of Light" [op-ed], *The New York Times* (January 25, 1989), 23.

"Attractive Human Qualities." In *Finding Values That Work: The Search for Fulfillment* (New York: Walker and Company, 1978), chap. 6.

"Building Coalitions, Collaborations, Alliances and Other Partnerships," Occasional Paper, Lincoln Filene Center for Citizenship and Public Affairs (Medford, Mass.: Tufts University, 1997).

"Citizenship and Community," *Bulletin, American Association of Higher Education* (November 1985). Washington, D.C.

"Civil Society: America's Invisible Colossus," in INDEPENDENT SECTOR's "Conversations With Leaders" series. (Washington, D.C.: INDEPENDENT SECTOR, 2002).

"Civil Society: Definitions and Descriptions," *Nonprofit and Voluntary Sector Quarterly*, vol. 20, no. 3 (September 2000), 471–478.

"Community Foundations: More of the Best," Invited paper and speech for the Council of Community Foundations conference, "The Community Foundation: A New Perception," Monterey, Calif., 1981.

"Compensation in Nonprofit Organizations," Occasional Paper (Washington, D.C.: INDEPENDENT SECTOR, 1993).

"Corporate Philanthropy: Getting Bigger, Broader, and Tougher to Manage," Keynote address, National Conference on Corporate Philanthropy, sponsored by the Public Affairs Council, and reprinted in *Corporate Philanthropy* (Washington, D.C.: INDEPENDENT SECTOR, August/September 1987).

"For Voluntary Organizations in Trouble . . . Or Don't Want to Be," Occasional Paper (Washington, D.C.: INDEPENDENT SECTOR, 1993).

"From Service to Advocacy to Empowerment, in Social Casework" and adapted from "Voluntarism: Today and Tomorrow," a speech presented at the biennial convention of the Family Service Association of America (Toronto, 1977).

"Future Leadership in America," keynote address, NOW Legal Defense and Education Fund's Tenth Anniversary Convocation, New York City, (1981).

"John W. Gardner: The Nation's Leader," (Afterword), in *Living, Leading and the American Dream*, ed. Francesca Gardner (San Francisco: Jossey-Bass/Wiley, 2003).

"Hurting Voluntary Agencies," [op-ed], *New York Times* (January 23, 1981), 25.

"To Remember the Dead," in *Philanthropy in Action* (New York: The Foundation Center, 1987), chap. 9.

"The New American Giver," keynote of symposium, and "proceedings." "The New American Giver." May 1, 1987, University of Akron (Akron, Ohio, 1987).

Nonprofit Management Series (Washington, D.C.: INDEPENDENT SECTOR, 1988): "The Role of the Board and Board Members"; "Finding, Developing, and Rewarding Good Board Members"; "Operating Effective Committees"; "Conducting Good Meetings"; "The Roles and Relationships of the Chief Volunteer and Chief Staff Officers, Board and Staff: Who Does What?"; "Recruiting, Encouraging, and Evaluating the Chief Staff Officer"; "Fund Raising"; "Budgeting and Financial Accountability"; "Evaluating Results."

"Origins, Dimensions, and Impact of America's Voluntary Spirit," Occasional Paper (Washington, D.C.: INDEPENDENT SECTOR, 1986).

"Our Heritage of Giving" [op-ed], *The Washington Post* (February 10, 1979), 21.

"Our Religious Heritage," in *America's Voluntary Spirit* (New York: The Foundation Center, 1983).

"Philanthropy: America's Extra Dimension," in *Give Me a Log With You at One End,* ed. Jack Shakely (Los Angeles: California Community Foundation, 2003).

"Philanthropy Checks Government Response," Guest Column, *USA Today* [Washington, D.C.] (December 21, 1987).

"Public and Voluntary Sectors: Future Responsibilities," Keynote, 25th anniversary celebration, University of Cincinnati School of Social Work, Cincinnati, Ohio, December 12, 1984.

"The Relationship Between Voluntary Organizations and Government: Constructive Partnerships/Creative Tensions," Paper presented to the spring meeting of the National Academy of Public Administration, Washington, D.C., 1986.

"Religion Is Central to the Nonprofit Sector," [op-ed], *Non-Profit Times* (1989).

"State of the Sector: With Particular Attention to Its Independence," prepared at the request of the INDEPENDENT SECTOR Annual Meeting Planning Committee for discussion at the Annual Meeting and Assembly of Members, Washington, D.C., 1987.

"The Strategic Links Between Business and the Nonprofit Sector," in *Corporate Contributions Handbook,* ed. James P. Shannon (San Francisco: Jossey-Bass, in cooperation with the Council on Foundations, 1991).

"Strengthening Philanthropy and Voluntary Action," *National Civic Review* (July/August, 1987). New York: National Civic League.

"Taking Our Civic Measure: Americans Care and Show It—But Strangely Not in Matters of Governance," Opinion, *The Christian Science Monitor* [Boston] (March 13, 2000), 21.

Voluntary Spirit Column Series (Washington, D.C.: INDEPENDENT SECTOR, 1992): "Guidelines for Giving"; "Rationale for Corporate Philanthropy"; "Controversial Grants That Achieved Universal Acclaim"; "The Common Sense for Sabbaticals or Project Leaves"; "The Roles and Relationships of the Top Volunteer and Staff Officers"; "Effective Planning Even in Voluntary Organizations!"; "Advocacy is Frequently an Organization's Best Service."

"What Colleges Ought to Do to Instill a Voluntary Spirit in Young Adults," Point of View, *The Chronicle of Higher Education* [Washington, D.C.] (August 15, 1987) 104.

"Work and Money," in *Finding Values That Work: The Search for Fulfillment* (New York: Walker and Company, 1978), chap. 5.

Index

Charles Stewart Mott Foundation, xii, 172

Charter meeting of INDEPENDENT SECTOR, 104–5

Chase, Irving, 203

Churchill, Winston, 74

Citizen participation: and criticism of voluntary organizations, 82; education for, 182–85, 199–201; international efforts, 144–52, 175, 193; need for literature on, 181; philosophy and role of, 157–60; summary of advice on promoting, 186–202

"Citizen Participation and Influence in America" (O'Connell), 181

Citizens for a Better Environment, et. al., v. Village of Schaumburg, 104

Civic Responsibility in Higher Education (Ehrlich), 200

CIVICUS: World Alliance for Citizen Participation, 144–52, 175, 193

Civil liberties: and independent nonprofit role, 127–29, 192–93; of mental patients, 61–63, 66–68; variations in international respect for, 62, 140–41, 143, 153. *See also* Advocacy programs

Civil Society (O'Connell), 183, 197

Civitas: A Framework for Civic Education, 199

CJF (Council of Jewish Federations), 189

Clymer, Adam, 195

Coalition building, 130–35, 137, 139–53

Coalition of National Voluntary Organizations (CONVO): charitable contributions deduction expansion, 107; formation of, 86; and IS formation, 94–96, 98, 99–102, 137; merge considerations with NCOP, 80–81; O'Connell's assessment of, 86–90

Code of Patients' Rights, 68

Colleges and universities, public service roles of, 117–18, 120–23, 160, 182–85. *See also* Research

Commission on Private Philanthropy and Public Needs, 82–83, 84–85

Committees in voluntary organizations, 18, 27–28

Communication: and importance of volunteer effort results, 8–9, 96, 110–11, 164–65, 179–80; as IS focus, 96, 111; MHA initiatives, 46. *See also* Professional education; Public education; Publicity

Community-level services: AHA role, 14; American tradition of, 158–60; CHA initiatives, 34–35; crime prevention by neighborhoods, 196; government vs. nonprofit responsibility for, 141; MHA initiatives, 63, 65–68; and O'Connell's early career goals, 5; pressure for IS to fill government gap, 106–7; and primary mission of voluntary sector, 83

Community Service Learning (CSL), 200

Conable, Barber, 2, 112

Congress, U.S., and advocacy restrictions battle, 113–14

Consumer/citizen orientation of O'Connell, 48, 49, 62–63

CONVO (Coalition of National Voluntary Organizations). *See* Coalition of National Voluntary Organizations (CONVO)

Corcoran, Lawrence, 105

Cordua, Harney, 26, 27, 203

Cornuelle, Richard C., 83

Corporations and nonprofits, 106, 124, 176–77, 189

Council of Jewish Federations (CJF), 189

CPR (cardiopulmonary resuscitation) training, 34–35

Craig, Stephen C., 194

Crime, community action to prevent, 196

CSL (Community Service Learning), 200

Decision making, sharing of, 17, 133

Deinstitutionalization of mentally ill patients, 66–67

Democracy. *See* Participatory democracy

Depression, 63–65, 69, 70–71, 72–75

Developmental disabilities and Worcester clinic experience, 3–4

22–24, 38–39, 40–42; and voluntary sector effectiveness, 83–84; and women's roles in voluntary organizations, 51–53. *See also* Board leadership

Legislation affecting nonprofits, 2, 82, 95, 107–8, 113–15

Libraries, philanthropic origins of public, 162–63

Lilly Endowment, 122

Limitations of nonprofit groups, importance of articulating, 56–57, 107, 118, 132–33, 148

Lincoln, Abraham, 74

Lincoln Filene Center for Citizenship and Public Affairs, 172–82

Lippincott, Earle, 32

Lipscomb, James, 89, 134, 203

Lobbying by nonprofits. *See* Advocacy programs

Lobbying by Public Charities Act, 2

Local voluntary association chapters. *See* Chapters; Community-level services

Lomask, Milton, 162

Los Angeles chapter of CHA, 22, 25–28

Luckow, Lynn, 179–80

Lyman, Richard W., 130, 204

Maimonides, 202

Malevolent Leaders (Craig), 194

Management consulting firms, services for nonprofits, 176–77

Mandel, Mort, 121, 141

Mandel Center for Nonprofit Organizations, 121–22

Marschall, Miklós, 145

Marts, Arnaud C., 163

Maryland Heart Association, 12–21

Mathews, David, 200

Maxwell School of Citizenship and Public Affairs, 4–5

McGuffey's Reader (1844), 158–59

Mears, Charles, 6, 7–8, 11, 13, 20

Measurement of nonprofit success, 124–25

Media: and CHA public education initiatives, 33–34; and deinstitutionalization of mentally ill patients, 66–67; and depression education, 63–64; and diversity in IS, 127; IS as important source for, 109–11; Maryland HA publicity, 16; and misconceptions about public service effectiveness, 195; and nonprofit independence, 113; and physical therapy training successes, 4

Medications, overuse for mental illness, 66

Meeting ground concept at INDEPENDENT SECTOR, 97, 127, 129

Meléndez, Sara, 175

Membership: at CIVICUS, 148–49, 150; commitment to, 135; at IS, 98–100, 103, 126–30; strategy for building, 132

Menninger, Karl, 71

Menninger, Will, 71

Mental Health Association (MHA): candidacy for national position, 38–39, 40–42; chapter vs. national issues, 6, 46, 75–76, 77; community services initiatives, 63, 65–68; crusade for government support, 1–3; macroanalysis of, 54–58; minority group issues, 53–54; O'Connell's departure, 77–79; O'Connell's orientation, 42–44; organizational issues, 44–50, 55–61, 76–77; patients' rights advocacy, 61–63, 66–68; pressures of job, 50–51; public education, 46, 63–65, 72–75; social revolution effects, 68–72; and women's leadership roles, 51–53

Mental Health Commission, 73–74

Mental health vs. mental illness focus, 40–41, 49–50, 71–72

Mental Hygiene, 46, 61

Mental illness: autism classification issue, 47–49; vs. mental health focus, 40–41, 49–50, 71–72; spectrum of, 43

Meyer, Cord, 94

Meyerson, Max, 59, 78–79

MHA (Mental Health Association). *See* Mental Health Association (MHA)